The Complete Guide to
METAL BOATS

The Complete Guide to
METAL
BOATS

BUILDING, MAINTENANCE, AND REPAIR

BRUCE ROBERTS-GOODSON

International Marine / McGraw-Hill

Camden, Maine • New York • San Francisco • Washington, D.C.
Auckland • Bogotá • Caracas • Lisbon • London • Madrid • Mexico City • Milan • Montreal
New Delhi • San Juan • Singapore • Sydney • Tokyo • Toronto

International Marine
A Division of The McGraw-Hill Companies

10 9 8 7 6 5 4

Library of Congress Cataloging-in-Publication Data
Roberts-Goodson, R. Bruce.
      The complete guide to metal boats : building, maintenance, and repair /
      Bruce Roberts-Goodson.
          p.   cm.
      Rev. ed. of: Metal boats. 1st ed. 1998.
      Includes bibliographical references and index.
      ISBN 0-07-136444-7 (alk. paper)
          1. Steel boats—Design and construction. 2. Aluminum boats—Design and construction. 3. Steel boats—Maintenance and repair. 4. Aluminum boats—Maintenance and repair. I. Roberts-Goodson, R. Bruce. Metal boats. II. Title.

VM321.R64 2000
623.8'43—dc21   00-040944

Questions regarding the content of this book should be addressed to
International Marine
P.O. Box 220
Camden, ME 04843
www.internationalmarine.com

Questions regarding the ordering of this book should be addressed to
The McGraw-Hill Companies
Customer Service Department
P.O. Box 547
Blacklick, OH 43004
Retail customers: 1-800-262-4729
Bookstores: 1-800-722-4726

All photographs and illustrations courtesy the author except as noted, with thanks to the many builders who have contributed photographs over the years.

This book is printed on 70# Citation at Quebecor Printing Co., Fairfield, PA
Design by Chris McLarty
Production management by Janet Robbins
Page layout by PerfecType
Edited by Jonathan Eaton, Alex Barnett, and John Vigor

Cor-Ten, De-Bug, Formica, Green Diamond, Heart Interface, Laminex, Lexan, Monel, Mylar, Plexiglas, Skilsaw, Styrofoam, Treadmaster, Tufnol, Vaseline, Viny-Lux, and West System are registered trademarks.

Contents

Centennial Spray 38. This round bilge steel design has proved popular and has been built as a sailboat, motor sailer and trawler yacht.

Foreword

Who is this book written for? If you have an interest in metal boats, and perhaps a desire to own one, this book is for you. Building a metal boat from the ground up is a technically challenging project. I haven't attempted to cover every aspect of the subject—and I doubt any one book could. In particular, this book will not teach you how to weld. Those of you with experience of welding and working with metal will have much to gain from my discussions of boat design and metal boat building techniques. In this regard, *Metal Boats* is intended to turn a welder into a boatbuilder.

On the other hand, you may come to metal boats with a solid background in boating and boat design but little experience of working with metal. If so, you may choose to subcontract out the welding portions of the project. Many novice builders have attended evening classes in welding and become proficient enough to handle the easier welds and assist an expert brought in for the critical welds. You can learn a great deal by watching over an expert's shoulder.

Or you may plan to buy a used metal boat, or oversee the construction of a new one. In this case, my intention is to provide an overview of the whole process so you can make informed decisions.

One of the most frequently asked questions is, "Which metal should I use?" I have compared the primary choices in some detail. Other major topics include choosing a suitable design, building from plans and precut kits, preventing corrosion, and selecting and installing an engine.

Finally, pride of ownership plays a big part in the pleasure of boating. I hope that by understanding the design and construction of your metal boat you will also deepen your enjoyment of it.

Good boatbuilding.

Bruce Roberts-Goodson
P.O. Box 1086
Severna Park MD 21146
www.bruce-roberts.com
bruce@bruce-roberts.com

Acknowledgments

My sincere thanks go to all those builders of metal boats in Europe, especially those in the Netherlands, who gave me such good advice when I needed it most, back in 1973. To Grahame Shannon, the developer of Auto Ship and other computer programs that have changed yacht design forever. To Carol A. Powell, a gracious lady, consultant metallurgist, and copper-nickel expert, who provided me with copious quantities of information about the history, properties, and handling of copper-nickel. To the Copper Development Association (CDA) and the Nickel Development Institute (NIDI) and their various consultants and experts for their help in furthering my knowledge of copper-nickel. To Max Pille and all the engineers at Heart Interface who provided me with additional information on things electrical. And to Del F. Kahan, of the Marinetics Corporation, Newport Beach, California, for his insights into the special requirements for electrical systems in metal boats.

To the many hundreds of builders of metal boats constructed from my plans who have sent photographs, asked intelligent questions, and offered valuable suggestions; these builders have made a great contribution to the development of our metal building techniques.

Special thanks are due to my wife, Gwenda, who has supported me in my work for over 30 years; as a very active first mate, she never hesitated to impose the woman's view when it came to designing items in which she was particularly interested. She certainly didn't restrict herself to the galley or other stereotyped areas of design.

My thanks to Andrew Slorach, my long-time partner and associate who is always ready to offer constructive advice; to George Love, my boatbuilding mentor, and to all those in the boating industry who, over the past 35 years, have helped me chart a course through the shoals that have claimed so many who have tried to turn a hobby into a business.

This Spray Trawler Yacht 52/58 has been built in steel and makes an excellent long-distance powerboat or motor sailer. (Steve Davis illustration)

Introduction

My first and later intense interest in metal boats came about almost by accident. By 1973, I was already established as a designer of custom fiberglass sailboats and powerboats, and fiberglass materials were inexpensive and readily available. Our building techniques were proven and widely accepted around the world; who needed any other building material? The oil embargo of the early 1970s changed all that.

Since our clients still wanted to build boats, we were forced to consider the options. Ferrocement was already thoroughly discredited as a boatbuilding material; wood-epoxy was established, but the materials were expensive and didn't have a wide enough appeal. By the process of elimination, we turned our attention to metal.

In 1973, there were relatively few designers and builders of metal pleasure boats apart from those in Europe, and especially in the Netherlands. Where to start? That was easy. The Dutch had been building metal, particularly steel, boats for a century, so I spent several weeks visiting many boatbuilding yards in the Netherlands. Fortunately I was able to study the building techniques and discuss construction methods with several established builders.

In chapters 16 and 17, you'll find a wide selection of designs for metal sailboats and powerboats. They range in size from 26 to 73 feet (7.9 to 22.2 m), and all are intended for amateur construction. Our first plan designed for steel construction was the Mauritius 43 sailboat. Over the following twenty years, 800 of this design were built by individuals and another 150 were constructed by professional yards around the world. This first plan designed especially for steel was quickly followed by several other sailboat and powerboat designs for steel construction, including the Roberts 34, the Offshore 44, and the Roberts 53. Early steel powerboat plans included the Coastworker 30, the Waverunner 34, the Waverunner 40/42, and the Waverunner 45. As of now, over 20,000 steel sailboats and powerboats have been successfully built to our designs.

Up until 1984, only a few boats of our design were constructed in round-bilge steel (these were built to modified versions of the fiberglass hull lines). At that time, most of the steel and aluminum boats built to our plans were constructed using the double-chine technique. In 1985, we switched to computer-aided design and this made it possible to draw radius-chine designs that were easy to build and had all the beauty of a round-bilge hull. At last we could offer metal hull shapes that rivaled their fiberglass sisters. These radius-chine hulls can be built by anyone with some welding experience, and are as simple to build as any hard-chine boat.

We were introduced to aluminum in 1974 when a client requested a design to be constructed in that material. Since that time, many aluminum boats have been built from our plans. My preferences will no doubt become obvious as this text develops, so I might as well state right off that I prefer the use of aluminum to be restricted to high-speed planing powerboats. In the latter case, the benefits of the material can be fully exploited. Fortunately for the sake of variety, not all builders agree with me. We often prepare plans for aluminum-hulled sailboats and semidisplacement powerboats, as well as for steel hulls and, more recently, for copper-nickel hulls.

Copper-nickel has been used to build several commercial vessels and a few pleasure craft. With increased interest in the ecology, higher costs, and restrictions on types of antifouling paint, you will find this material has a lot of advantages if you can manage the much higher basic material cost.

1
WHY METAL?

HISTORY

Metal boats have a long and distinguished heritage stretching back 200 years. The first recorded instance of a small metal boat was a 12-foot (3.66 m) iron hull built on the banks of the River Fosse, in England, in 1777. Ten years later, the next known example, a 70-foot (21.33 m) iron canal boat, was built using ⅝-inch (13 mm) riveted plates laid over a timber frame. In 1818, the first all-metal commercial boat was built in Scotland. The *Vulcan* was 63 feet (19.20 m) in length overall (LOA) and had a beam of 13 feet (3.96 m). This boat, with its flat-bar frames and riveted iron plates, was the forerunner of hundreds of boats and ships built using similar techniques.

As suitable timber for boatbuilding became increasingly hard to find, designers and shipbuilders turned to metal. In 1834, a violent storm drove hundreds of wooden boats and ships ashore in England, marking a milestone for metal boats. Most of the boats were totally destroyed, but one exception was the 125-foot (38.10 m) all-metal *Gary Owen*. After being driven ashore, this boat was able to withstand the severe pounding until the storm subsided. It did not go unnoticed that the *Gary Owen* suffered only a few scrapes and scratches, and that she returned to port under her own power. Another boost for metal ships occurred when the first all-metal liner, *Great Britain*, came to grief on the Irish coast and was later floated off to resume active service. These incidents did much to popularize all-metal vessels, so that gradual acceptance turned into a flood of orders for builders of metal ships.

Shipowners soon found that metal ships were more resistant to the stresses of the sea in all weathers, and better able to keep schedules. Many wooden ships had been lost with all hands because some of the fastenings let go under extreme weather conditions. Shipowners found that although fire can occur in boats and ships constructed out of any material, metal vessels are better able to stay afloat, giving the crew more time to control the fire. As early as 1853, a survey of sailing ships operating in the Far East trade revealed that to build and operate metal ships cost as little as 80 percent of the cost of wooden ones. Comparing equal-sized vessels, it was proved that metal ships, because of their greater interior volume, smaller frames, etc., were able to carry as much as 25 percent more cargo than otherwise identical wooden vessels. The published results of this extensive survey gave a great boost to metal shipbuilding, and no doubt helped Great Britain become the largest builder of commercial shipping until World War II.

In 1858, the all-metal *Great Eastern* was built in the U.K. and at the time this was the world's largest ship, 700 feet (213 m) in length with a beam of 85 feet (25.91 m). In a world where trade was increasing at a great rate, this proved that there was virtually no limit to the size of ship that could be built using metal. It's interesting to compare this early metal ship with the longest wooden ship ever built, the *Dunderberg*, which was a mere 377 feet (114.91 m) long.

METAL SHIPS

Steel

Up to the early 1860s, all metal ships were built of wrought iron, but thereafter a new material became available: steel. Steel was lighter than iron, but this new wonder material had one major drawback: it cost four times as much as the iron it would soon replace. Economy of scale soon prevailed, however, and steel became affordable. That, together with the fact that it was available in large sheets, soon established steel as the premium shipbuilding material. The giant liners of the past were built from steel, including the *France*, which was 1,035 feet (315 m) long and displaced over 70,000 tons. The liner *United States* holds the fastest passage time for a North Atlantic passenger ship, having made the trip between Europe and North America in only 3 days and 10 hours, averaging 35.59 knots for the crossing. High-speed ferries and other similar vessels are challenging this record. More recently, a large number of new giant liners entering the charter trade have spawned a great revival of steel shipbuilding.

Steel warships and oil tankers dwarf the famous passenger ships of the past. The aircraft carrier USS *Nimitz* displaces 95,000 tons, and the oil tanker *Seawise Giant*, which is 1,504 feet (458.52 m) long and 225 feet (68.58 m) wide, weighs in at 564,763 tons.

This steel Spray 40, Mirounga, *was built in Germany by Ulrich Kronberg.*

While this revolution in building large ships moved almost all construction of commercial shipping out of the timber era and into steel, small boats continued to be built of wood, except in Europe—and there, mainly in the Netherlands.

This situation prevailed until the early 1960s when the advent of fiberglass changed the pleasure-boat scene forever.

Aluminum (or Aluminium)

This metal is refined from the natural material bauxite. Although it was discovered early in the

The Tom Thumb 26 is ideal for building in steel, aluminum, or copper-nickel. It would make a great first project for the novice metal boat builder.

nineteenth century, it was not until 1886 that the first practical refining methods were developed in France. As early as 1894, an aluminum alloy was used in Switzerland to build the power yacht *Alumina* for Prince Wilhelm zu Wied.

The designers of the liner *United States* made extensive use of this metal, saving over 27,000 tons compared to a similar-sized all-steel vessel. Today, aluminum is used to build sailboats and power yachts of all sizes. This material is especially useful where weight saving is the most important factor.

Copper-Nickel

In electro-chemical terms, copper is one of the most noble metals in common use. It has excellent resistance to corrosion in the atmosphere and in salt water. The British Royal Navy introduced copper cladding to wooden warships in the eighteenth century to prevent the hulls from being eaten by marine borers and fouled by other marine growth. The hulls of the *Cutty Sark* and other famous clipper ships were clad with copper. These vessels were required to

make fast passages, and the copper ensured that their bottoms remained smooth. In 1893, the America's Cup defenders *Vigilant* and *Enterprise*, and other Cup defenders of the period, had hulls of Tobin bronze, fastened with rivets of the same alloy.

The practice of cladding the hulls of wooden ships and pleasure boats with copper was common until the mid-1950s, when modern antifouling paints came into common usage. Copper cladding was the forerunner of modern copper-nickel alloys that combine superior resistance to corrosion with excellent antifouling properties. Today, copper-nickel can be used to clad the underwater sections of commercial and pleasure boats of all types.

SMALL BOATS

It is only in recent times that steel, aluminum, and copper-nickel have been considered mainline boatbuilding materials. Metal boat building has come a long way in a few years, and even as recently as 1965 very few small craft were built from these materials.

In the early 1960s, at the start of my own career in Brisbane, Australia, I knew every small craft in the area. Out of some 200 boats, only 3 were built of steel. By 1973, when I started to design in metal, there were still fewer than 10 steel boats in the area. What a difference today, when metal boats are much more widely accepted, and even regarded by many as the best for serious offshore cruising. It's common for our office to receive from cruising people letters that read: "We are anchored off [a popular cruising area] and there are 20 boats here, and 12 are built from steel." A rare dash of modesty prevents me from quoting the percentage of these boats that are to my design!

Steel

Steel is the most commonly used boatbuilding metal. It has many advantages including great strength, low cost, and ease of fabrication. There are great numbers of experienced welders in all parts of the world. Add to this the ease of repair, and the availability of a wide selection of suitable plans designed especially for building in steel, and it's easy to see why steel has become so popular with the cruising fraternity. Successful steel cruising boats can be small, too—as little as 25 feet (7.62 m) in length. The Dutch even build steel dinghies of around 15 feet (4.57 m) and use them as tenders on their barges and other commercial craft.

Steel is heavier than other boatbuilding materials, but that hasn't proved to be a disadvantage in cruising sailboats or powercraft. Steel still needs

care and attention, but modern coatings have greatly reduced the chances of rust forming. As the owner of several steel boats, I must confess I have found it hard to find any serious disadvantages in building, owning, and maintaining a steel boat.

Aluminum

Now widely accepted as a boatbuilding material, aluminum has the advantage of being about one-third the weight of equal-size steel, although this is partly offset by the fact that you need a thicker material for boatbuilding. Aluminum is easy to work with. In fact, you can use hand tools on aluminum, even some woodworking ones. It's ideal for decks and superstructures where its light weight and malleability can be used to advantage. In some areas of the world, aluminum has become extremely popular for building commercial craft and fishing boats because when the correct marine grades are used, the entire boat can be left unpainted.

This tidy pilothouse would look equally attractive on a sailboat or a powerboat.

Aluminum was the material chosen by Leuder Kerr for his Spray 33 Brass Loon. *This strong hull has successfully withstood contact with many deadheads (near-submerged floating logs) in the Gulf Islands of British Columbia, Canada.*

When it comes to repairs, experience won't be a problem if you have built your own aluminum boat.

Copper-Nickel

In 1938, a 45-foot (13.72 m) motor cruiser, *Miss Revere*, was built in the U.S. using an alloy of 70 percent copper and 30 percent nickel, welded over framing of the same alloy, and fitted with aluminum bulkheads. Between 1938 and 1965, many U.S. Coast Guard motor whaleboats were sheathed at the waterline in copper-nickel. In 1968, the pleasure yacht *Asperida* was built, using 70-30 copper-nickel hull plating over framing of the same material; this boat is still in service today.

The first of several copper-nickel commercial fishing boats was built in 1971. The hull of the 67-foot (20.42 m) *Copper Mariner* was constructed from a ¼-inch (6 mm) alloy containing 90 percent copper and 10 percent nickel, installed over steel framing. More recently, several other trawlers and general-purpose fishing boats have been built using copper-nickel alloys.

One interesting example of copper-nickel construction is the sailboat *Pretty Penny*. I inspected this boat in Faversham, England, after she had been removed from the water for the first time in 16 years. *Pretty Penny* was also scrubbed once a year, and there were only a few barnacles present when she was hauled. I was most impressed with her condition. (See sidebar *Pretty Penny: A Copper-Nickel Boat* on pages 23–24.)

The disadvantages include greater cost and relatively greater susceptibility to galvanic corrosion. Aluminum requires expert fabricators and experienced welders who are used to handling it.

All the advantages of steel accrue also to copper-nickel, which has the additional benefits of being resistant to corrosion and fouling by marine organisms. Copper-nickel requires neither painting nor anodes. It's a natural antifouling element. These benefits may make it the choice of those who can afford the costly material. Another advantage is that you will never be short of conversation with your peers if you choose copper-nickel.

The disadvantages of copper-nickel include the shortage of boatbuilders with experience in handling this metal, greater cost, and the sense of being a pioneer when you decide to build a copper-nickel boat.

The Cost of Metal Boats

Steel is the cheapest metal suitable for boatbuilding. It's considerably cheaper than fiberglass or the materials used in wood/epoxy construction. Steel is definitely today's bargain boatbuilding material. Aluminum comes next in price, then fiberglass or wood/epoxy. Copper-nickel is the most expensive of all.

Another attractive pilothouse. This one graces the steel Roberts 370 Tensile.

But you have to remember that the cost of the hull (meaning hull, deck, and superstructure) represents only 25 percent to 33 percent of the total cost of the vessel. Thus, a good argument can be made for ignoring the cost of the hull. If your budget allows this, then choose the material that is most suitable for your needs. After you have examined the building techniques explained in later chapters, you will be in a better position to make an informed decision.

2
BOAT AND BUILDING CHOICES

CHOOSING A SUITABLE BOAT

Before your decision-making process gets into top gear, you would be well advised to get your partner and family involved. Over the past 30-odd years, we've seen many boating projects come to grief because the senior family member failed to consult with, or listen to, the wishes of the others. You'll have to forgive us if we repeat this advice elsewhere; we feel it is worth the telling.

You'll find many fine designs for sail and power in chapters 16 and 17. But don't be tempted to buy or build a boat that is larger than you need. Reaching this decision is harder than you may imagine. If you have children who will accompany you throughout your boating adventures, make sure you think through the options. For instance, if you have teenagers, the chances are that within a few years they will be doing their own thing and not interested in accompanying their parents. It's a fact, though, that many families cruise with young children. Home schooling, and other concessions to your young crew, can turn cruising into a wonderful experience for the entire family.

What breed of boat is right for you? Power, or sail, or a 50/50? That's a decision you may already have reached before you discuss the options with your spouse and other family members. Age has a bearing on this decision; if you're under 40, then you will most probably opt for sail; up to 55, it may be a tossup; and over 60, power may be your choice. There are many ex-ceptions to the above but it's my experience that the happiest boaters fall into the age/sail/power categories outlined above.

Many people enjoy the comfort, convenience, "level playing field," and perceived safety of powerboats. They don't particularly like preparing meals and generally keeping house at varying degrees of heel. If more sailors chose nonplaning powerboats, or at least comfortable sailboats like the *Spray* type, they and their families would be (and would remain) more enthusiastic about serious boating.

That's our idea of the comfortable cruising lifestyle. In the many years we've spent designing and supervising the construction of hundreds of boats of all types, we have met many families before, during, and after their boating adventures. Our suggestion is that you give stability and comfort some serious consideration before you make a decision about which boat will suit you and your family.

If you're new to boating, you may want to consider a boat that's suitable for weekend and holiday cruising as opposed to a fully equipped liveaboard cruiser. That would be jumping in at the deep end. Again, your age will have a bearing on your decision; the younger you are, the more time you will have to correct any mistakes of judgment you may make when choosing your boat. Most people who enjoy boating will own three or more boats in their lifetime. You'll need to consider if your first boat is truly "the boat" or just a stepping-stone in that direction.

This Roberts 43 hull and deck was built by Custom Steel Boats of North Carolina.

A metal weekend cruiser can be as small as 25 feet (7.62 m) in length or as large as you can afford or handle with your family for crew. *My advice is never to own a boat that cannot be handled by a crew of two.* Most boats that are used regularly, as opposed to those that languish in the local marina, are crewed by a couple. How big is too big? We have many Roberts 53 sailboats successfully cruised by healthy and active (not necessarily young) couples. Neither crew member is required to have an outstanding physique. Modern equipment makes it possible for small persons to handle the sails and associated gear comfortably.

Before deciding on the size and type of vessel that will best suit your needs, you may wish to read more on the subject. See appendix 1 for a list of books that can help you to make an informed decision.

BUYING NEW

If you're considering a powerboat in Europe, you'll have a wide choice of metal boats. There are many builders of fine steel cruisers in

Holland, Britain, and elsewhere in the European Union. The off-the-shelf motor cruisers built by the Dutch are mainly intended for coastal and canal work. The quality of hull construction, interior joinery, and general finish is first-class.

Frank Ozannes built this steel Roberts 36 from scratch.

In the U.S. and Canada, there are a few builders of stock metal boats, most of whom build fine boats. Fortunately, the shoddy builders soon disappear; but make sure you are not one of their customers before they quit the scene. You may wish to contact one of our offices for a list of builders and kit manufacturers in your area. Visit our website at www.bruceroberts.com.

BUYING USED

Buying a used metal boat is another option, but the purchase of a secondhand boat can be fraught with traps for the unwary. The term "buyer beware" is never more apt than when buying a used boat. With any boat, age has its potential problems, so the younger the better. Naturally, there are cases where a well-built and maintained older metal boat is superior to a jerry-built nearly new vessel. Nevertheless, try to consider only boats that are less than five years old. This advice applies to any boat, no matter what material was used to build the hull.

Older boats with teak decks are to be viewed with added suspicion. Assume you may have to replace or extensively repair the decks, and factor this into your offer. Remember that a boat that needs extensive repairs and renovation will cost you nearly as much as building a new one, and the result will still be an older boat with a doubtful resale value.

Now, having painted that picture of doom and gloom, let us say that there are some fine used metal boats out there, but you'll have to sort through a considerable number of undesirable examples before you find your dream boat. We have owned many boats, mostly new, but the last two were used steel boats. Both these boats had been only lightly used before we purchased them. With one of our previous boats, *K*I*S*S*, a 28-foot (8.53 m) steel Spray design, we were able to recover all of our investment after two years' use.

If you're able to deal directly with the owner, you may avoid some of the pitfalls associated with this type of purchase. You must make sure you are absolutely satisfied *before* you hand

Radius-chine Roberts 64 built by Richard White and family of Québec, Canada.

over your money. Always hire a qualified surveyor to check out your boat before you part with any substantial amounts of cash.

In the U.S., boats are often documented with the coast guard, which proves ownership. Another way to check ownership is to contact the yacht's insurers and the harbormaster where the boat is kept. It's as well to remember that if you buy a boat from someone who doesn't have legal title to the vessel, and it's later reclaimed by its lawful owner, you may lose both the boat and your money. There's always a chance that the boat you're considering buying may be subject to a loan agreement, or it may form part of a legal dispute, or there may be some impediment in the title. Carefully check builders' certificates, bills of sale, and any other documentation that's offered to prove the current ownership.

Build carefully if you wish to emulate this Spray 40 sailed to the Antarctic by her owner-builder, Alan Sendall.

Surveys are essential when you're buying a used boat. You'll have to bear the costs of hauling for a full survey, but before you commit to that, here's a tip. To cut your potential costs, conduct a very detailed inspection of the interior, galley equipment, pumps, heaters, batteries, mast(s), rigging, sails, dinghy, and electronic equipment before you commit yourself to a full survey. Do it yourself, and don't be rushed. Take your time, and don't be afraid of being a nuisance. If you have trusted and knowledgeable friends, seek their help and advice at this early stage. Don't ignore advice because you've fallen in love with the boat. Assemble your facts, and on no account part with your cash before you are in possession of all the information about the boat's condition.

CUSTOM BUILDING

Many of you will be considering having your metal boat fully or partially built by professionals.

But most owners of metal boats are better informed than owners of vessels built from other materials, and many are capable of building or supervising the construction of their new vessel.

If you opt for a custom-built metal boat, you'll need the services of a competent naval architect or boat designer who is familiar with your chosen material. Fortunately, there are several designers who have either specialized in, or had experience in, designing boats in steel, aluminum, and (more recently) copper-nickel.

A custom-built boat need cost you no more than one from a production run. One way to save money is to act as your own contractor. You rent the building space and hire local workers to do the work. And here you reap another benefit of building in metal: any competent welder with experience in your particular metal can build a metal boat, given a detailed plan. All the materials and equipment, engines, electrical gear, and everything you need to build and equip your vessel can be purchased locally. If you go about this in the right way and buy most items at trade prices, you can save a great deal of money; perhaps this will enable you to

Starting with a precut kit can get your building project off to a good start. These kits are preshotblasted and primed.

"Tack and weld" kits allow you to form up a hull in days rather than weeks. The special weld primer used on many kits has many desirable features; see text.

afford a larger boat. A letterhead with your "Boatbuilding Company" name and address will go a long way toward convincing suppliers to give you trade discounts; make no mistake, they want your order, so make it easy for them to supply you at trade or discount prices.

STARTING FROM A KIT

In some areas, it's possible to purchase a kit of parts that have been precut from plate. Your job then is to assemble them into a hull, deck, and superstructure. Some designers (including this one) have the ability to prepare a special computer disk with the parts "nested" to allow more economical cutting. It's necessary, of course, for the company producing the kit to have the automatic, computerized cutting devices.

This service obviously costs a little more, but if you can afford it, you will find this a practical and perhaps even economical way of getting your project off to a quick start.

You alone can tell if the additional cost is justified; discuss these matters with the designer and with the company supplying the kit. The best of these precut kits are cut from shotblasted and primed steel coated with a specially formulated "weld primer." This coating doesn't give off fumes when you're welding. Another benefit of the weld primer is that there is little to clean up after welding.

HULL AND DECK OPTIONS

Many metal boat owners start with a hull, deck, and superstructure that have been built to their order and delivered to a suitable site for them to complete. Again, the owners buy all the equip-ment and finishing materials and then undertake as much of the labor as they wish. It's still a good idea to print your letterhead, as mentioned ear-lier, and buy at trade prices.

There are many books for those who want to build or partially build their own boats; you'll find some suggestions in appendix 1. If you don't want to do some jobs yourself, you can hire local electricians, mechanics, and other tradesmen to do them for you. You're in charge; you decide just how much or how little you want to do yourself. One thing is for sure: you'll save a great deal of money, and end up with a boat that you can eas-ily maintain. If you plan any extensive cruising, it's imperative that you be familiar with every as-pect of your vessel. What better way to learn about your boat than to work on the construc-tion? After studying all of the options, you can personally select all the equipment you need to complete your vessel.

A Voyager 493 radius-chine steel kit being assembled in Canada. Any competent welder can assemble one of these kits.

BUILDING FROM SCRATCH

Many thousands of owners have built their metal boats from scratch. These determined individuals have selected a design, purchased plans and basic materials, and built their own hulls, decks, and superstructures. Depending on the size of your boat, and whether you are building part-time or full-time, this process will add about 9 to 12 months to the overall building time.

There are many of you who have some welding experience. If you feel you would like to build from the ground up, don't be put off by the size of the project. Choose a design that has been especially drawn for the less-experienced builder; there are many designers who can provide you with suitable plans. Some designers, including us, provide full-size patterns for the frames and other parts of the hull structure.

We're often asked how long it takes an amateur to build a boat. Here are a couple of extremes. One Roberts 53 steel sailboat, including the hull, deck, and superstructure, was built and equipped ready for sailing by one Australian man and an occasional helper in the unbelievable time of 10 months. One has to assume that this person purchased many items ready-made. Another builder of the same design took 10 years part-time, but he made everything himself, including the sails. This tenacious builder even made patterns for his cast winches, and then finished them himself. Photographs taken while he was sailing his 53-foot (16.15 m) boat off the Australian coast show a happy couple enjoying their boat and cruising far from home. In fact, this builder has now completed a circumnavigation of the world and is back home in Germany. In our records there are hundreds of letters from builders who fall between these two extremes.

There have been many attempts by others and us to try and calculate building times for individual boats. In most cases this has proven a futile exercise. Factors such as starting from scratch versus buying a ready-built hull, the amount of help available from your partner and friends, how many hours a week you can devote to the project, and just how badly you want to get the job done all play a part.

This radius-chine aluminum Bermuda 385 was assembled from a cut-to-size kit by Robert Downie, of Ohio.

This steel Spray 40 shows several attractive and sensible features, including substantial pipe guardrails (stainless would have been nice) and a nicely laid teak deck. Note the wide covering board around the edge, a sturdy pair of stainless-steel bollards on the foredeck, a timber rubbing strip "stood off" the hull, a pair of stainless-steel bow fairleads, and a well laid out fore-cabin top.

FINANCE, OR PAY AS YOU BUILD?

Unless you are financially independent, you'll have to consider how you're going to pay for your new boat. If you buy a new or a used vessel, you may decide to finance *part* of the purchase. Many finance houses will give you a loan. Of course, you'll pay for this in interest, loan set-up fees, and so forth. You'll usually get a more favorable interest rate if you obtain a marine mortgage, as opposed to a simple bank or finance company loan. Many banks, savings and loan associations, and similar lenders will give you a loan for 10, 15, or 20 years to purchase a new boat. But before you sign any finance agreement, make sure you're aware of all the interest and other expenses involved.

Paying as you build will mean that not only will you save on the overall cost of the boat, but you'll also avoid interest and other associated charges. We've seen thousands of fine boats built or completed by owners who, on launching day, have had the extra thrill of knowing that their pride and joy was debt-free. Some builders even have it both ways—they build as much as they can afford (paying cash), and then they raise a loan, using the partly built boat as security.

BUILDING SITES

If you decide to build your own boat from a hull-and-deck package, or from scratch, you'll need a suitable building site. If you live in a warm area, a simple shelter will suffice. If your boat is to be built or completed in a cold climate, you'll need to consider a heated structure. In any case, you'll need some form of secure building in which to keep your tools and valuable supplies. Fortunately, when you're building a metal boat the lower perceived value of the materials will mean the need for security is relatively less than if you were building in fiberglass or plywood. This benefit lasts only until you start on the interior. Even if you're working outside, it's a good idea to keep your more valuable items out of sight, or maybe in more secure storage, until they can be properly installed in the boat.

Part of the advantage of building in a place that's secure, comfortable, and weatherproof is purely psychological; it will be easier to make the effort to work on the boat. Also, if you're paying rent on a building, you're more likely to get on with the job. If you're building outdoors, exposed to the elements, then you'll often have to stop work because it's rainy, cold, or windy. The disadvantages of building outdoors can add months to your building program.

To determine how much space you'll need to house your boatbuilding project, plan for a space 50 percent longer and 100 percent wider than the finished boat. For instance, if you're building a boat 40 feet long by 13 feet wide (12.19 by 3.96 m), your working space should ideally be 60 feet long by, say, 26 feet wide (18.29 by 7.92 m). When it

This Roberts 342, built in Europe, is a fine example of what you can achieve using the radius-chine technique to build in either steel or aluminum.

comes to handling plate and other construction members, you'll need plenty of space for tools and materials, as well as room to move around.

For maximum efficiency, plan your building site so that you spend as little time as possible walking from one area to another. The positioning of benches and frequently used tools will play a part in making a comfortable and productive workplace.

Your boatbuilding project should not be too far from home; this becomes even more important if you're only working part-time on the boat. Travel time can eat into valuable work time, and distance can be a deterrent to getting started evenings and weekends. Make sure also that your work site is accessible to the large trucks needed to deliver long lengths of plate and other necessary supplies. If you're working outdoors, be sure you have a flat, level site. Carrying tools and materials up even the smallest gradient can soon become a tiring exercise. And you'll be getting plenty of that already.

One obvious choice is to build your boat beside your house. Many fine boats of 65 feet

(19.81 m) have been built to our designs beside the owners' homes. To make this a practical proposition, you need to live on a large lot or in an isolated area.

Local building ordinances may govern just what you can do in your own backyard. Check them before you start building a shelter or erecting boat frames beside your house. Generally speaking, the farther you live from the center of town, the better chance you have of being able to build or complete a boat on your own property. If you're not committed to a mortgage, you may consider renting a suitable house away from the town center and building your boat on the grounds of your rented property. Obviously, you need to check with the owner first and get permission in writing before you sign the lease.

If you start with a hull and deck, all you may need in the way of a building is a toolshed; the hull can be heated, and the outside work can be completed in fine weather. Another advantage of starting with a ready-built shell or kit is that you may be able to complete the boat in your own yard. Metalworking is noisy, especially when you're

The Dutch love to build everything out of metal, as is evidenced by this attractive steel dinghy.

building the hull and deck. If you're building in a residential area, make sure the noise that can be heard outside the boat is kept to a minimum.

Here are a few suggestions for boatbuilding locations: your own yard; unused corners of marinas and boatyards; fenced in, but unused, industrial sites; beside or in an engineering business; inside old warehouses; inside or beside an old storage barn. These are just a few of the many possibilities and these locations can often be rented cheaply.

Make sure you think ahead to the day that the boat is completed and ready for launching. Can a low-load trailer and lifting crane get to your site and move your boat to the water? Have you surveyed the route? Check for low overhead wires and sharp corners in narrow streets. We've seen it all; there are hundreds of stories about boats being lifted over houses and hoisted from mountain sites by large helicopters. Some boats have been literally dragged through villages by willing helpers.

The ultimate metal boatbuilding project! This Waverunner 106 can be built in aluminum, steel, or a combination of both materials.

3
THE MATERIALS

STEEL

It bears repeating: steel is today's bargain boat-building material. If possible, you should choose preshotblasted and primed materials. The terms *sandblasting*, *gritblasting*, and *shotblasting* have similar meanings. The process for all three involves blasting the steel plate and bar stock with a grit to remove the impurities from the surface and preparing the material to receive the prime coating (see chapter 9, Gritblasting and Priming). If you're building outdoors, you'll lose some of the precoating. But the benefits of preprime coating are so positive that it's worth your consideration. It not only provides a cleaner working environment, but it will encourage you to arrange a temporary cover. When you're welding prime-coated steel, you should wear a protective mask to avoid inhaling the fumes released as the prime coating is burned off around the weld.

One of the main benefits of using shotblasted and primed materials is that when you have completed the hull and deck, you should not need to shotblast or gritblast the interior. This part of the blasting process is the most time-consuming and expensive. If you can avoid it by using primed, painted steel, it's worth the cost and effort of obtaining this material. You may wish to consider shotblasting and priming your metal before you start construction. Make sure you use weld primer that is specially formulated for use on the plate to be welded. One brand is

Sigma weld primer; other manufacturers should have similar products.

We used to think that building outdoors and using unprepared steel was a good idea, the theory being that the weather removed some of the mill scale and other surface impurities. But, as you will have gathered, we've changed our mind. You may take longer than you originally planned to build a boat with unprepared steel, and the wastage of metal through rusting could be a sizable factor in its life expectancy.

Steel Plate

When ordering the plate, make sure you specify "plate-mill" and not "strip-mill" plate. Plate-mill stock is plate that has never been coiled. Strip-mill is plate that has been rolled into large coils after manufacture; later, the steel is unrolled and sold as flat plate. But it has a "memory," so it won't be absolutely flat and unstressed before you start to bend it. If you're forced to use strip-mill material, try to ascertain the natural curve of the plate, and use it to your advantage.

Our choice for steel boat building is plate with a low-to-medium carbon content. You'll find there are many different grades of steel, but we recommend low-carbon steel with a carbon content of between 0.15 and 0.28 percent. The highest carbon content acceptable to most classification authorities is 0.28 percent, so we recommend you stay within the range quoted above. Low-carbon steel is available in various shapes, strips, and plate, and has good welding characteristics. As code numbers vary from country to country, you should seek advice from your steel supplier to ensure that you receive the correct materials as suggested above. Lloyd's A-grade shipbuilding steel will be one of your preferred choices if you live in Europe, or build from a precut kit.

The plate thickness will be specified in your plans. Remember that it's harder to avoid distortion when welding materials that are thinner than ⅛ inch (3 mm). Even this thickness should be restricted to decks and cabins, as well as to hulls on boats under 35 feet (10.66 m) in length. Your designer will specify the plate thickness recommended for your boat. When you're building small steel boats, it's better to reduce the amount of framing than to reduce the plate thickness.

Some builders increase the plate thickness without consulting the designer, which, in a steel boat, can have disastrous results. If you are unable to obtain plating as specified in your plans, always contact the designer for advice. Changing the plating thickness may require rescheduling the spacing and sizing of the framing.

As you may be responsible for the quality of the steel being used in your boat, you should be aware of the common defects. Check for "wavy" areas in the sheet. This defect can appear as small, uneven areas of a "wavy" appearance. Another defect is "rolled-in mill scale," which is caused when impurities on the surface of the plate are rolled into the surface. Buckles or kinks in the plate can be caused by improper handling after manufacture. You may also find thin areas in the center and ends of pipe.

Cor-Ten

Avoid materials such as Cor-Ten or high-tensile steels; they have limited or no boatbuilding applications. Some designers have recommended Cor-Ten in the past, but this steel contains traces of copper, which tends to encourage corrosion in salt water rather than inhibit it. Cor-Ten was developed for use in industrial applications such as

Table 3-1. Mild steel plate in pounds per square foot and kilos per meter.		
Thickness	Pounds per sq. ft.	Kilos per sq. meter
3 mm	–	24.5
⅛ in.	5.10	–
10 gauge	5.52	–
9 gauge	6.10	–
⁵⁄₃₂ in.	6.37	–
4 mm	–	33.5
8 gauge	6.75	–
7 gauge	7.30	–
³⁄₁₆ in.	7.65	–
6 gauge	7.97	–
5 mm	–	39.5
5 gauge	8.70	–
⁷⁄₃₂ in.	8.92	–
4 gauge	9.14	–
6 mm	–	48.5
3 gauge	9.77	–
¼ in.	10.20	–

water tanks on farm properties. While it resists corrosion in a salt-free atmosphere, it doesn't have good corrosion resistance when it's immersed in water, especially seawater.

Cor-Ten is more expensive than mild steel and it needs to be welded using copper-clad, continuous-feed electrodes and argon-arc. We do *not* recommend Cor-Ten or other specialty steels for boatbuilding.

Stainless Steel

Occasionally, we're asked about the possibility of building a boat of stainless steel; the simple answer is: Don't! This material has no place below the waterline on most boats. The problem is "shielding" corrosion caused by oxygen starvation, which, in turn, will promote crevice corrosion. The important factor is the amount of oxygen in contact with the surface of the steel; one part of the steel must not be starved of oxygen while another part has it available. This phenomenon is known as the "oxygen differential," and it will set up an electrochemical cell that will lead to rapid deterioration of the metal.

Stainless steel is ideal for deck fittings, chainplates, and stanchions. Stainless is also required as a liner in areas where dock and anchor lines would soon wear off the paint. Always paint 2 inches (50 mm) onto the stainless to prevent galvanic action between any defects in the painted mild steel and the uncoated stainless fitting.

The types of stainless steel most commonly used in boatbuilding fall into the 300 series, namely 302, 304, and 316. The 316 grade is considered the best for marine use and should be used wherever ultimate strength and freedom from corrosion are required.

When the quoted number is followed by the letter "L," it indicates a low carbon content; this feature allows welds with good corrosion resistance by avoiding loss of chromium at the grain boundaries. The free-machining grades, type 303 or 303e, should never be used in seawater because they corrode. These specialized steels contain sulfate particles that facilitate the machining operation; however, the particles create a surface with numerous built-in alloys to particle galvanic cells. (See chapter 12, Corrosion Prevention.)

Buying Plate

The price of steel plate varies from supplier to supplier, so shop around. Generally speaking, the more you buy, the lower the price, by weight. We recommend that you order all the plate, stringer materials, other flat bar, and angle at one time. Many designers supply a material list with the plans and it's wise to compare this list with the drawings, so you'll have a better understanding of the construction procedures. Use your material list to obtain quotes from as many suppliers as possible. In most cases, 20 percent should be allowed for wastage.

Stock sizes of sheet are 8 by 4 feet (2.50 by 1.25 m) and 6 by 3 feet (2 by 1 m) but some stockists can supply sheets 10 or 12 feet (3 or 3.50 m) long. (Note that the metric sizes here are rounded

out to the most likely available sizes.) Another consideration is that the steel supplier may make additional charges for larger or unusual sizes of plate, and the delivery costs may also be higher. The size of your boat and the steel-handling equipment you have available may decide the sheet sizes for your project.

It's better to tack-weld your plates into as long a length as practical before installing them on the hull—you'll achieve a much fairer hull by following this practice. The same advice applies to stringers and other longitudinal framing.

Steel Framing

Framing includes the transverse frames, stringers, stem, and backbone. For small-to-medium-sized boats, you can make the framing from flat-bar stock. For the deckbeams and cabintop beams, it's preferable to use L-angle or T-bar (flange down) as this provides a suitable cavity for the insulation material. It allows the lining materials to be fastened to the underside of the flange.

Hull frames may be flat bar or L-angle. Our objections to angle used to be that it was more difficult to keep the rust out of the angle. More recently, however, we recommend that all hulls have sprayed-in foam insulation. Where the spray-in-place foam is installed, there's much less chance of rust forming around the frames. Because of weight considerations alone, we would not recommend angle frames in boats under 40 feet (12.19 m). Heavy-displacement boats and larger vessels can carry the extra weight and also will benefit from the extra strength of the angle frames. We have just completed plans for a new Spray Pilot House 40, and in this case I have suggested L-angle or T-bar frames as an option. The presence of the flange will assist in the lining and fitting out process. On flat-bar frames, timber strips are screwed to the frames to accept the lining materials.

As mentioned above, the stringers, stem, and backbone will almost always be fabricated from flat-bar stock. Occasionally, solid round bar is used for the hull chines; there will be more on this subject elsewhere in this text. Web floors (otherwise known as "solid floors" or gussets at the bottom of the frames), are best formed using plate that is the same thickness as the frames.

BRONZE

Bronze is an alloy of copper, tin, and varying small amounts of other elements. It's a fine boatbuilding metal and it has been used in marine applications from time immemorial. In Roman times, bronze was a prized alloy and had many uses. The exact combination of metals used to make the bronze alloy will depend on its intended use. Copper is the main ingredient, and tin usually accounts for 5 to 10 percent of the mix. Bronze will often take its name from the third metal in the alloy; for instance, phosphor bronze contains about 5 percent tin and 0.5 percent phosphorus, and it is suitable for use in the marine environment. Alloys of aluminum bronze, or nickel-aluminum bronze, are often used for propellers.

ALUMINUM

Aluminum has been available for over a century, but it's only in the past 40 years that it has been widely used for boatbuilding. Pure aluminum is a soft metal and not suitable for most commercial applications, let alone boatbuilding. There are many aluminum alloys for various applications but only a few suitable for marine use.

Some of the metals alloyed with aluminum are chromium, copper, iron, manganese, magnesium, and zinc. Small amounts of these metals are used to improve the industrially pure aluminum. For marine use, the main addition to pure aluminum is 4 to 5 percent of magnesium.

Because there's no universal grading system for aluminum, you should check your local suppliers for advice. At right are some type numbers and their recommended usage. We have grouped them into U.K. and U.S. areas; most of the rest of the world follows one system or the other.

The 5000 series and, in particular, material with the 5086 designation, is the metal most commonly used for boatbuilding. There are several different numbers in the 5000 series and it's

worth checking with the aluminum manufacturer in your country so you get firsthand advice. Don't be fobbed off by unscrupulous suppliers or merchants who may try to sell you what they have in stock.

The 5000 series has excellent resistance to salt water, is ductile, and retains its high strength when welded. In some cases, you may choose aluminum with one designation for hull plating, another for framing, and still another for decks and superstructure.

When you're ready to order your aluminum materials, it's always recommended that you make one bulk purchase. As with other metals, and indeed all your boatbuilding requirements, it's always best to buy in bulk. If you can find another builder with similar requirements, then a group order is recommended.

At the same time as you are ordering your aluminum plate and framing materials, you should order the filler wire for your MIG welder. The most common wire is 5356, which is compatible with most aluminum alloys used in boatbuilding including 5052, 5086, 6061, and 6063. The 5386 wire can be used to weld these alloys to themselves or to dissimilar alloys. (See notes about spool sizes in chapter 5, Welding.) It's most

---

Table 3-2.
Weights of aluminum plate, etc.

UK.	hull plate	BS 1477 NP8
	frames and stringers	BS 1476 NE8
	superstructures	BS 1470 NS6

U.S.	hull plate	5086 H116
	frames and stringers	5086 H116
	decks cabin structures	5086-32

Weights of aluminum plate in pounds per sq. ft.

$1/16$ in.	0.90
$1/8$ in.	1.76
$3/16$ in.	2.64
$1/4$ in.	3.52
$5/16$ in.	4.53
$3/8$ in.	5.44

Table 3-3.
Comparative strengths of different materials.

	Steel	Aluminum	Copper-Nickel	Fiberglass	Wood
yield strength in PSI	36,000–42,000	18,000–40,000	15,000	10,000–15,000	12,000–20,000
tensile strength in PSI	60,000–70,000	23,000–47,000	40,000–78,000	15,000–34,000	16,000–27,000
compression strength in PSI	60,000	32,000	45,000	Fair	2,000–13,000
shear strength in PSI	23,000	17,000	20,000	Low	700–3,000
modulus of elasticity ($\times 10^6$)	30	10	19.6–22	2.8	0.7–2.3
hardness (Mohs' Scale)	7	4	5.5 approx.	1	1–3

important to keep your welding wire clean and to use the spool as soon as it is opened. Store the wire in a dry area, and discard any dirty or contaminated material.

In this book, we'll mainly consider welded aluminum, as this covers the method by which most boats are built from this material. There are other building methods, however, including small boats pressed out of a single sheet; these are popular in Australia, where they're affectionately known as *tinnies*. Riveted construction is still used to build some smaller aluminum boats. Aluminum boats have also been formed by explosive techniques, but this and other offbeat methods are outside the scope of this book.

For transverse frames you may choose either flat bar, L-angle bar, T-bar or flat/round-top bar. The latter is sometimes used for longitudinal stringers. For longitudinal framing, stringers, and chine bars (if fitted), we prefer flat bar, but the final choice of scantling sections should be left to the designer of your particular boat.

COPPER-NICKEL

Copper, one of the most noble metals, has excellent resistance to corrosion in the atmosphere and in freshwater. When combined with nickel to form copper-nickel, it has superior resistance to saltwater corrosion. These features, coupled with its excellent antifouling properties, make it ideal for building hulls.

Copper-nickel is readily available in sheet form and generally is produced in two main grades. The two copper-nickel alloys with good track records for boatbuilding are 90-10, an alloy of 90 percent copper and 10 percent nickel, and 70-30, which contains 70 percent copper and 30 percent nickel. Both these alloys include small amounts of iron and manganese. Generally, these alloys are nonmagnetic but in the 90-10 alloys some magnetic response may be detected, depending on how the alloy is processed by the manufacturer. For most marine applications, including framing and plating, the 90-10 alloy is recommended.

Copper-nickels are ductile and have excellent resistance to fracture under impact-loading conditions. Both the above-mentioned alloys are single-phase, solid-solution alloys that cannot be hardened with heat treatment; they can, however, be strengthened by work hardening. Both alloys are easily fabricated and welded. When welding, a 70-30 consumable is preferred for the 90-10 alloys because it gives a weld that is galvanically nobler than the base metal. Copper-nickel can be welded to steel, and in that case a consumable of 65 percent nickel and 35 percent copper is preferred. Throughout the book, the term *consumable* refers to the welding rods, wire,

Pretty Penny: A Copper-Nickel Boat

Pretty Penny was designed and commissioned by Alan Beckett, an engineer and sailing enthusiast whose aim was to create a maintenance-free sailing yacht. The material chosen for her construction was 90-10 copper-nickel. She was built by Arma Marine Engineering Co. Ltd., in the U.K., and launched in 1979. In October 1995, 16 years after she was built, she was hauled and thoroughly surveyed for the first time since her launch. An invitation was issued to C. A. Powell, a consultant metallurgist, to examine the boat. The salient facts from his subsequent report are given below in condensed and, in some cases, paraphrased form.

The boat is 31 feet (9.45 m) in length overall, with a beam of 9 feet (2.74 m) and a draft of 5 feet (1.52 m). Its gross tonnage is 7.66 tons. The framing, hull, and superstructure plating were fabricated using 90-10 copper-nickel. The hull is slightly magnetic, which indicates not all the iron and alloy composition is in solution. The hull is plated in $1/8$-inch (3 mm) plate, and the same materials were used to form the L-angle framing material.

This boat has never been painted inside or out. The liferails, pulpit, and propeller shaft are made from stainless steel. The propeller is a regular off-the-shelf bronze version, so the exact composition of the metal is unknown. The deck was originally covered with Trackmark, but the adhesive failed and this was replaced with regular marine deck paint.

Since the launch, she has been afloat continuously and moored for the greater part of the time in the River Swale, at Uplees, off the Thames Estuary. For the first three years, she remained free of fouling, but since then her owner has found it necessary to scrub her at least once a year. For the most part, the form of fouling was weed and barnacles, mainly concentrated at about 6 to 12 inches (150 to 300 mm) below the waterline, and quite easily removed by a scraper. She has a 10 hp Volvo single-cylinder engine and sails well with a clean bottom, managing 5 knots in Force 4 to 5 conditions.

In 1995, the yacht was removed from the water for the first time since her launch 16 years previously and inspected. Prior to inspection, Beckett cleaned the hull for the first time during the year. There was a grass layer, but hardly any barnacles were noticed. The grass was loosely adhered and a piece of wood cleaned this away in a few minutes. The yacht had been sailed very little during the previous 12 months. At the time, the surveyor concluded that the craft could be considered in "almost new condition, with the hull plating in the same condition as when she was originally built."

Overall, the *Pretty Penny* was in excellent condition. The hull is a unique testimony to the corrosion performance of copper-nickel in a marine environment over 16 years, both above and below the water. The stainless-steel rails and rigging seemed in excellent condition and were still looking bright and shiny. There did not appear to be any galvanic problems with the copper-nickel connections. Esthetically, the copper color above the waterline might not appeal to all when compared to painted vessels. The original concept was to produce a maintenance-free hull and, without doubt, this area is in perfect condition.

The owner was concerned that he might be getting thinning of the hull around the waterline, so he asked a firm of specialists to take ultrasonic measurements. This survey report showed that there appeared to be some thinning of the original 3 mm down to 2.7 mm at the waterline on the main part of the hull, and 2 mm near the bow. The owner speculated that some of the material in the bow area was lost by overzealous grinding during the construction stage.

When considering the waterline, and ignoring the grinding effects during fabrication, the corrosion rate of the hull at the bow averaged 0.019 mm per year. The general corrosion rate for immersed copper-based alloys, given for guidance, is generally in the range of 0.025–0.0025 mm per year. In practice, immersed corrosion rates would be expected to reduce *(continued next page)*

Pretty Penny, an unpainted copper-nickel sailboat. After 16 years on a tidal mooring in England, this boat shows little fouling. For the first three years she remained free of fouling, but subsequently she was scrubbed once a year.

(continued from previous page) with time as the surface films matured. The thinning near the bow appears to be in excess of the norm. The speed of the vessel would not suggest the possibility of erosion. The thinning at the waterline and particularly at the stem and bow has been noticed in other boat studies for copper-nickel and will need to be examined more closely in future and verified. In this case, I would suspect that the thinning near the waterline was due to natural wastage of the material, while the thinning near the bow was probably due to grinding during the construction. It is, however, a useful observation for perhaps incorporating greater thickness for the bow waterline area in future boat design.

The antifouling behavior is ideal: the boat was free of fouling for three years and thereafter required a scrubbing once a year. The vessel is not very actively used of late, and such behavior is in line with observations of fouling build-up in quiet waters. The sailing speeds may also have been too low to effectively remove the fouling once it had occurred. It is encouraging to note that the fouling, once formed, was easily removed by using a wooden scraper.

Pretty Penny created a lot of interest at that time, and we, too, were invited to inspect the interior and make a detailed study of the construction techniques used to build the hull, decks, and superstructure. Our enthusiasm grew as we inspected each detail of the methods used to frame and plate the vessel. The interior framing was not covered, and this made a detailed inspection possible. The framing was angle that had been simply bent from strips of the same material as was used to build the hull, namely ⅛-inch (3 mm) plate. We were very impressed with this boat and it, together with other experiences with this material, has inspired us to prepare preliminary calculations on existing designs to enable them to be built in copper-nickel. If you're considering copper-nickel, you'll need deep pockets. The cost of the material is about 10 times the price of steel. General fabrication and welding is also more expensive.

or strips that are used to join two or more parts of the metal structure.

Because copper-nickel has good corrosion resistance, it's best to use angle for frames and deck beams because this makes it simple to fasten the interior linings. These and other framing members can easily be formed out of sheet material that has been cut into suitably sized strips. By adjusting the frame spacing, it's often possible to use the same thickness of sheet material for the plating and the frames.

The protective surface film that forms naturally and quickly on copper-nickel exhibits excellent corrosion resistance in seawater. This feature, together with its natural antifouling properties, means that no paint or coatings are required below the waterline.

Although it's more expensive than other metal boatbuilding materials, copper-nickel is worth consideration if you're planning extended cruising in areas where fouling is prevalent. If you consider metal's ease of working, low maintenance costs, and other desirable features, you may find that it suits your requirements.

BRASS

Brass has no place as a structural member on any boat, and should never be used in place of bronze. You may have a few decorative items—lamps and the like—that are made of brass. You will know what they are because you will be continually polishing them to remove the tarnish that quickly forms in the marine environment. Brass is an alloy of copper and zinc.

Brass made of 60 percent copper and 40 percent zinc loses all its surface zinc in saltwater, and is soon reduced to a useless mess. Beware of cheap fittings imported from the Far East. They may be sold as bronze, and look like bronze, but more often they aren't bronze. If in doubt, select only materials from known U.S. manufacturers.

OTHER BOATBUILDING METALS

Monel Metal

The ultimate marine metal is Monel metal. It's rather expensive, otherwise it would be more widely used. It's not used for building complete boats but it's perfect for fittings where ultimate strength and machinability is required. There are two main alloys, including the regular version that contains 67 percent nickel and 28 percent copper. This alloy is ideal for propeller shafting, where its corrosion resistance and hardwearing qualities are best appreciated. There may be some doubt about the use of Monel shafting in steel boats, however, and it may be better to use 316 stainless for your shafting requirements.

The variant "K" is nonmagnetic and is often used for special purposes. Often, Monel is used as the main propeller shafting on minesweepers. They can afford it. It's also used to protect compasses on boats and aircraft. When more boats were built of timber, and before the wood/epoxy technique was developed, Monel screws were sometimes used on the finest craft, either to fasten the hull planking or in other important parts of the structure. The alloy contains aluminum

Two young men looking for adventure built this steel Roberts 38 in New Zealand. The interior is as attractively finished as the exterior you see here.

and titanium as well as nickel and copper. It's a great metal, but it's not important to amateur builders of metal boats.

Magnesium

Freshwater anodes are made from magnesium. It may surprise you to learn that protection from galvanic and other corrosion is necessary in *all* types of water, including salt-free environments. Anodes of zinc are not as effective as those of magnesium in freshwater. Conversely, if you move your boat from freshwater to salt water for more than two or three weeks, you will need to change to zinc anodes; the magnesium ones will rapidly disappear. Copper-nickel hulls do not require galvanic protection in freshwater or seawater.

Zinc

In its pure form, zinc is used for anodes. In salt water, it's the ideal material for this use. In freshwater, as mentioned previously, magnesium is better. A small quantity of zinc is present in many metals. Zinc is also used in paint primers, paints, and other coatings.

LEAD

With its dense consistency and very low melting point, lead has many uses for the boatowner. The most obvious use for this material is for the ballast, but don't be tempted simply to pour molten lead into the keel of your metal boat. Even heavy steel keels can buckle if lead is installed in this manner. (See Ballast and Trimming in chapter 15.)

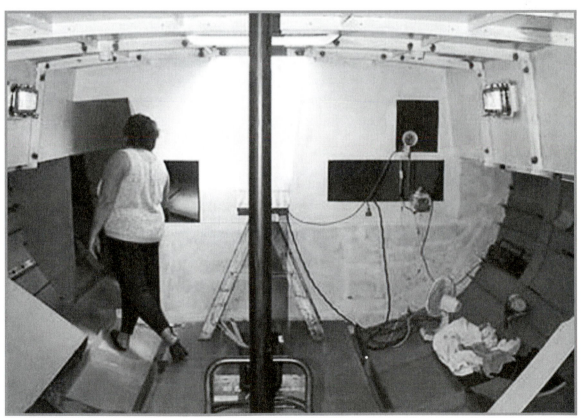

Make sure to thoroughly paint the interior of your metal hull before you start the fit-out. Most corrosion in steel boats starts on an unprotected interior surface. Pre-prime-coated steel can give your hull a great start in life.

4
TOOLS AND SAFETY EQUIPMENT

Because of today's emphasis on working safely, you'll want to consider what tools and equipment you need to build, maintain, or repair your metal boat. One of the best and least expensive safety items is a clean work area. Avoid leaving anything lying about that is not in use or needed in the immediate future. These are the things that can trip you up, slash you, or otherwise cause bodily injury. Working with metal naturally produces hazards of varying degrees, but you can protect yourself by having the correct safety equipment. Under no circumstances sell yourself short in this area.

PROTECTIVE CLOTHING

Always wear a proper industrial safety helmet. You never know when something may fall, or be dropped on your head. Safety goggles are a must. They should have side guards to protect you against flying metal particles when you're cutting, grinding, or chipping. You'll need a face shield and the various lenses. Don't forget your ears; remember that good earmuffs are essential. A respirator is required. Invest in good coveralls or a boiler suit. A leather apron and gloves with cuffs are definite requirements. One of our customers built a steel Roberts 38 in a Florida nudist colony. We often wondered how he dealt with the weld splatter. Wear steel-toed shoes or boots, not sneakers, around your metal boat building project.

Protective hand cream and an adequate first-aid kit are essential. Have the first-aid kit handy because you can't anticipate when it may be required in a hurry; its presence may save your life or at least prevent a minor injury developing into a major one. Make sure you have plenty of eyewash on hand. A good-sized fire extinguisher and an industrial vacuum cleaner are other essential items of safety equipment.

Arc welders are relatively safe pieces of equipment, but potentially lethal alternating-current electricity powers them, so you can't afford to treat them casually. Your alternating current (AC) supply will be 110-volt, 220-volt, 240-volt, or perhaps a larger three-phase supply. Make no mistake: all these voltages can be lethal.

This builder of a Tom Thumb 26 found an angle grinder ideal for cutting the plates. Accuracy of $1/16$ inch (1 mm) was achieved with most cuts.

Watching the arc with the naked eye is not recommended. Even if you look at the arc for a short period with unprotected eyes, you can get "arc eye," which is very uncomfortable and feels like sand around your eyeballs. Assuming that you, as the welder, *always* use a mask, then it must be the assistant or casual onlooker who will need protection.

TOOLS FOR BUILDING STEEL BOATS

Many of the tools you'll require for building in all types of metal are those common to steel boat building, so we'll look at this list first. Later, we'll follow up with information on the additional tools you'll require for building in aluminum or copper-nickel.

If you have more-than-adequate funds, no doubt you'll find many exotic and expensive labor-saving devices to keep you happy. Fortunately for the rest of us, a modern metal boat can be built with relatively few inexpensive tools, most of which are readily available in all parts of the world. The metal used to build a steel, aluminum, or copper-nickel boat is relatively thin, so it can be easily handled, cut, formed, and welded. Many tools are common to the three main metals. The few specialized tools required by each type are available and familiar to those who possess the necessary skills to work with that particular material.

A check of the yellow pages of your telephone directory will provide sources for all

For bending deck beams, stem, and frames as required, you can make this simple device from a hydraulic jack and an H-frame formed from angle bar.

the tools and equipment you need. Another source is the "For Sale" sections of local newspapers. Perhaps a "Wanted" advertisement in the correct classified section will bear fruit. Flea markets, jumble sales, and "yard" or "garage sales," are all good sources of reasonably priced tools.

In the case of radius-chine hulls, we recommend that you have the relatively small amount of radius plating rolled by a professional metal shop. This service is available in most areas.

John Reid built this Centennial Spray 36 in England. Reid used a garden roller to roll the plates— no mean effort, even considering his considerable boatbuilding experience. This perfectly fair hull was being fitted out at Iron Wharf Boatyard, in Faversham, Kent, England.

Our plans include details of tools that you can make yourself. Most builders make many of their metal-handling tools, often inventing new ones as required.

A simple tool that you can make yourself will serve well to bend deck beams, the stem, and other smaller parts that need to be formed. This bending device is made up of a suitably powerful hydraulic jack and a simple H-frame formed from angle bar.

Included in the list of small tools you'll need, are a variety of metal-working hammers and mallets, (including chipping hammers), an assortment of clamps (some of which you can make yourself), bolt cutters, a metal-worker's vise and a selection of sawhorses. A good portable drill is essential and a drill press will be useful. You'll need a large selection of high-quality metal bits, cold chisels, and metal files. Other tools include a bench grinder, a crimper, a power hacksaw, a jig saw, a straightedge, and tinsnips.

Oxyacetylene Equipment

There are several ways to cut steel and most other metals. Steel was traditionally cut with the gas torch, or oxyacetylene torch, and although this method is still widely used, more sophisticated and affordable methods are now available. Nevertheless, the oxyacetylene torch and its associated bottles and gauges will find many uses around a metal boat building project, although it's not a necessity. The gas torch is quick, efficient, and low in operating costs. With this equipment you'll need a light-to-medium-duty kit with a 90-degree angle, and specialized cutting tips.

The basic oxy kit consists of the cutting torch, tips of various sizes, a set of gas regulators, a flint lighter, goggles, a special wrench, couplings for oxygen and acetylene tanks, and two lengths of hose to lead from the tanks to the torch. This package could cost less than $300 (£200) if you're able to pick up used equipment at a favorable price. A small cart to hold the bottles would be useful; you can either buy one or make one yourself. The cylinders are usually

leased from the gas supplier and you'll only need to pay for the refills.

The oxyacetylene torch cuts metal through a rapid oxidization process in two continuous steps. While the torch heats a small area of metal to a cherry-red color (about 1,500 to 1,600°F), a small stream of pressurized oxygen is directed from a central tip within the torch against the hot metal. The stream of oxygen causes the metal to "burn" rapidly and the metal separates as the torch is moved along the line of the desired cut. There are many different cutting tips and they can be used to influence the size, speed, and accuracy of the cut. A special plate-cutting, drag-step tip can cut steel plate from ⅛ to ¼ inch (3 to 6 mm) thick with precision at the rate of about 2 feet (61 cm) per minute. The resulting cut using this tip will be between 1/16 and 3/16 inch (1.5 and 4.5 mm) wide. Using this equipment is something of an art form and considerable experience is required to achieve the type of fine cutting that is required when plating your hull.

The main drawback is that torch cuts are rough around the edges and usually need some cleaning up before they are suitable for welding to other parts. You should avoid the disgusting habit of some low-cost builders who plate the hulls oversize and simply torch off the overlaps at the chine. The oxyacetylene torch can also be used for some specialized welding operations, but for boatbuilding it's better to use the other equipment discussed below, such as arc (stick), metal inert gas (MIG) or tungsten inert gas (TIG) welders (see chapter 5). Reserve the oxy equipment for cutting where precision is not required.

Angle Grinder

You should buy the best-quality angle grinder you can find; it will get a lot of use. This is a much-used tool in boat construction and can perform a variety of jobs, ranging from cutting lengths of flat and round bar to smoothing out the edges of torch-cut plate. You can use this tool to bevel thicker plates by grinding off the excess metal before welding. Fitted with wire brushes, it can be used to clean off rust, mill scale, and weld splatter. Another use is to smooth off the welds on the hull topsides and superstructure. (Take note, though, that we, along with most classification societies, do not recommend grinding welds below the waterline.)

When you fit your angle grinder with a special wheel, it can be used to cut the slots in the frames to accept the stringers. Another use is to make many small cuts in metal bar. This feature is useful for making frames, sniping off the ends of stringers, and similar tasks. Don't use your grinder for heavy-duty cutting; the grinding/cutting wheels don't last very long. For instance, when you use it to cut ⅛-inch (3 mm) plate, you can expect to get only about 12 to 15 feet (3.5 to 4.5 m) from a single blade. When you use it for cutting, consider your angle grinder to be more of a convenience tool than a fully fledged cutting device.

Buy a 7- to 9-inch (178 to 228 mm) heavy-duty, commercial-grade angle grinder. Make sure it has heavy-duty switches and a high-efficiency cooling fan. Don't order this item by mail. You need to hold the grinder, see how it balances in your hands, and feel the weight.

You'll be holding this tool for many hours, so make sure it feels right if you want long and trouble-free service.

Nibbler

A nibbler will cut thinner plate, but it's an expensive tool, especially considering its limited use on most boatbuilding projects. You could rent one if you really find it useful. This tool is like a pair of electric scissors, and it slices through thin metal by taking small nibbles, hence the name. The nibble is an up-and-down punching action and makes a cut about ¼ inch (6 mm) wide. When it's used by an experienced operator, this tool can produce a smooth cut with clean edges. The cutting rate will vary, depending on the thickness of the metal, but on ⅛-inch (3 mm) steel or copper-nickel it can cut about 2 to 4 feet (60 to 120 cm) per minute.

Plasma Cutter

A plasma cutter is ideal for cutting plate and other steel and metal sections, so rent or buy the best you can afford. This device cuts without

This radius-chine Roberts 434 was built by Topper Hermonson, in Florida. This boat has cruised extensively, including a complete circumnavigation and several Atlantic crossings.

distortion and can be used to trim plates in position. In the hands of an experienced operator, the plasma cutter produces a clean, sharp cut without any sign of distortion. The cutting action is very fast, and steel or copper-nickel plate up to $\frac{5}{16}$ inch (8 mm) in thickness presents no problems for this device. It is not suitable for aluminum, however. The narrow cut of $\frac{1}{8}$-inch (3 mm) makes for neat and efficient cutting. Be forewarned, however, that the plasma cutter uses a fair amount of electricity, and the cutting tips do not have a long life. This tool is especially suited to cutting plate, and it finds angle and other shapes something of a problem, so alternative cutting methods should be used for those sections.

In the U.S., Hypertherm manufactures the portable Powermax 800, which, it is claimed, can cut all metals up to $\frac{1}{2}$ inch (12 mm) thick. (See appendix 2.)

TOOLS FOR ALUMINUM BOAT BUILDING

You can usually cut aluminum either by sawing it or by shearing it. For straight cuts of material up to $\frac{1}{4}$ inch (6 mm) thick, you can use the same power guillotines used for cutting steel. Remember to replace the holding-down pads with plastic ones that won't mark the softer aluminum. Pay particular attention to keeping knives sharp;

blunt cutters will burr the edges of the metal. Nibblers can be used to cut aluminum up to $\frac{1}{4}$ inch (6 mm) thick.

Band Saw

A deep-throated band saw fitted with a narrow (say $\frac{1}{2}$-inch or 12 mm) blade will be capable of cutting a wide range of thicknesses. The band saw should be set to run at 2,000 to 5,000 feet (600 to 1,500 m) per minute; the slower speeds will be needed for the thicker plates. A band saw with variable speeds is preferred, but the older heavy types used for cutting timber are satisfactory.

Table Saw

For cutting straight lines, a regular table saw fitted with carbide-tipped blades will give perfect results. Be sure to provide lubrication with a kerosene-oil mixture or suitable vegetable oil; this will make the cuts easier and also increase the life of the blade. A portable jigsaw can also be very useful for making on-the-job cuts. Remember, a spray of lubricant will make the cutting go easier for most tools.

Power Handsaw

A hand power saw or Skilsaw can be a most useful cutting device when working with aluminum. Fit your saw with a special blade designed for cutting this metal. This blade will have a tooth face rake angle of zero degrees. If you use a guide clamped in position, you can make long straight cuts with this saw. For cutting sheet or framing to length, and in fact for almost all shell and frame cutting, this is a most versatile tool. Treat the hand power saw with utmost respect; the chips thrown off the sawn material are not only hot, but also sharp. Always

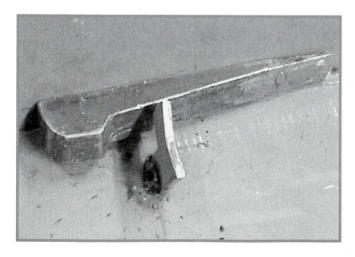

Many tools you'll need for building in metal can be made or converted from other uses; wedges and steel dogs like these will find many uses.

Pieces of metal tacked and stitched across a join in the plates can help you produce a fair seam weld.

wear a full-face mask when working with this tool. Make sure that the remainder of your body is suitably protected from flying chips. Use kneepads if you're kneeling while operating this saw. You'll need to take extra care when you're cutting ³⁄₁₆-inch (4 mm) or thinner plate; the blade will tend to jump out of the cut, especially at the beginning. It's best to do a plunge start just inside the first part of the cut. This allows the blade to enter the material along the line of cut, and can avoid the kickback.

Router

You'll find a router fitted with a single-flute, carbide-tipped cutter useful for cutting uniform holes such as lightening holes. You'll discover that this tool has many uses in the building of your aluminum boat. As with all powered equipment, though, it has to be handled with care. A small electric router, or an air-powered one, is usually used for gouging out the back of welds or removing contaminated ones.

Planes

Planing is possible with either a carpenter's hand plane or an electric hand planer with carbide-tipped cutters. Any edge can be planed, and this is a useful feature where a sawn edge would show on the finished boat and planing will provide a superior finish. A plane can also be most useful in beveling the edges of plate.

Press Brake

For forming aluminum, hand folders will handle the thinner gauges, but for serious bending you need a press brake with a bed of about 8 feet (2.4 m). The press brake is a strong, hydraulically or mechanically powered forming machine used to crease or bend metal. This machine comes in a variety of sizes and is found in most professional metal shops. The benefit of using this machine is that it can reduce the number of welds required. For instance, a cockpit bottom and sides could be formed in one piece. If you're building a one-off aluminum boat and you don't own a press brake, you'll need to find a subcontractor to handle this work. Never forget that when you're building in aluminum it makes sense to take advantage of the easier handling of this material. Forming up large multisurfaced parts by bending sheet into various angles can save a lot of welding and grinding.

Plate Rolls

Bending rolls are used to form plate into a permanent curve and can be operated by hand or power. A typical roll consists of two lower power-driven rolls and one adjustable upper idler roll. As the shape suggests, this type of roll is called a pyramid roll and is widely used in building round-bilge boats. The method of operation is that the metal is inserted between the upper roll and the

The Waverunner 38 has been built in many different versions; this one was built in Ireland for use in a local charter operation.

lower two rolls. By adjusting the pressure on the upper idler roll, you can vary the resulting amount of curvature in the plate. Although these rolls operate at slow speeds, remember that loose clothing or carelessly placed limbs can get caught. This could be extremely dangerous especially in the power-driven versions.

Explosive Forming

This method has been used to form various aluminum shapes including boat hulls. Briefly, the process consists of making a concrete or steel mold and using explosives to force the metal into the correct shape within the mold. This method was used in the U.S. as far back as the 1960s and in Australia as recently as the late 1980s. As with many other exotic building methods, government money (taxpayers' dollars) was used to pay for these experiments. The process proved not to be cost-effective, however, so explosive forming has passed into history. We include it here because occasionally a client will inquire about the viability of this method.

5
WELDING

It is beyond the scope of this text to teach you how to weld. The suggested uses of the various welding equipment and actual welding techniques are included to show what is involved, rather than to teach you the art of welding. If you're not already a proficient welder, and you intend to undertake this work yourself, then you should seek instruction and advice from an appropriate local source. There are many full- and part-time teaching institutions where the craft of welding can be learned from experts.

Nevertheless, if you're a complete beginner, you might find it easier to understand this book if you know a few basic details about welding.

First, when metal is heated to the melting point for welding, it distorts. So most metal boats are not welded continuously. They are mostly "tacked" together with small, intermittent welds at intervals. The exception, of course, is the plating of the hull, decks, and superstructure, which must be absolutely watertight. Tack-welding is perfectly strong. In fact, too much welding locks in the stresses caused by distortion, which can actually make your boat weaker. Typical tacks are 2 inches long and spaced at 10-inch intervals, but your plans will give you precise instructions.

Tack-welds are usually laid down in two ways. The first is called a chain weld and the second a staggered weld. If you were welding a vertical plate to a horizontal plate, you could lay down tack-welds along one side of the join, and then back them up with identical tack-welds on the exact opposite side of the join. That's a chain weld.

Alternatively, you could lay down tack-welds along one side of the join, and then space other tack-welds alternately on the other side, not backing up the original welds, but falling in between them. That's a staggered weld.

In boatbuilding, you'll need two basic types of welds. Butt welds join material end-to-end. Right-angle welds, as their name implies, join two pieces of metal touching at right angles, or nearly so. The bead of weld laid down in the right angle is known as a fillet. Really heavy plates are often ground off at an angle of about 45 degrees on each side where they are to join, and a V-groove weld replaces the simple fillet weld.

To control distortion of the metal during welding, you have to lay down your welds in the correct sequence. For instance, if you tried to butt-join two steel plates by starting at one end and working straight across, you'd find the plates spreading apart as you did so. There would be a large gap between them by the time you reached the far end. So you have to start with a tack-weld in the middle, then lay down other tack-welds to the left and right of the center alternately. It also helps to alternate the direction of your welding each time. This is known as *back-step welding*. It's a very important principle, and one that's followed throughout the building process on a larger scale. Thus, after you've welded a frame to the shell on the port side, your next move would be to weld a frame to the shell on the starboard side. And, of course, you'd start in the middle of the boat and work outward toward the ends.

At this stage, you don't have to worry about what kind of weld goes where. Your plans will tell you.

ARC WELDING

You can use arc welding for steel and copper-nickel construction. In this method, an electrode is used to create an electric arc that melts the metal to be welded. The electrode is a metal rod that simultaneously produces the arc and is melted to contribute filler metal for the joint. There are many different types of arc welders, and it's difficult to decide which one to buy. It's important to make sure that the welder has sufficient capacity for your project. Don't make the mistake of buying a welder that's too small. The difference in price between a welder of adequate capacity and one that is underpowered for your job won't be great, but the irritation certainly will be enormous if you make a mistake and obtain a lightweight machine.

If you're building your boat on a nonindustrial site, you'll need a welder that will run off your normal domestic electricity supply. In the case of the most powerful machines, a higher input voltage will be required, but with good fortune on your side you should be able to obtain a suitable machine to run off the local power source.

Welder Amperage

You must consider the output rating of the welder, which is measured in amps. The higher the amperage, the thicker the plate that can be welded by that machine. The thickest plate you are likely to be using will be in the order of ¼ inch (10 mm), and this thickness can be handled by an arc welder with an output rating of 140 amps. If you are using thicker plate, say for the bottom of the keel, you can manage by beveling the edges of the thicker plate and using more than one run of weld. You may think that because your plans call for ³⁄₁₆-inch (4 or 5 mm) plate that you can get away with a welder that puts out only 110 amps. Don't be tempted. As a minimum, choose between a 140- and a 200-amp machine.

Arc welders of greater than 140-amp capacity cannot be run from the normal 15-amp domestic supply, so you'll need an alternative supply. If possible, you should try to arrange a 30-amp input supply. Heavy-duty supply is obtainable in the U.S. by way of the three-phase wiring supplied to domestic washing machines and electric dryers. No matter where you are planning to build or undertake a major refit on a metal boat, you will need to ensure an adequate power supply of the correct voltage and amperage for your particular needs.

The maximum input required can usually be obtained from the welder instruction manual and is often quoted in kilovolt/amps (kVA), which equals 1,000 volt/amperes times a power factor of 0.8. For example, the amperage calculation for a 140-amp welder with a maximum input of 4.2 kVA at 240 volts would look like

$$V \times A \times 0.8 = kVA$$
$$240 \times A \times 0.8 = 4,200 \text{ VA}$$
$$A = 22$$

So, in this case, a 25- or 30-amp input supply is recommended. Some better-quality welders are capable of being run at varying input voltage; this feature may be appreciated when you consider the voltage drop resulting from a long lead. As part of your selection of the boatbuilding site, you should consider this possibility and make allowances for any deficiencies in the power supply. A voltage meter can be used to test the voltage at the actual location where you'll be operating your welder. A 10 percent drop in voltage could put paid to a successful welding job. Input wires will need to be heavy, and a single run of cable is best because joins at outlets and sockets can result in a considerable voltage drop. As mentioned above, the alternative is to equip yourself with a welder that will accept varying voltages.

While we're on the subject of leads and cables, you'll find that the output cables supplied with your welder will seldom be long enough for your type of work. You'll most likely have to replace them with longer leads. Make sure the replacements are of good quality and thick enough to carry the loads without an accompanying and unwelcome drop in power. The earth clamps are usually spring-loaded. You may find it advantageous to replace them with the threaded-clamp type, which has a more positive grip. Also along the same lines, your electrode holder will most likely be spring-loaded; be warned that it should not be too heavy. The many hours you will spend welding can put a strain on your wrist and arm. This is especially so if this is your first major all-welded project. A little weight saved in the holder can make all the difference.

Air or Oil Cooled

Arc welders come in two main types, either air-cooled or oil-cooled. The oil-cooled version has the advantage of being capable of long continuous usage without overheating. This advantage also means that the oil-cooled version will have a much longer working life than its air-cooled counterpart. Even if you're building only one boat, you may want to take your welder with you when you go cruising as a means of earning additional funds. The oil-cooled version will also have a higher resale value. Against these advantages, you'll find that the oil-cooled version is much heavier and it needs to be stowed with care as the oil can drain out of the vents if the unit is not kept upright.

The air-cooled version is about half the price of the oil-cooled welder, so you'll need to make your own value judgment. This is only one of many you will be making throughout your boatbuilding project. Make sure the unit you select has some form of automatic thermal cutout, so that if it overheats it will shut down before it self-destructs. Summer and winter temperatures will have an effect on the amount of time during which you can use your air-cooled welder before you have to take a rest and let it cool down. If there's more than one person welding and using the same unit, extra thought will have to be given to the selection of a suitable unit.

On some of the better air-cooled models, you'll find a dial to control the amperage setting. This works throughout the output range, and this "choke control" can be handy when you're tackling a variety of welding conditions. A proficient welder can "tune" the output to suit the job in hand. Finally, no matter what type of arc welder you choose, don't buy a cheap unit; it's unlikely to remain in working condition long enough for you to complete your boat.

Electrodes

Although electrodes are consumables, rather than tools, it seems practical to include them here with arc welders. There's a wide range of electrodes in all appropriate materials. In some cases, there's more than one type of rod available to suit a particular job. You'll need to undertake some experimentation to find the rod that gives you the best results. The choice of electrode will be governed by the sequence of the work, your welding position, the equipment powering the electrode, and of course, the material you're welding.

The electrodes must be compatible with the base metal. The low-hydrogen variety is recommended for better quality and a stronger weld. This type reduces porosity and prevents the hydrogen embrittlement that causes hairline cracks. Porosity would allow water to pass through the weld and promote corrosion and the cracks caused by hydrogen embrittlement would have the same result. Although I do not feel that is necessary to dye test every weld, it is important to make sure that you don't rely on filler to keep the elements out of your boat.

There is some disagreement between various experts as to which rods, electrodes, or consumables (these terms mean the same thing) are best for a particular job. You may need to study this subject and perhaps seek local advice from those more experienced than yourself. Running practical tests with different types of rods will often assist you in choosing the correct rods.

Low-hydrogen electrodes require a little more skill on the part of the operator. Avoid electrodes that are promoted as high-speed, single-pass types; they produce a weld that has low ductility and should not be used in important parts of the boat. If you are building "to survey," or to pass U.S. Coast Guard inspection, then certain rods may be *required*. Check this out if you are building to a Classification Society rule, or under similar circumstances. No matter what rods you are using, you must store them properly. Ensure that the rods are kept in their sealed packets, dry and free from all contaminants.

As this book covers boats built all over the world, it's difficult to recommend specific brands of welding rods. For those of you building in Europe, the Swedish Oerlikon rods (made in Northern Ireland) have a good reputation among many steel boat builders. When you're fabricating a steel boat you'll be using mild-steel rods, but it may be useful to have a few "gouging" rods on hand. They let you cut plate with an electric welder, and although this will not, and should not, be your common cutting method, there may be times when these rods will come in handy. The method of using gouging rods for cutting is to heat the plate using high amperage and then the rod is pushed through the plate and drawn along the desired line, thus effecting the cut—and a surprisingly accurate one.

If you are not already familiar with the terms *slag*, *flat beads*, *fillet welds*, etc., that appear in this chapter, please refer to appendix 3 for a complete glossary explaining these and other welding and boatbuilding terms.

For North American readers, here are details of a few of the more popular rods and their uses. Note that each number in the letter designation has a special meaning. For instance, the E signifies electric welding; the first two numbers relate to tensile strength, and the next number shows the welding position. One equals all positions, and the final number signifies the special manufacturer's characteristics. Unless you already have considerable welding experience, make sure to seek local advice.

Mild Steel

E6010: A good beginner's rod, use it in all positions for general applications; good for tacks; will give good penetration, flat beads, and light slag.

E6011: OK for all positions; can be used on galvanized steel; produces light slag and is a good beginner's rod.

E6012: A general-purpose rod for all positions; moderate penetration, medium slag, recommended where fit is poor.

E6013: Another rod recommended by some builders.

E6020: Use for flat and horizontal positions; ideal for single-pass, deep-groove welds.

Note: All of the above 6xxx series electrodes are subject to hydrogen embrittlement.

Low-Hydrogen Mild Steel

E7014: Can be used in all positions; produces medium-to-heavy slag and is useful for high-speed work.

E7024: Especially good for down-hand welding and fillet welds. Is high-speed but produces very heavy slag.

E7018 AC: This AC electrode produces little slag and can be used on either low-, medium-, or high-carbon steels.

E7028: Can produce X-ray-quality welds. A very fast rod that is preferred for welding very heavy sections.

Special-Purpose Rods

E9018s: For high-tensile steels, medium penetration, low hydrogen, and porosity; often used for welding castings, fittings, and pipes.

E308, E309, E310, E312, E316, E317, E320, E330, E347, and E410 are all for welding stainless steels.

MIG WELDING

Because aluminum is more reactive than steel, arc welding doesn't provide enough protection against contamination. In many cases, aluminum boats are built using metal inert gas (MIG) welding, in which an inert gas such as argon is blown over the surface to shield the weld and prevent oxidation. MIG welding is fast and has the lowest distortion of any method; it can also be used to weld steel and copper-nickel. With the availability of less expensive machines, this method is becoming more popular for metal boat construction. The electrode for MIG welding consists of a thin continuous wire led from a spool. Many welders claim that this type of welding is easier to learn than arc (stick) welding, and better results can be achieved. You should give this system your consideration.

MIG welding machines operate on DC current and can be adapted for use under water. The usual output is between 200 and 300 amps, and this is sufficient for most operations. The dials on the machine are used to set amperage and wire speed. An easily handled gun is used to feed the wire and deliver the current.

There are many advantages to MIG welding, including a smaller (and consequently lower) heat-weld puddle, low distortion, and a slag-free bead. Its main disadvantage is its higher initial cost, but less-expensive machines have recently appeared on the market. As with the better-quality, higher-priced arc welders, you can recoup more of your investment if and when you decide to sell the equipment. MIG can be used to weld stainless steel to mild steel, a common requirement when building a good-quality metal boat.

Generally, the standard equipment as purchased has only a 12-foot (3.66 m) main lead to the gun. You can overcome this by rearranging the equipment so that you can use the gun with the machine up to 50 feet (15.24 m) away from the main unit. With all gas-shielded welding you must ensure that the workplace is free of air movement, including wind. This almost makes it mandatory that you are in a fully enclosed workplace when using MIG equipment.

The MIG welding filler wire comes in rolls of two readily available sizes. The smaller roll, generally about a 1-pound (450 g) spool, is designed to fit on the special gun. The larger, 10-pound (4.5 kg) spool runs off the normal wire feeder. The smaller spools are much more expensive but some builders consider the convenience outweighs the extra cost.

TIG WELDING

In tungsten inert gas (TIG) welding, an alternating-current (AC) or direct-current (DC) arc is struck between a nonconsumable tungsten electrode and the material being welded. The filler rod is fed independently. Flux coatings are unnecessary, as the arc itself cleans the electrode and the weld, and a shielding inert gas prevents reoxidation. The operator has control of the amount of heat and wire feed and has better control of penetration than is obtainable with MIG or other methods.

TIG can be used to fabricate aluminum as well as steel and copper-nickel. However, for various reasons, including cost and degree of difficulty, it's often the last choice associated with boatbuilding. TIG is favored for unbacked joins, where welding is possible only from one side and where good penetration is required. Where complex welding is needed, it's possible to make some passes with TIG and complete the job using MIG.

WELDING STEEL

The great advantage of welding is that the weld has the potential to be stronger than the materials it joins. Make sure your welds always fall into this category. Good welding requires proper preparation, correct weld joints, careful use of welding positions, correct weld size, and perfect root. Inadequate root penetration, the presence of slag, porosity, and cracking are common faults. When you're using arc welding, you're more likely to have these problems and you'll also find it harder to control these faults. MIG welding, with its shielding gas, will give you a cleaner and stronger weld.

Cracking is caused by excessive local stress brought about by improper conditions such as voids, not enough allowance for shrinkage, and rapid cooling. This latter problem can occur in colder-than-usual weather. Poor or inadequate back gouging can also result in cracks appearing in an otherwise healthy weld. Preventive measures include preheating to slow down the cooling rate, back-step welding, and the use of low-hydrogen electrodes.

Slag trapped in the weld consists of nonmetallic material separating the weld metal from the base metal. It's the result of improper location of the weld, inadequate cleaning, or chipping of slag from previous passes of weld. It's virtually impossible to eliminate this problem altogether, but there must be no more than a minimal amount of foreign material in the finished weld.

Porosity is the result of improper welding current and length of arc. Low-hydrogen electrodes require a relatively high welding current and a short arc. Porosity can be found in the base metal itself, so carefully examine your materials for this and other defects.

Light steel plate of ⅛ inch (3 mm) thickness should be spaced with a gap similar to the thickness. The ³⁄₁₆-inch (4 to 5 mm) plate will need to have its edges beveled at around 30 degrees. In the heavier plates, where the 30-degree "V" bevel

is required, you'll need to make one or more passes; one or two outside the "V" and one inside to complete the weld. This should not be done consecutively; to avoid excessive heat and the resulting distortion you must use intermittent welding techniques.

When you're welding steel plates whose edges fall on a longitudinal stringer or chine bar, you can weld them more robustly than you can weld other thin plates that merely butt against each other. In any case, plates should be welded from both sides; as with all rules there are exceptions to this one, but keep them to a minimum. Each weld must fully penetrate the joint. Where plates fall on a stringer or chine bar, they should either be spaced or beveled, depending on thickness, so that the weld achieves good penetration from the single side that is available for welding. You should weld plate butt joints, and plates to stringers and chines, with staggered welding techniques, using short staggered passes and then returning to fill in the spaces.

We don't recommend welding the frames to the plate. It may be desirable to allow the stringers to stand proud of the frames by about the thickness of the plate, then you may weld using 2-inch (50 mm) long welds on 8-inch (200 mm) centers. Overwelding the frames to the plating will surely spoil the fair line and overall appearance of the finished hull.

Where the plates butt together, they should be joined vertically. Any one of several techniques can be used to keep a fair line in the plating at the join. The surest way is to assemble and weld the plates into long lengths on the shop floor. You'll want to be very careful when you're fitting these long plates; you do need proper lifting equipment to handle them safely.

WELDING ALUMINUM

To weld aluminum, you need MIG or TIG equipment. In the case of MIG equipment, a special gun is required. Argon or oxygen, rather than the less expensive carbon dioxide must be used as the shield when welding this material. Even if you only plan

The neat welding on the transom of this aluminum Roberts 370 will need little grinding before the initial prime coat.

to use your MIG or TIG equipment for welding steel, it's worth considering the possibility of later using it to weld aluminum. For this reason alone, do not stint on quality, when purchasing your welding gear.

Experts who work with aluminum on a daily basis often disagree about the merits of MIG and TIG. If you have only minimum experience in handling this metal, you should seek advice locally. If you have no previous experience in working with aluminum, then you should either build in steel or seek professional help with the welding. You can solve a lack of experience in handling aluminum by acting as your own laborer while you hire an expert to undertake the welding. You could handle the cutting, fitting, and patterning work as required.

In the U.S., a wide range of DC inverters used to power MIG units is manufactured by PowCon and by Miller. You will most likely need equipment equal to the Miller XMT300 CC/CV that can be set at 230-volt or 460-volt single or three-phase. This unit, when used with three-phase power, can weld aluminum in excess of ³⁄₁₆ inch (4.5 mm). As there is a wide choice of units, you'll need to investigate all possibilities before making a final choice. In the U.K., the Kemppi PSS 5000 AC/DC multisystem welding machine is suitable for both MIG and TIG welding.

WELDING COPPER-NICKEL

Most normal cutting processes are acceptable for copper-nickel. Shearing and cutting with an abrasive disk, or by use of plasma arc, are equally ac-ceptable. Oxyacetylene cutting is not appropriate for this material.

As mentioned earlier, copper-nickel can be welded using arc, MIG, or TIG equipment. The alloys have been specified for use in seawater for over 50 years. Copper-nickel has been used in saltwater-pipe work and condenser service for many of the world's navies and merchant fleets. Copper-nickel has been and is still used where fouling must be prevented and where longevity is of utmost importance. This metal has the potential to be the premier boatbuilding material and it is expected that with an expanding market, copper-nickel will become more affordable. The choice of welding methods often depends on the availability of equipment.

The arc-welding process, using flux-coated electrodes, is widely practiced and requires only existing equipment and a suitable power source. The gas-shielded processes, MIG and TIG, are capable of producing welds of high quality. These processes have the advantage of greater control over all stages of the welding. In all cases, the persons actually undertaking the welding of copper-nickel should be familiarized with the special characteristics of this metal. Test pieces should be checked for weld integrity. If inspection authorities are involved, they will in any case wish to approve procedures and the competence of the welders involved in the project.

General preparation of the copper-nickel surfaces to be joined will include removing all dirt and other contaminants. Contaminants such as lead, sulfur, phosphorus, and residues from marking crayons, paints, cutting fluids, oil, and grease that can cause weld cracking must all be removed. Use clean cloths to apply fresh organic solvents to the joint area, and dry it off. If the drying cloth shows any residue, repeat the process until the cloth is clean. By now I am sure you get the picture: areas to be welded must be scrupulously clean.

In general, a 70-30 copper-nickel filler material is used for joining both 90-10 and 70-30 copper-nickels. Using this material ensures the weld metal is at least as corrosion resistant as the parent material and thus avoids the concentrated attack that might occur if the relatively small area of weld metal were more susceptible to corrosion than the substantially larger area of parent metal.

If copper-nickel is to be welded to steel, the standard weld metals tend to crack when de-

posited, due to the effect of the steel, which is fused into the weld joint. In this case, a nickel-copper of 65 percent nickel filler material is used; this composition remains sound when diluted by the fused steel.

Copper-nickels are relatively simple to fabricate, and given the correct information and conditions any competent welder can handle the material. This material is naturally ductile and does not undergo any significant metallurgical changes requiring special treatment. Copper-nickel can be cold-formed up to 50 percent deformation, before any stress-relief heat treatment is required. The machinability of this metal is similar to that of aluminum bronze, phosphor bronze, and other copper alloys.

It's important to bear in mind two important requirements when you're welding copper-nickel: cleanliness, and protection of the weld from the atmosphere. The first ensures that none of a number of detrimental minor contaminants can cause cracking. The second prevents the absorption of gases and the formation of porosity in the weld metal. It's preferable to set up a dedicated area when building in this material, as this makes it easier to avoid undesirable contact with other materials. It's essential that tools used in the fabrication and handling of copper-nickel are not contaminated with the residues of other metals.

For de-scaling, the surface-oxide films on both 90-10 and 70-30 alloys can be very tenacious. Oxides and discoloration adjacent to the areas to be welded can be removed with very fine abrasive belts or disks. If pickling is required, a hot 10 to 15 percent sulfuric acid solution containing 2 percent

Copper-nickel is more difficult to fabricate than other metals but, given the correct information and conditions, a competent welder can handle the material.

sodium nitrate or dichromate is satisfactory. Before pickling, oxides can be broken up by a light gritblast. The pickled components should be rinsed thoroughly in running water, then preferably in 2 percent ammoniacal water, rinsed again, and finally dried in hot air.

In general, you can weld copper-nickel of up to ⅛ inch (3 mm) thickness with a square-butt preparation. Butt preparation for thicker copper-nickel involves forming beveled edges; the angle of the V should be larger than is normally used for steel and should be 70 degrees or more. This is because the molten weld metal is less fluid, and some manipulation of the electrode or torch is necessary to ensure fusion with the sidewalls of the joint. Whenever possible, it's desirable to weld in the down-hand position. Welding in other positions requires greater skill if defects in the weld, particularly porosity, are to be avoided. It's worth the effort of manipulating the fabrication into the most favorable location, rather than attempting to operate in an unsuitable position. All of the foregoing points toward building the hull upside down. In our opinion, the upside-down method is recommended no matter what metal is being used for the hull. The main exception to building upside down is when assembling a hull from a precut kit. The kits are designed to be built upright and as the are built in a special jig that forms part of the kit. This system works well because the complete kits were designed to accommodate this method.

In the case of arc welding, the flux-coated electrodes are designed to operate with direct current, electrode positive. They require no special pretreatment unless they have been exposed to the atmosphere for some time—which is not recommended in any case—when they'll need to be dried in an oven for about an hour or two at 480°F (250°C). Taking into account the need for manipulation, it may be helpful to select a rod size slightly smaller than that of a carbon-steel electrode that would be used under comparable conditions. Any finished weld, however, should not be more than three times the electrode diameter. A long arc should be avoided, since this results in weld porosity through reaction with the surrounding atmosphere. Where start positions are found to be unsound, reversing the electrode direction to re-melt initially deposited weld metal or the crater at the end of the run can help to avoid problems. The joint temperature should not be allowed to rise excessively after successive runs; it's usual to restrict the interpass temperature to 300°F (150°C).

Many manufacturers of consumable rods offer electrodes for welding copper-nickel. The brand selected should conform to a recognized standard. Generally, coated electrodes meet the requirements of both American (*AWS A5.6 ECuNi*) and German (*DIN 1733 EL-CuNi30Mn*) specifications, and contain the appropriate amount of deoxidizers to ensure sound welds in normal conditions. Because of these deoxidizers, any quoted copper content will be a little less than the nominal 70 percent. The welding currents recommended by the electrode manufacturer should be followed.

TIG welding of copper-nickel employs methods similar to those for other metals. Separate control of heat input, via the arc, and filler metal addition, gives this process a degree of flexibility that's an advantage when welding shaped joints or inserting root runs in thicker joints. It's essential, nevertheless, to ensure that filler material is incorporated and that the simple fusion of the parent metal is avoided. The latter is important because substantial amounts of deoxidizers in the filler materials are necessary to prevent porosity. Bare filler wires are produced to the American *AWS A5.7 ERCuNi* specification, and to *DIN 1733 SG-CuNi30Fe* and *BS2901: part 3 Grade C18* in Europe. Argon, or argon plus 1.5 percent hydrogen, is used as the shielding gas and once again the need for a short arc is emphasized. Direct current should be used and the current should be adjusted to suit the wire size and material thickness.

MIG welding of copper-nickel can be operated over a range of currents to provide low-heat-input dip transfer or the relatively high-heat-input spray transfer, which is suitable only for thicker materials, say above ¼-inch (6 mm) thickness. While dip transfer is used successfully

The use of metal need not restrict shapes on your boat. This stern arrangement was built by Almarine, of the Netherlands.

for thinner materials, a more advanced technique, pulsed-arc transfer, provides a better combination of low overall heat input and adequate fusion of the parent material. This requires a power source designed for the purpose. They're available at different levels of sophistication and price. Pulsed-arc welding has substantial advantages for the operator and gives greater assurance of good quality welds than the dip-transfer process. Advanced synergetic welding power sources control the detachment of the droplet from the wire effectively while reducing the number of variables to be set by the welder.

Argon, or a mixture of argon and helium, is preferred as shielding gas and the spooled filler wire must be kept dry and not exposed to contamination. Because of the higher capital cost of equipment and the cost of buying spools of wire, this process is more appropriate for extensive welding, such as when one or more complete hulls are to be built. This last condition applies no matter what material is being welded by the MIG or TIG process.

Filler wires for both tungsten-arc and gas-shielded metal arc processes are available to American, German, and British standards. For reasons given earlier, the 67-30 copper-nickel alloy is preferred as a filler material for both 90-10 and 70-30 copper-nickel alloys. Wires of this alloy conform to the same specifications as for tungsten-arc welding. Because of the relative softness of the wire, it's important to feed it through low-friction liners.

Because of the range of transfer conditions possible in the gas-shielded metal-arc process, welding parameters can vary widely. In all cases, they should be set for the equipment, position, and thickness of the material by careful welding procedure trials directed toward stable transfer conditions and welds of good appearance. It's not desirable simply to reproduce published welding conditions, since indicated current not only depends on transfer mode but on the type of indicating instrument and power source in use.

Copper-nickel has been used extensively to clad large container ships, oil tankers, and similar merchant vessels. This process has proved most successful in preventing corrosion and virtually eliminating marine growth on the underwater surfaces of the hulls. The obvious advantages include the fact that these ships are able to continue to operate without the need for bottom cleaning and repainting—a valuable asset in today's competitive market. Information on this process is available from the Copper Develop-

6
BUILDING FROM A PRECUT KIT

Precut metal boat building kits have been around for several years. The first kits consisted of frames and a stem cut from plate. This left the builder to make patterns and cut the plating for the hull, deck, and superstructure in the traditional manner. The first attempts at complete precut hull, deck, and superstructure kits showed a varying degree of accuracy and a few were so bad as to set the whole progress back by several years.

ADVANTAGES OF A KIT

You can get your boatbuilding project off to a great start by using a precut steel or aluminum kit for a sailboat or powerboat. Modern kits contain accurate precut parts that you can easily assemble into a complete hull, deck, and superstructure. The latest computer software allows the designer to model the boat in such a way that extremely accurate computerized files can be prepared to direct the cutting machines. These files contain all the information to facilitate computer-controlled cutting of all the metal parts for your boat. It may not interest the average builder, but a huge amount of work is required to turn a boat plan in to a cut-to-size boat kit. Every part has to match that of its neighbor exactly, the slots need to be in the correct locations, and everything must fit perfectly together. All this is necessary to enable you to complete the assembly of the hull, deck, and superstructure with the minimum of problems. We're always amused when we

receive a request from an uninformed customer that goes something like this: "By the way, now that I have the plans for your design, just send me the cutting files."

The amount of careful and intense work required to turn a design into a set of cutting files far exceeds the expense in creating the original design. It's only possible to justify these costs if one can expect to market several kits of similar design. Often, we've been able to make cutting files for a particular design in such a way as to give several customers the custom items they desire. Some custom items are relatively easy to incorporate in the cutting files, while other more complex changes require redesigning the basic boat and remaking all the cutting files.

The metal-cutting shop uses the NC files to produce your kit. The kits are cut from preshot-blasted and primed steel (or aluminum) and are delivered ready for easy assembly by any competent welder. The primer used on the steel kits is especially formulated so that it doesn't give off harmful fumes as you weld the kit together. This primer doesn't burn off on the reverse side of the metal in welded areas. It's truly a remarkable coating used to protect the steel until additional paint is applied.

The parts are all nested, including all of the hull, deck, and cabin plating. You can easily assemble the hull, deck, and superstructure. All you have to do is to match each part to the special assembly plans you receive with the kit.

Computer-controlled automatic cutting machines can cut a complete 50-foot (15 m) boat in about 12 hours, but hundreds of expert operator hours are required to prepare the cutting files on computers.

The "tack-and-weld" method described below is in many ways similar to the stitch-and-glue procedure used with plywood. It's a practical and economical way to get your boatbuilding project off to a great start. You can achieve a professional result, especially if you already have some welding experience. If you lack welding experience, then any local person with suitable welding knowledge can help you assemble your kit. Of course, many thousands of boats have been built from a set of plans and frame patterns, so if there isn't a kit that meets your requirements, building from plans is the way to go. Nonetheless, if you can afford a kit, you'll have a hull in the least time and this alone may justify the modest additional expense. The resale value of your boat will be enhanced if you can show that the hull was built from preshotblasted, primed, and computer-controlled precut metal parts.

Steel Kits

In high-quality kits, all steel plates are shotblasted and primed with a zinc-rich primer before cutting. Cutting of plates is carried out with computer-aided lofted surfaces on an "NC"-driven plasma-oxygen cutting machine with a maximum plate size of 82 by 10 feet (14 by 3 m). The best material is of Lloyd's-approved, "A" grade, "shipbuilding quality," or equivalent

The kit includes a setting-up jig as well as detailed assembly plans. All required steel profiles are shotblasted and primed with a zinc-rich primer before being cut. Kits are constructed from the steel product specifications mentioned above.

Normally, all the plate material is supplied as a flat pack with marking lines engraved in the plate surface (a zinc line) and part numbers painted on the surface. The maximum size is usually 19 feet, 6 inches, by 6 feet, 6 inches (6 by 2 m). All steel profiles are supplied in sufficient length to ensure the minimum number of joints in the plating. Those who prefer aluminum as their basic building material will be pleased to learn that kits are available precut from marine-grade materials.

Bottom plates, supported by jigs, are in position ready to receive the first frames. Note preassembled frames at rear.

YOUR FIRST MOVES

The first thing to realize is that the kit differs in many ways from the methods you would use to build a metal boat from scratch. The kit is far superior to anything you could achieve by starting with the plans and a delivery of raw steel plate and profile bars.

Most metal boats built from scratch are built upside down and most boats built from cut-to-size metal kits are built upright. Not only is this a more appropriate way to assemble the kit, it also saves the cost and inconvenience of having to turn the hull. And here's one very important piece of advice: *You must tack-weld the complete hull, deck, and superstructure together before you run any final welds.*

If you don't follow this advice, you'll almost certainly end up with an un-fair boat requiring a considerable amount of filler. In any case *do not overweld* or try to run long welds at one time.

Your kit may arrive on a flatbed truck or in a container. Kits are normally packed on pallets and can be lifted off the transport by a small

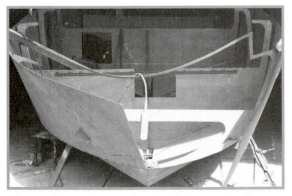

The topside plates are simply pulled around to be tacked together at the bow.

crane, front-end loader, or similar equipment. Provided your kit is on a pallet, you may find it more convenient to drag your kit from the truck or container, using a pair of planks as a ramp. Once you have unloaded your kit, you must keep it covered until assembly is under way.

With your kit, you should receive a packing list and large-scale assembly drawings. The drawings will show all the parts as flat surfaces grouped together as they will be assembled to make the finished hull. There will also be a number of drawings showing the assembly of the frames. Each part will be numbered, so that you can check it against the packing list and the corresponding drawing.

One of your first jobs will be to tack-weld the frames together, so make sure you sort the parts and store them in the order you'll need them. On larger frames, it may be easier to tack only the bottom sections of the frames together at this time.

Once you've tacked all the frames together, it's time to prepare the building jig. The transverse profile jigs will be supported by the metal "castles"

Sort and check the content of your kit as soon as possible after delivery.

Most kits come with three or four setting-up jigs as part of the cut-steel package.

Another view of one of the setting-up jigs that supports the bottom plates.

that come as part of your kit. The setting-up jig is merely intended to start things off. It's *not intended to support the boat* during the entire building process. Usually, however, you leave the jig in place for the entire building program so you can weld a flat strip on the top of each web to spread the load of the plate where it rests on edge of the plate web. After you have both sides of the bottom plates tacked together you should consider adding extra support and bracing to the jig structure.

Set up two parallel I beams as shown in the instructions that come with your kit. These beams must be long enough to accept the number of support jigs mentioned above. Cross-tie I beams should be installed at the same location as indicated to install the support webs. Obviously, the whole support structure must be level in all directions and well braced as it will play a part in supporting the boat during construction.

Keels are assembled either in place or separately, as shown here; your plans will advise you.

Don't attempt to fully weld the plates into one length on the floor. The plate joins should only be tack-welded in three locations, one weld at the each of the ends of the join and one in the center of the join. These tacks should be no more than a ½ inch (12 mm) long. If you weld the plates on the floor, you'll end up with a hard spot in the hull plating. Some plates of ¼-inch (6 mm) or heavier material may need to be beveled before you tack them in place. You may prefer to make the bevels after you've tack-welded the plates and before you run the final welds. In all cases, good metal boat building practices should prevail. After you have both sides of the bottom plates tacked together, you should consider adding extra support and bracing to the structure.

Sailboats with long keels, such as our Spray designs, as well as most powerboats, should have the keel structure assembled at the same time as the bottom plating. Take care that you don't "squeeze in" the tops of the keel; use the webs as spacers. After you've positioned the bottom plates, the keel sections, and the transverse profile jigs, you may start to tack-weld the bottom plates to the keel sides. Sailboats with deep fin-style

The "heel" that supports the rudder on a long-keeled sailboat or semidisplacement powerboat is formed into a box shape as shown. Alternatively, your kit or plans may call for a square-sectioned box tube to be "spliced" onto the aft end of the keel.

Assembling the setting-up jigs will be one of your first jobs.

keels may have the keel installed after the hull is completed. The canoe body should be built from the bottom of the hull upward in a manner similar to that used to assemble a powerboat hull. The webs can be arranged so that they can be added along with the rest of the keel after raising the hull to the correct elevation.

The benefit of using this method is to allow you to work on the hull, deck, and superstructure while the boat is lower and thus more accessible. The exact method and order of assembly depends on the availability of lifting equipment and your general work environment. Details given below are valid for the general assembly of all hulls.

With most powerboats, you can start by laying the bottom plates in the transverse profile jigs that come with your precut metal kit. The frames will soon be added at the locations indicated by the transverse lines marked on the plates.

With any hull, the first step is to set up the bottom plates and tack them along the centerline. Next, start to install the pretacked frames on the appropriate transverse lines marked on the plating. From now on, the whole structure will grow upward. The better equipped your workshop is with overhead lifting and handling gear, the eas-

ier and more smoothly your job will proceed.

If you're in doubt about your welding skills, seek the help of a suitably qualified person at the earliest stage. There is a great deal even the most inexperienced person can do to assist a qualified welder to assemble the kit. Generally, two people are required to handle the larger pieces of metal, so acting as laborer to your hired professional may be the best route for you.

If you have moderately good welding skills, you'll find that the kit comes with enough scrap material to allow you to get in some practice before tackling the assembly of the kit. Don't try to weld aluminum or copper-nickel unless you have the proper knowledge and considerable experience in handling these materials.

The metal kits are constructed so that the strength of the finished hull comes from the build-up of the frames and stringers in interlocking sections. Heavy and continuous welding of frames and stringers should be avoided at all times. After the hull and deck is tack-welded together, the process of finish-welding can proceed without fear of distortion.

The secret of creating a fair hull and deck is to use a welder of high enough amperage for the

The Voyager 495 cruising sailboat was developed especially for the range of cut-to-size metal kits. These radius-chine sailboats are available in sizes ranging from 38 to 65 feet (11.58 to 19.81 m).

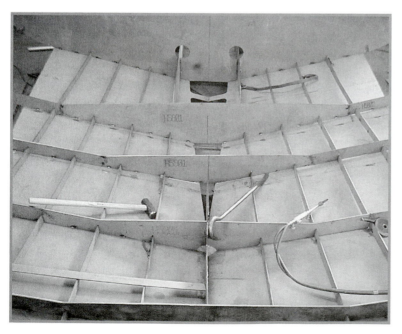

The frames are set on the bottom plate at the premarked station lines and tacked into position.

job. Welding with too little amperage, and too slowly, will create lots of heat on the spot and less penetration of the weld material in the seam. This may make for a weak weld and additional grinding to remove excessive weld material. This, in turn may further weaken the weld.

ASSEMBLING THE HULL

For those of you who are new to this type of boatbuilding, there is an early shock in store. Having placed the bottom plates on the jig, you may think they're not going to fit. Keep the faith! Start tack-welding in the middle of, or somewhat aft of, the middle of the plate. Make sure the marks on the plates are lined up at all times. As you work forward and backward from the tack-welded position, you can form the plates to shape with some human help or by using a trolley jack underneath the area of the plates where they are to join. When they touch, tack-weld them together and move along to the next position.

At the bow, you'll probably need a block and tackle to pull the sides of the plates together. Some tension will be experienced in this area. Don't forget to secure the positions of any clamps, so that they cannot unexpectedly let go.

Having finished tack-welding the bottom plates together, start placing the frames in position on the bottom plates. Lines on the plate will indicate the location of the frames. You may use the scale drawings as a reference. Depending on the layout of the bottom stringers on your particular design, you may have to install some of them as you are installing the bottom frames.

The frames are set up on the premarked station lines.

Frames have been assembled and erected. You'll find that you'll reach this stage in a few hours.

Close-up of frames shows web floors with T-bar longitudinal supports installed to accept the plywood cabin sole.

Study the layout of the bottom framing on your boat plans and it will become apparent which sequence will work best for your hull.

Pull up the bottom plates toward the frames until they fit snugly, and tack-weld them. Start with a frame where the plates are least shaped, and work backward and forward from there. If you've assembled the complete frames, as opposed to the bottoms only, use temporary braces, as necessary, to support the top portions of the frames. Once all the frames are installed, you may fit some of the side stringers into the slots on the frames. These stringers will assist in stiffening up the structure at this stage. Once again: only tack-welding must be used at this stage of the assembly process.

The next step is to install the side plates. This is best done by using a simple overhead gantry or a forklift truck. Pick up the side plates with a plate clamp on a chain connected to a block and tackle made fast to a forklift leg. Make

The transom in place; the next step will be to install the radius stringers. Photos on pages 53 through 58 taken by Brian Smyth of Intertec Marine, Nova Scotia, Canada.

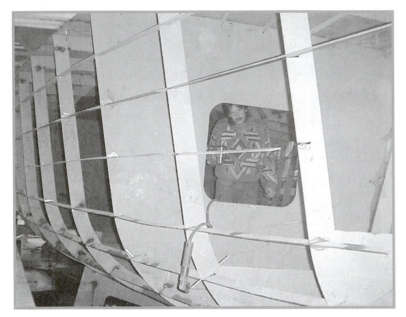

Note the fair line of the stringers as they are installed into precut slots.

and tackle until the entire side is in position and tack-welded in place. Place some tack welds on the side frames-to-plate joint as well as on the chine seam.

The side plates near the bow and the underside of the bow will show some tension, and can be pulled into place by attaching a chain on the outside of the plates. To attach a chain or a block and tackle to a plate, tack-weld a temporary eye or similar piece to the plate. By welding only one side of the eye, you can easily remove it after use.

sure the plate is more or less in balance while it's hanging free of the ground before you lift it into position. Use a helper to locate a matching line in the right position and tack-weld it. Continue to move the plate up or down a bit with the block

Next, the transom plates, bathing platform, stern plates, and all other plates that go into forming the hull are now installed and tack-welded in position. Note that with radius-chine boats, the

With radius-chine hulls it's best to install both the bottom and topside plating before fitting the radius sections.

A prefabricated long keel is installed on a Voyager 495 hull.

The transom can be assembled separately and installed later, as shown at right.

The preassembled transom is lowered into place.

Deck stringers help stiffen the structure while the hull is being plated.

Optional twin cockpits, cockpit coamings, and sidedeck plating installed on a Voyager 495.

*View of pilothouse looking forward
from cockpit and poop deck.*

radius panels are installed later. Remember to refer to the drawings frequently.

Now the deck plates, superstructure, and items like a flybridge are installed and tack-welded into position. Any deck stringers and cabintop intercostals in your design may need to be installed before the applicable areas of plating. In some cases, it may be possible or preferable to tack-weld the superstructure together off the boat and then install it as one unit. Some of the more recently designed kits allow for this option by providing special "landing areas" at each frame. These landings make it simple to line up the completed superstructure with the hull and deck.

RADIUS CHINES

After you've tack-welded the entire boat together, it's time to tackle the radius chines. We've always maintained that radius-chine hulls should be built upside down. For one-off boats built from scratch, this advice still stands. But, because all kit boats are built upright, a special approach is required to enable the radius chines to be fitted without blemish. At first, we supplied the radius plates rolled in one direction only; this is the same rolled plate you would use in one-off radius construction. We soon discovered why we had always insisted that these radius-chine boats should be built inverted. Fortunately, we were able to solve the problem. The radius-chine boats built from these kits are still built upright, but with one important difference: we now supply

On kit boats, the radius plates are usually installed in one piece; however, if the plates are only rolled in one direction, then some longitudinal cutting will be necessary to get a perfect fit.

Owner Ricardo Menendez stands beside his plated Voyager 495 hull. Assembly by Intertec Marine of Nova Scotia, Canada.

fully formed radius plates. They are rolled in all directions to ensure a perfect fit. This improved arrangement is available because it is now possible to have the plates fully formed and rolled from the information supplied in the original modeling files. The forming cannot be accurate right to the edge of the plate, however, so each section is a little oversized at the edges, which allows for exact fitting and trimming. Your kit will contain the appropriate amount of prerolled, numbered sections to fit the area covered by the radius chines.

Now you can carefully place the appropriate prerolled section against the position on the opening in the hull. Using a helper, scribe the edges of the plate with a sharp tool or pencil and then cut, grind, or nibble the edge for a perfect fit. Tack-weld it in position and continue until you have all the radius panels in place.

FINISHING THE ASSEMBLY

The first job is to complete the welding of the frame sections and then intermittently weld the frames and stringer to the hull plating using 2-inch (50 mm) weld spaced at 6 inches (150 mm). Do not overweld and do not continuously weld on one side of the hull. Weld on a reasonable amount on one side then switch to the other side, back and forth until the entire hull is welded. Constantly working from side to side will avoid the plates pulling out of shape and general distortion that can be caused by overwelding or welding entirely on one side at a time.

You should have made a 60-degree V between the plates, 30 degrees on each plate, but if you haven't previously prepared the heavier plates in this manner, you may do so now by running an angle grinder along the appropriate seam.

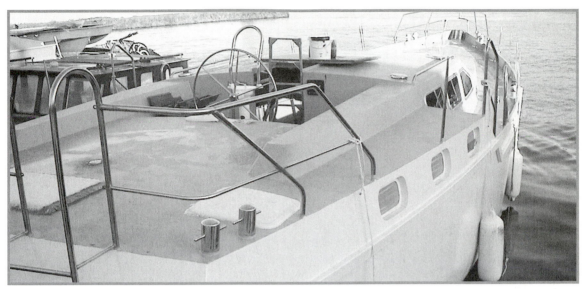

Bermuda 480 built by Almarine, Holland, from a precut kit.

Now you can proceed to run the final welds on the outside of the plates. The hull below the waterline must be welded both inside and out. Again, work from one side of the hull to the other, frequently changing sides.

You can grind off any excess weld material by first using a coarse disk and then finishing up with a softer, more flexible disk. Take advice from your materials supplier about these items.

Lastly, apply a minimum of filler to the seams and apply a coat of primer to the ground areas. You're now ready for final finishing and painting. The remainder of the painting and fitting-out work is the same whether you build from a kit or from scratch. One big difference is that by using a precut kit you'll have saved over 75 percent of the time required to build a similar hull from scratch.

On a well-designed kit you can preassemble some parts off to one side and install on the hull when convenient. Transport height restrictions may make this a necessity.

7
GETTING STARTED

This is a good time to mention that the professional who designed your boat may have spent many hours over some small detail believing that it will have an important bearing on the performance, appearance, or resale value of your boat. Respect his or her efforts, and please don't make changes casually without consulting the designer.

Making and erecting the frames is one of the most exciting parts of building any boat. Having built a few boats myself, I know the thrill of seeing the frames erected for the first time, and of standing back and admiring the line of the hull. Of course, the addition of the chine bars (if present) and a few stringers gives a better idea of the shape of the hull, but the initial thrill of seeing the frames erected is still a most memorable occasion.

MATERIAL LISTS

You will get a better price if you order in bulk, so we recommend that you order all of the basic hull materials in one combined package. Your building plans may include a material list and, if so, it usually consists of the main items required for building the hull, deck, and superstructure. On some occasions, if you calculate the total weight of the metals, you may find that there appears to be too much material. Your list should include an allowance for offcuts and other wastage. The list may also include details of the temporary bracing required to set up the hull.

Even if your plans include a material list (including the lists included in our plans), go through the drawings carefully and "take off" the list for yourself. Don't forget to allow for wastage; 15 to 20 percent is about right. Some of this wastage material will be used to make tools, including clamps and tags. The time required calculating the quantities will be a good investment, and it will prove invaluable in your better understanding of the plans. "One hour of study can save two hours of work" is an oft-quoted truism.

Most lists do not include the materials required for the interior joinery. In some cases, this list isn't included because there may be several alternative accommodation plans. It's better to compile a timber and plywood list after you've made a definite decision as to which interior you will finally select for your boat.

BUILDING UPRIGHT OR INVERTED?

The shape of the boat, the metal being used to construct the hull, and the particular building method you choose may all contribute to your decision to build the hull upright or inverted. Another factor could be the space and facilities available for turning the hull. There are many simple systems for turning hulls over, so this factor shouldn't play too big a part in your reaching a decision. You could decide to build two or

The framing shown here is one of several methods used to set up a hull that is built upside down. This Spray 33 was built by John and Joan McDermott in Oman, Arabia, from where they set sail around the world.

more rings around your hull, thus facilitating working on the hull and other areas of your boat.

Advocates of the upside-down method like it because most of the important hull welding can be done in the down-hand position. In any case, some of the welding must be done from inside the hull, including tacking the intermediate stringers to the hull plating. Unfortunately, this may be a bit awkward, but at least some of this welding will have to be done while the hull is still inverted. Leaving the transom off the hull until after turnover will be of some help in gaining access to the interior of the hull. There is some justification for not installing the transom until immediately before the deck is installed.

In the case of radius-chine construction, I consider it imperative that the hull be built upside down. Building inverted makes it easier to install the radius plating. In our opinion, it's much simpler to lay the plate onto the framework from above than it is to draw or hold the plating from below until it is tacked in place. At the risk of repetition, you must always build radius-chine hulls upside down. Our preference for building upside down extends to round-bilge hulls as well.

To be fair to those who prefer to build the hull upright, the stated advantages of this method include the fact that the hull is already in a position to complete the deck superstructure. In other words, it doesn't have to be turned over. Building the hull upright offers easy access during the entire welding operation. You can overcome some of the disadvantages of not being able to lay the plate on by employing the use of adequate scaffolding. There are also many tricks, such as drilling a hole in the plating and pulling it into position with chains, wedges, and threaded bolts. As mentioned earlier, whether you build upright or upside down will largely depend on your circumstances and personal preference.

USING FULL-SIZE PATTERNS

Let's get this straight right from the start: the only people who decry the use of full-size patterns are those who either don't have access to them or those with masochistic tendencies. Under no circumstances try to "improve" on the patterns by using the offsets (if available) to re-loft the boat completely. Today, most boats are designed, drafted, lofted, and provided with full-size patterns plotted from computer-generated offsets. You can't improve on that, even by completely re-lofting the boat by hand.

The patterns you receive will most likely contain full-size shapes for all of the frames for one side. This is all you'll need unless you are building an asymmetrical hull. In addition to the frames, other full-size shapes should include the stem, the developed transom (the full-size transom shape when the curved transom is laid out flat—the radius will be included in the plan details); and the deck and cabintop beam cambers. Also, patterns may be included for the rudder, window patterns, and other items. These extra patterns are included when the designer feels that they will ensure that you interpret his ideas as intended. If possible, use these patterns. Usually any "improvement" in the designer's work will result in a less attractive boat.

Paper patterns are quite satisfactory, provided they are handled properly. These patterns should not be exposed to a damp atmosphere before being transferred to a more durable surface. If your plans come with paper patterns, don't open or unroll the patterns until you're ready to start building the boat. The patterns that come with our plans arrive in a plastic bag. Mylar patterns are a nice luxury, but they're expensive, usually costing about $800 to $1,300 (£500 to £800) per boat.

You'll need a suitable surface on which to lay out the patterns. You can work either directly from the patterns (not recommended) or you can transfer them to plywood or steel plate. This working area is variously known as the loft floor, the master plate, or any one of a dozen other locally inspired names. If you are transferring the frame shapes and other patterns to plywood, you can use a dressmaker's wheel to mark the shapes through the patterns onto the surface of the plywood. This plywood could be later used in the

fitting-out process, so it won't represent an additional expense. If you're transferring to steel plate, you'll need to center-punch the main points onto the steel plate and use a batten and straightedge to scribe in the shapes of the frames. In the case of shaped frames and the stem, you'll need to center-punch several points along the curve and then join the marks with the aid of a batten and the drafting weights known as "ducks." We find the plywood surface has many advantages.

The advice above applies to multi-chine sailboats, single-chine powerboats, and round-bilge boats of all types. In the case of radius-chine hulls, you'll not need to transfer the radius sections from the patterns; transfer only the straight sections. You should have the radius-frame parts bent to the radius specified on your plans, and the length (as measured around each radius) that will be needed to match up to the straight sections of the frames. Allow a little extra for trimming.

LOFTING

If the plans for the boat of your choice are not available with full-size patterns, you'll need to arrange for the hull to be lofted by computer or by hand. To enable the hull to be lofted by computer, you'll need to supply the lines and offsets to be entered, faired, and then plotted as full-size patterns. Computer-lofting is available from several design offices, including ours.

Lofting by hand involves actually drawing out the entire hull of the boat full size. Don't be trapped into drawing only the frames or stations, without actually drawing out the complete boat. You'll need a loft floor that can consist of several sheets of plywood. The sheets are laid out to form an area of say 3 feet (1 m) longer than the overall length of the boat, or longer by half the beam if you plan to develop the transom. The floor will need to be wider than the height of the stem above the keel or baseline, or more than half the beam, whichever is the greater. You should paint your loft floor with flat white paint; this will enable you to see the grid and other lines more clearly.

You'll need at least one long timber batten of about ¼ by ½ inch (20 by 12 mm). You'll also need some smaller battens, a builder's square, string or chalk line, and a set of loftsman's drafting weights (*ducks*), plus suitable pencils. The information included here is very basic and if you haven't lofted a boat before, you'll need a good book containing detailed instructions.

MAKING THE FRAMES

It's usual to assemble the frames over patterns that have been lofted by the builder or supplied with the plans. As mentioned earlier, you may prefer to use a plywood or steel area for this purpose. Make sure the area is level and that it will provide a firm base on which to assemble the frames.

A boat has two basic types of framing: transverse framing, generally referred to as the *frames*, and longitudinal framing, usually known as the *stringers*, which also includes chine bars, deck stringers, and the like. Here we are discussing the *frames*.

In steel or copper-nickel boats, transverse-framing material may be flat bar, L-angle or T-bar. Your plans will most likely stipulate which is appropriate. For many years, flat-bar frames have been favored in steel boats. Many designers have given this advice. The reason usually quoted is that L-angle is hard to protect from corrosion, and that the angled portion adds unnecessary weight. More recently, however, we have considered angle in a more favorable light.

Against the above objections, an argument can be made for angle. The flange will provide an excellent place to attach the lining material. Corrosion problems can be overcome by using prime-coated materials and spray-in-place foam insulation, which is now common practice in metal boat hulls. Regarding the extra weight of angle, I believe that this is not a problem in larger and heavier displacement boats. All that has been said about angle can also be applied to T-bar frames. Aluminum boats will have transverse frames made of angle, T-bar, or a proprietary extrusion that has some type of bulb or flange. Copper-nickel can have L-angle frames or angle frames that are bent from stock cut from plate.

Some builders may prefer to have the deck beams included as part of the original frame construction. If you prefer this arrangement, you'll find it's best used when you're building upright. Those of you building the hull inverted will find that the deck beams interfere with access under the boat. My experience is that the deck beams are best installed after the hull is fully plated and already turned upright. It is easier to check for a fair sheerline before installing the beams. In some cases—for instance, if your boat has a bulwark—this last objection may not apply, To summarize, if you're building upright, then you may consider installing the deck beams as part of the original frame, but if you're building inverted, don't install the beams until after the hull is upright.

After you have established how many frames you'll need, and which material you'll be using, L-angle, flat bar or T-bar, it's now time to start cutting the correct lengths of material to form each frame. An angle grinder fitted with a suitable wheel can be used for cutting the frame material to the correct length and angle. Some builders prefer to use their oxyacetylene equipment for making these cuts, and no doubt you have your own preference. Cuts made with the angle grinder are more accurate and will be preferred by many builders. A neat trick is to make up strips of cardboard as templates for the angle joins on the frames. Use cardboard that is the same width as your frame material. Lay two cardboard strips directly over the joint on your patterns, ensuring that there is sufficient overlap to allow you to cut through both layers of cardboard using a straightedge that bisects the angle. You have now created a pattern that forms the angle required for both parts of the framing material. Transfer these angles to your lengths of framing material and now you can neatly cut each angle to provide the basis for a perfect join. You may prefer to use a carpenter's bevel-gauge or a plastic protractor to obtain the correct angles. You can always clean up your angles by using the grinder, but it's preferable to make the correct cuts in the first place.

Next, tack-weld the frames together. After checking against the patterns, make the final welds. It's worth noting that a very small incorrect angle at the chine can become a large error at the sheer or keel. The frames may be made up in two halves, or one half on top of another, and then opened up like a clamshell to form the frame. You must carefully check the fully assembled and welded frames against the patterns and one half against the other. Accuracy is vital at this stage. It's not a good idea to tack the various parts of the frame to the steel master plate or loft plate. Frames assembled in this manner can have built-in tension that will cause them to change shape when released from the loft-plate floor.

A good way to avoid distortion is to follow the same sequence for assembling each frame. For instance, place a tack-weld at the center of each angle joint and let it cool for a few seconds before tacking either ends of the angle. Several frame sections can be done in sequence, ensuring that minimum time is lost through waiting for welds to cool, before proceeding to the next step in the assembly process. The object is to keep the job moving forward, without setting up stresses in the frames, and avoiding unnecessary delays in the work schedule.

Once you've tacked the frame together, you should be able to move it about and check the accuracy against the master patterns that have been scribed on the metal or plywood loft floor. When one side of the frame is tacked together, you should turn it over and tack the other side. Again, check the accuracy against the master patterns.

You'll be installing some form of headstock across the frame. This headstock may be used to support the frame on the strongback or bedlogs (see below). Make sure you install other bracing between the headstock and the sides and bottom of the frame, otherwise it will be too flexible and impossible to set in position on the strongback.

Mark all of the important reference points on all frames. Include such points as the load or datum waterline (LWL or DWL), the sheerline,

the deck line (if this is below the sheer), and any other points indicated on your full-size patterns. Finally, please follow the designer's specifications for making your frames; never overlap the ends of the frame bar where they join, in the misguided belief that you're making the boat stronger. Overlapped metal can harbor moisture and promote corrosion. It also adds unnecessary weight and looks unsightly, as well as giving your boat an amateurish appearance. On the same theme, don't add extra reinforcing plates or permanent gussets at the frame joints; these items were necessary for frames in wooden boats but add extra unnecessary weight in a metal hull.

There are several ways to make the various cuts in the frame to accept the stringers, deck shelf, and sheer stringer. One method is to divide each area between the chines into equal spaces and, using a square, mark in a notch for each stringer. These notches may then be cut while the frame is still on the loft floor. If you prefer this method, it may be better to cut the notches before tacking the frame together; cutting the notches will probably distort the frame part, so this is best corrected before you assemble the frame.

We recommend standing up the frames and then marking in all of the stringer locations on the frames, using a batten to simulate the fair curve of each stringer. The next step is to take the frames down and cut the slots. Finally, check each frame for accuracy before reinstalling it in its correct location. This method is time-consuming but it does ensure that you get a fair set of stringer notches and, in turn, a fair set of stringers. This method also makes sure that the final frame is still the shape intended by the designer, and in due course it will contribute to building an attractive and fair hull.

Drainage

This is a good time to think about drainage inside your hull. When the hull is in its correct position, there will be low points on the stringers. Careful observation will enable you to locate them at this stage. This is the area where moisture can collect inside the hull and cause rust.

If you're intending to install foam insulation, especially the spray-in-place variety, you won't have this problem because the foam should come at least to the inner edge of the stringers. The foam will provide a flush surface and leave nowhere for moisture to collect. In foam-insulated boats, any condensation that does occur will drain into the bilge. As your boat will need insulation, this is the obvious answer to a known problem.

If you're going to install preformed insulation, instead of the spray-in-place variety, you may wish to grind small semicircular holes in the low point of the stringers. Arrange them so they leave a drain hole between the stringer and the hull plating.

Some frames, too, will require limber (drainage) holes, but there's no point in cutting limber holes in the areas of the frame or keel webs where the hole will be later filled with ballast. The forward and the aft frames will need limber holes to allow water to flow to the lowest point. Check our plans and give some thought to this drainage situation.

Avoiding the "Starved-Cow" Look

In Europe, many designers and builders prefer to have the stringers stand proud of the frames by say ⅛ to ³⁄₁₆ inch (3 to 5 mm). This practice stops the frames touching the hull and causing the "starved cow" look that spoils the appearance of an otherwise fine metal hull. If your boat is large enough, say over 36 feet (11 m), then consider using ³⁄₁₆-inch (5 mm) hull plating, as this will result in a fairer hull.

Radius-Chine Frames

Do not confuse this type of hull with one that simply has pipe chines. True radius-chine hulls have a radius of between 24 and 36 inches (600 and 900 mm). The radius-chine hull has many benefits, including all of those attributed to a round-bilge metal hull. The fact is that the radius-chine hull is one of the easiest hull forms

At last it is possible to build a round-bilge steel boat without the great amount of time and effort (not to mention experience) that used to be required for traditional methods. Radius-chine building techniques are developed through computer fairing, which provides you with full-size patterns of all the frames, a full-size stem, and a full-size expanded transom. The secret of radius-chine lies in fairing the radius through to the bow. Most other attempts at this type of hull form have tried to fade out the chine before it reaches the bow. This usually results in a flat spot, or unfair area, up forward. Previous methods have been, and still are, more difficult to build than the multi-chine method. Our radius-chine is very easy to build because of the exact way we develop these hulls on our in-house computer programs. The full-size patterns are plotted on Mylar film.

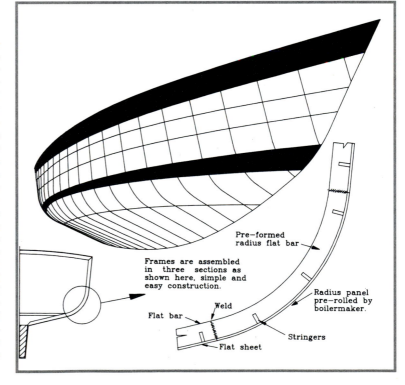

Pre-formed radius flat bar

Frames are assembled in three sections as shown here, simple and easy construction.

Weld

Flat bar

Radius panel pre-rolled by boilermaker.

Stringers

Flat sheet

On smaller frameless designs like this one, it may be simpler for the less-experienced steelworker to build a frame from timber.

to build in metal. This ease of construction applies from making the frames right through to the final plating.

All true radius-chine hulls are designed, faired, and lofted in the computer, so you'll almost certainly have accurate full-size patterns. Naturally, it's most important to have accurate patterns from which to make your frames, and computer lofting is the best way to achieve this end. As the radius sections are all of the same radius, it's only the amount of arc around the curve that will vary. This means that you won't need to transfer all of the radius curves to your loft floor. Transfer only the straight frame sections. Make sure that the ends of these lines are clearly defined. Use a check mark to give a clear definition to the ends. Next, simply cut the straight lengths of framing and place them in position. Now, cut the exact lengths of curved frame material that have been prebent to the correct radius.

You can either bend the radius-frame material yourself, or have it bent by an outside metal shop. Assuming that you farm out this work, we recommend that you have the radius-frame sections, stem bar, and lengths of plate all bent to the correct radius section at the same time (see Radius-Chine Hulls in chapter 8, Plating Your Hull). The remainder of the techniques used for assembling the frames of your radius-chine hull are virtually the same as those used for the other hull forms.

Frames for "Frameless" Hulls

If you're building a "frameless" boat, that is, a hull with only a few frames, or one that has no transverse frames, then you may use angle frames as a mold, and these will not remain in the boat. When you're building the "mold" for a frameless boat, you may find it possible to eliminate every second frame when setting up the shape of the hull. When the designer prepares computer-designed lines, it's usual to have only 4 to 6 control sections (similar to frames) and the remainder of the hull is faired through these sections. Most light-to-medium-displacement steel-chine hulls (not radius-chine) under, say, 40 feet (12.19 m), are suitable for building with the frameless technique. Contact the designer of your boat if you're interested in using this method. Ask if some frames may be eliminated, either in the finished boat or in the setting-up mold. Some frameless hulls are built over a timber framework; this may be helpful if you're building a metal hull under 35 feet (10.66 m) and have limited metal-working experience. You could build the timber framework yourself, and then hire an experienced welder to weld up the hull.

PREPARING TO BUILD

Stem, Backbone, and Keel

You'll find that metal boats use many different sections for building the stem. Some boats feature a stem that is a flat bar on edge. This, in fact, is the material specified for many of our sailboat designs. Other designers favor solid round bar, round or rectangular tube, or rolled plate. In many of our powerboat designs, we favor stems that incorporate rolled plate above the top chine. Your homemade bending machine will come into use for bending the flat-bar stem if part or all or the stem is to be formed from this material. Some stems may include a conical section of rolled plate.

The aft section of the backbone may be installed on-edge without your having to form it in a bending device. Some stems, such as those used in the Spray designs, may be constructed using a box section of similar construction to that used to fabricate the keel. You'll need to make plywood or hardboard patterns for the sides of the box stem, and trial-fit them before cutting any metal.

The leading edge of the keel will be flat bar, split pipe, full pipe, or rolled plate. Flat-bar leading edges for the keel are satisfactory for very small powerboats. In most cases, a rounded leading edge will not only be stronger and less liable to damage, but will also offer a better passage through the water for the hull. The aft end of the keel is usually formed of flat bar on edge.

Bedlogs and Strongbacks

For hulls built upside down, your plans should include details of preparing the base needed to set up the hull frames. This base can have one of several names including bedlog or strongback. In our plans, a set of bedlogs consists of a framework of suitably sized timber or steel I beams placed on a prepared surface. The surface can be concrete, packed earth, or other similar base. If a packed-earth floor is used, you'd be wise to install strategically placed concrete pads capable of supporting the bedlogs and the completed hull. You're building a foundation, albeit a temporary one, and it has to support the hull until it is plated. In the case of a hull built upright, the strongback or setting-up bedlogs will be required to remain true until the boat is completed.

The strongback is a framework that's usually about 3 feet (910 mm) off the ground or floor. It's used to support frames on a hull being built upside down. The idea of the strong-

An overhead gantry set on rails can make the handling of plate a much easier and safer operation.

back is to have the inverted hull set up far enough above the floor so the builder could easily climb underneath the hull to undertake the necessary tack-welding of the stringers to the inner hull plating before the turn-over stage. More recently, however, we've found it easier to simply extend the frames to a common headstock or upper baseline. Using this method, we ensure that the hull will be far enough off the floor to clear the stem, and allow a welder to have easy access to the interior of the hull. In all setting-up methods, a wire stretched tightly down the centerline will be an essential part of the procedure.

Gantry

You may consider installing a gantry that can be used to erect the frames and assist in installing the plating. If you're assembling your hull inside a commercial building, you may be fortunate in having an overhead gantry already available; otherwise you'll have to arrange your own. The track will consist of a pair of channel rails made from some U-section steel that run full-length each side of the hull. Two sets of A-frames set to run on wheels in the channel and an I beam rigged with one or more chain blocks, chain falls, or a chain hoist (all the same device), will complete the arrangement. An even simpler gantry is a tripod with an attachment point for a chain hoist. You can use it to lift the plates and other large metal sections.

Building Upright

Professional builders have many methods of setting up the frames, transom, and stem, to build a metal hull upright. These methods, while suitable for the professional, could in some cases cause problems for less experienced builders. For instance, they could allow errors to creep in, resulting in a less-than-fair hull. It's the responsibility of the designer, especially when dealing with a less-experienced builder, to ensure that the method of setting up the hull is well detailed in

the plans. This will make things easier for the first-time builder who otherwise may be unsure of how to proceed. Experienced welders, metal workers, and fitters who had no previous boat-building experience have built many fine metal boats.

For the less-experienced builder, the secret is to have a well prepared building frame, strongback, or similar arrangement to allow the frames to be set up in their correct locations and to avoid errors. One method we have used is to build a framework for a shed-like structure, and support the frames from overhead rafters. Another way is to build a set of bedlogs and use pipe supports to hold the frames in position until the keel, stringers, chine bars, and stem are installed. With a hull built upright, once the keel is plated the structure can be more or less self-supporting, with the weight mostly on the keel. Additional supports should be installed under the ends and sides of the hull to avoid sagging during construction.

Building Inverted

By now you will have constructed and assembled all of the elements of the framework. Now you can start to install the frames on the strongback or bedlogs. A tensioned wire marks the centerline of the building jig. This wire will remain in position until the hull is turned upright.

You'll need a carpenter's rule, a steel measuring tape (at least as long as your boat), a plumb bob, a large carpenter's square, a spirit level about 3 feet (1 m) long, and a line spirit level. Each frame must be square off the strongback, and must be parallel with its neighbor. Use the plumb bob to ensure the frame is vertical.

After you've marked out the strongback or bedlogs with the correct station spacing, you can start with station 5 or the midsection frame (the same frame in most cases) and install it firmly in position. Work alternatively fore and aft, installing the frames until they're all in place. Needless to say, you should check everything several times until you're absolutely sure the whole structure is true and fair. We have seen boats with stems that are crooked and keels whose leading edges are out of line; it's really a sad sight. Your eye will be one of your best guides to fairness; use it, and then check again by measuring and use the level, square and plumb bob to ensure you have everything set up true and fair.

Next, install the stem, the aft centerline bar, and the centerline transom bar. The transom may be left off at this stage and not installed until after the plating is completed on the remainder of the hull. Generally, you don't install the keel sides or the bottom of the keel plate until after the hull is plated up and has the strength to support the heavier plating that is usually specified for the keel.

In some designs, a few of the bulkheads may be included as frames; this works fine, providing you do not change your interior plan after the bulkheads have been installed. The bulkheads at

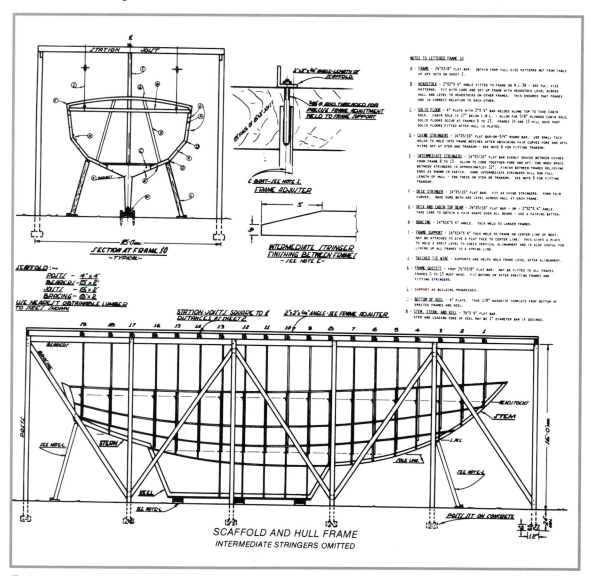

Typical section of plans, illustrating one of several ways used to build a hull upright.

the forward and aft ends of the engine room will be metal, as will the anchor locker bulkhead (sometimes called the crash bulkhead). The aft bulkhead of the main cabin and the forward bulkhead of the aft cabin (at least above the deckline), will all be metal. In our designs, we prefer to install at least some of the bulkheads after the hull is turned over. In most cases, the bulkheads will fall on a frame. It's no problem to deal with intermediate bulkheads. Some bulkheads will be metal and others are best built of plywood.

In our designs, the web or solid floors form part of the frame structure. It's like a mini-bulkhead at each frame. These web floors generally extend up from the keel to the cabin sole, and can be used to contain and divide up tanks and ballast, and to support engine beds. There is no need to ring these web floors with framing bar; in fact, it's a bad idea because corrosion can form between the bar and the web. The material for the webs should be the same thickness as that used for the flat of the framing; this way, there will be no change in thickness where the framing and the webs are butt-welded to the remainder of the frame.

Stringers and Chine Bars

Longitudinal framing plays a very important part in maintaining the strength of your hull. After you've set up the frames, it's time to install the stringers and chine bars. We prefer flat bar for stringers. For chine bars, both solid round bar and flat bar have advantages and disadvantages. We don't recommend closed pipe for chine bars. Steel pipe can rust inside, and it's difficult, if not impossible, to paint or otherwise protect the interior of the pipe. When it's used in the leading edge of the keel, you can fill the pipe with lead.

Many designers and builders prefer to have the stringers stand proud of the frames by ⅛ to ³⁄₁₆ inch (3 to 4.5 mm), thus avoiding every frame showing through the plated surface. If the frames are not touching the plating, it will be impossible to weld the plating to the frames; in our opin-

ion this isn't a problem, especially in boats under, say, 40 feet (12.19 m). Using this method, the stringers are welded to the frames and the plating is welded to the stringers. This ties the structure together and provides adequate overall strength.

If the frames are away from the plating, you can paint behind them when you're painting the interior. As most hulls now have sprayed-on insulation, however, this benefit may be academic. The main benefit is to keep the hull fair and not to allow any frame to show through onto the plating.

Check with the designer of your particular boat before welding or not welding frames to the hull skin; his calculations may require one or the other practice. In any case, the frames should have been set up in such a way as to avoid their showing through the plating; frames 0 through 5 (midsection) are set so the forward edge is on the station mark; frames 6 to the stern are installed so the aft edge of the frame is on the mark.

When installing the stringers, only tack-weld them into the slots. In most designs, the plating will take a fair curve and the stringers may need to be "relieved" so they'll make contact with the plating throughout the hull. It is a fine judgment whether to pull the plate into the stringers or let the stringers out to lie neatly against the plating. By now your eye should be developed sufficiently to make it obvious which course to follow. In some places, the stringers will need to take the strain while the plating is pulled into place; again your eye will help you to make the right decision.

The order of installing the stringers and chine bars (if present) can be as follows. Firstly, install the sheer or deck stringer, making sure that you keep the ends of the frames equally spaced and square off the centerline. Next, in the case of a chine or radius-chine hull, install the chine stringers (chine bars). Although there is room for discussion as to whether you should fit flat bar, round bar, or have no chine stringers at all, your practical choice is limited: follow the recommendations shown in your plans.

The alternate deck stringer shown here would double as a rubbing strake. It's best used on smaller boats, say under 35 feet (10.5 m).

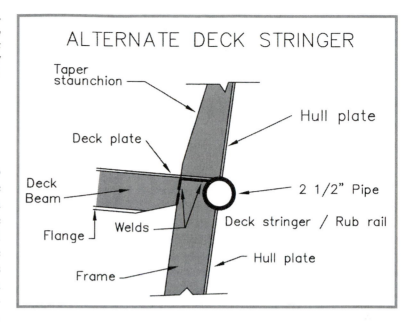

ALTERNATE DECK STRINGER

Taper staunchion

Deck plate

Deck Beam

Flange

Frame

Hull plate

2 1/2" Pipe

Welds

Deck stringer / Rub rail

Hull plate

Radius-Chine Stringers

In a radius-chine hull, fit two stringers, one each side of the radius. They should be just a little inside or outside of the radius-flat joint; and as you'll need to be able to weld the plates from inside as well as outside, the stringer must be a small distance from the intersection of the radius-flat line. One reason for having these two stringers, one each side of the radius-flat intersection, is to provide a fair guide for the radius-flat intersection. See your plans or full-size patterns, where this line should be clearly marked.

Some builders may prefer to have the radius-chine stringers right on the line that intersects the flat and radius section. If you choose this last method, you'll need to make sure that the plate-to-stringer weld attains full penetration from outside. A few short welds either side of the stringer from inside the hull may be advisable.

Intermediate Stringers

After you have installed the sheer, deck stringer (if it's present as a separate item), and chine stringers, check your hull for fairness. Again, use your eye (and perhaps the eyes of other more experienced builders) to ensure that the hull is progressing without being pulled out of line. Now install the intermediate stringers. The number of intermediate stringers in each chine panel will depend on the size of the hull and the particular metal being used. In most cases, a spacing of 12 inches (305 mm) will be adequate.

Under no circumstances should you perma-nently weld the intermediate stringers into their slots at this time. You may want to release them later, to allow the stringers to take up the same line as the plate.

When all the chine bars and stringers are in position, the next job is to check over the structure again to ensure that it's fair in all aspects. A timber batten, sized approximately 1 by ½ inch (25 by 12 mm) and about 6 feet (2 m) long, can be laid diagonally across the hull at various locations, and your eye will probably give the best indication of the overall fairness up to this point. Check over the whole structure and make sure there are no unfair areas. On a round-bilge hull a longer batten will be needed to achieve the same results.

Stern and Rudder Tubes

Before you start plating you'll need to decide if you're going to install the stern and rudder tubes at this stage. It's reasonable to install the rudder tube(s) before the plating is in place. The stern tube(s) for the propeller(s) are more difficult to place correctly at this stage. If your hull is upside down, you need some very accurate calculations and measurements to get the correct angle and position for the stern tube. It may be better to

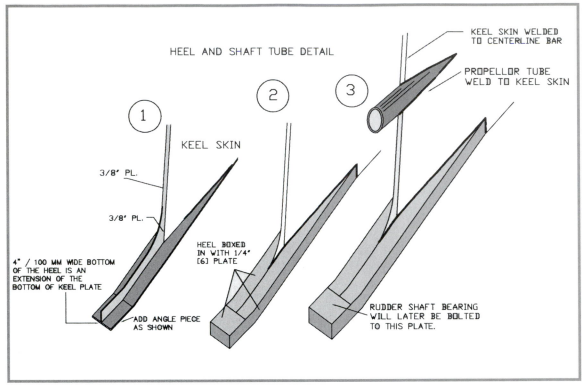

HEEL AND SHAFT TUBE DETAIL

KEEL SKIN WELDED TO CENTERLINE BAR

PROPELLOR TUBE WELD TO KEEL SKIN

KEEL SKIN

3/8" PL.

3/8" PL.

4" / 100 MM WIDE BOTTOM OF THE HEEL IS AN EXTENSION OF THE BOTTOM OF KEEL PLATE

HEEL BOXED IN WITH 1/4" [6] PLATE

ADD ANGLE PIECE AS SHOWN

RUDDER SHAFT BEARING WILL LATER BE BOLTED TO THIS PLATE.

These sketches show a simple way to build a "heel" to support the rudder and incorporate the tube for the transmission shaft in such a way as to allow the maximum amount of water to reach the propeller.

leave it until you've completed the plating and turned the hull. In hulls built upright, it's easier to figure out where the engine beds are located and where you should install the stern tube.

Just a note on stern bars. If your plans call for a stern bar that is, say, 2 to 4 inches (50 to 100 mm) wide, then you may be better served by using a flat bar placed in the fore-and-aft plane and cutting it to take the tube. When you plate the hull, the plating will have a half-oval shape around the stern tube, and the water flow to the propeller will be much cleaner and less turbulent than it would be with a wide stern bar.

This stern tube arrangement is recommended and will allow adequate flow of water to the propeller.

8
PLATING THE HULL

On a well-designed metal boat, many of the potential problems associated with plating multi-chine, radius-chine, or round-bilge hulls have been eliminated by the naval architect preparing your plans. If the plans and patterns for your hull have been faired by a computer, conically developed, or specially prepared for round-bilge construction, then you can lay the plating on, or pull it, or raise it into position without undue problems. The curvature in all directions should be gradual, to allow the bending of the plate by methods and devices employing simple mechanical advantages.

This also is a good time to review your safety procedures; this is especially important in the case of steel and copper-nickel, where you may be handling heavy plate. Make sure of the integrity of the weld when you're using various pad eyes, "dogs," and other devices to lift heavy plate and other sections.

If you're building upright, plating the keel and installing part of the ballast may be one of the first operations you'll consider before plating the hull. If you're building the hull

inverted, you should leave the plating of the keel until you've plated the remainder of the hull and built up sufficient strength in the structure to support the heavy keel.

PLATING TOOLS

You'll need a variety of special tools and devices to assist you to plate the hull. Fortunately, most of these labor-saving tools are simple in nature. You can make them from scrap plate and bar. As mentioned earlier, a simple gantry from which to suspend your chain-block lifting device will save you many hours of lifting plate and other materials by cruder methods. In the case of steel and copper-nickel, while the material is still on the shop floor the heavier plates can be moved about

Your plating pattern should lie flat on the plate; this is a test of its ability to lie evenly on the hull framing.

on pipe rollers. Aluminum, being softer and lighter, will need to be handled more carefully to avoid scratching the face of the plate. Lifting eyes can be tack-welded to the plates, but make sure there's sufficient strength in the weld to take the load.

Plate can be moved sideways using a "come-along" or a pipe lever. Every time you have to move a plate, there's a mechanical device or aid that can help you. These simple devices multiply your muscle power many times and will take much effort out of installing the plating and other heavy parts of your boat. In metal boat building you should try to work smart rather than hard. We have on our records the case of one builder with no previous metal boat building experience who, with the assistance of a simple tackle and gantry, successfully installed full-length plates on a 53-foot (16.15 m) sailboat that he built to our design. A great deal can be achieved with a little forethought and preparation.

PLATING THE KEEL

One of the many advantages of a metal sailboat is that the keel will almost certainly be of the "envelope" type, and your ballast will be fully enclosed and protected within the hull. Needless to say, there are no keel bolts to worry about.

If you're building upright, you may plate the keel first. We recommend that you install a percentage of the ballast during the construction of the keel. It's much easier to install a fair proportion of the ballast in the keel now, while you simply have to lift it into the partially plated keel. This is a good time to remind you that the sides and bottom of the keel form part of the ballast. Remember to deduct the weight of the keel structure from the overall recommended ballast before proceeding further. In our designs, we recommend you install 75 percent of the total ballast (including the weight of the keel structure) before launching. The remaining 25 percent can be installed as trim ballast after preliminary sailing trials are completed.

You can use inexpensive plywood or hardboard to make patterns for the sides of the keel.

The leading and trailing edges, and the keel webs, will already be installed. It will depend on the actual type and design of your keel as to whether you can plate the sides in one piece. In a deep keel, you may have a problem reaching down far enough to weld the lower ends of the webs and the inside side-to-bottom intersection. In this case you may prefer to have a longitudinal join, say 12 inches (305 mm) above the bottom of the keel, or some other suitable distance. On occasion, you may find it necessary to cut slots in the keel side plating so you can plug-weld through to the webs. Your plans should give you some guidance in these areas. If you're building the hull inverted, you'll follow similar procedures for building the keel, but you'll undertake this work after the other parts of the hull are fully plated.

PLATING HULL CHINES

After you've carefully checked over your hull to ensure that it's fair, you may start to prepare patterns for the plating. The plating patterns or templates are made from a number of 6-inch (150 mm) strips of inexpensive ¼-inch (6 mm) plywood or hardboard. The outer edges of the templates represent the outer edges of the plate. Seldom is it necessary to use a complete sheet of plywood or hardboard for a template. Usually, these patterns are made up of straight strips and corner gussets, like a frame, and made to fit the particular area to be plated. To strengthen large areas, cross-brace your templates by nailing on reinforcing pieces where necessary. The templates are built right on the hull by clamping the strips in place in between the chines. The length of each panel may vary; you want the patterns as long as possible, but not so long as to be unmanageable. Do not end a template on a frame, otherwise your plate will have a bulge in that area; always end a pattern between two frames. The ends of the patterns are always vertical; this helps in getting one pattern to join to the next with the minimum of error.

After you've formed the outline of the pattern, you can trim it to exact shape with a grinder

Radius-chine panels around the center of the hull need to be split lengthwise before being fitted.

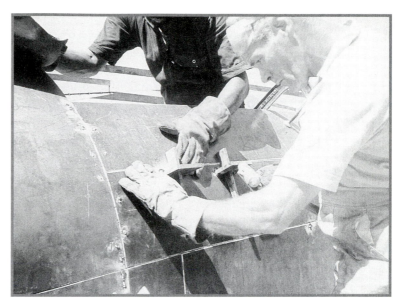

or jigsaw, or, in fact, any tool that will help you achieve a perfect pattern. Check and double-check the template to ensure that it's a neat fit. After you're satisfied with the pattern, you can mark in the frame locations and use them as guides when you're positioning the sections of plate. See the welding details on your plans to decide on the welding gaps between the various plate edges. After you're satisfied that you have an accurate template, lay it on the floor. It should lie flat if the plating is to lie on your hull in a fair manner. Successive sections of patterning templates can be joined to make a pattern for one long plate. The longer the section of plate you intend to have in one length, the more accurate your patterns must be. Small discrepancies are greatly magnified over the length of a long plate. The patterns can contain other information, including stringer locations and any other information that you feel will help you to match the plate precisely to your hull framework.

It's usually best to pattern the largest panel first, then the pattern can be trimmed and used for the next section. This will save on patterning material. You should start at the keel and work either downward or upward, depending on the aspect of your hull. Make the patterns as sturdy as you can, and they will serve you well.

PREPARING THE PLATE

You must decide how long each plate will be before it is installed on the hull. Some builders prefer a plate as long as possible. The actual length will depend on the size of your hull, your previous experience, and the capacity of your scaffolding and lifting gear. Panels that are welded to full

length on the shop floor where they will lie flat will be easier to install in a fair curve. This helps in eliminating any humps and hollows in the finished hull plating. On smaller boats, say under 30 feet (9.10 m), you should be able to plate the full length in one operation. Larger boats will require more sections. For instance, one man with a helper plated a 75-foot (22.86 m) hull using three 25-foot (7.62 m) panels. In general, use the longest sections you can comfortably handle. Builders of aluminum hulls will have some advantage here, as the material weighs only about one-third that of steel or copper-nickel and is therefore much easier to handle. You can transfer the outline of the template to the steel plate by laying the pattern on the plate, (it must lie flat), clamping it in position, and then carefully scribing around the edge. Mark in the frame and other pertinent locations on the plate.

Start plating at the keel and work either up or down, making sure that you work on alternate sides of the hull: that is, never plate up one side completely before plating the other. Keep the plating balanced so no undue stresses are placed on your hull framework by the plating pulling one way or the other. This can result in a twisted or otherwise deformed hull. The transom is best installed after the remainder of the plating is completed. The open transom will provide access inside the hull for the welders and let in light. Once you have marked the template outline onto the plate, you can cut it to shape. The method of cutting will depend on the hull material, and is covered in detail in chapter 4, Tools and Safety Equipment.

Once you've cut the plate, you'll want to serve the panel up to the correct area. Using the alignment marks you've previously marked on the boat, pattern, and plate, clamp the piece in position. If there are any discrepancies in the fit, take the panel down and make the necessary adjustments before reinstalling the plate. It's worth noting that professional boatbuilders often find it necessary to "serve up" the plate several times before they achieve the desired fit. It's obviously easier to trim off excess than to put back areas that are over-trimmed. Keep this in mind when making patterns and cutting the plate.

On no account try the sloppy practice of installing an oversized plate and then trimming it by simply torching off the excess. If you plate your hull in this manner it will clearly show in the finished job. Buckles, hollows, and other large imperfections will tell all who care to look at your boat that you were indeed a sloppy builder. Always remember that one day you may want to sell your boat, and an unfair hull is one of the greatest factors in reducing the value of any used boat.

Before the plates are finally installed, make sure you have ground off any imperfections on the edges. Unless your plate is shotblasted and preprimed, which we recommend, make sure you clean up the face of the plate as well. It's easier to clean the plate before installation than when it's in place, especially in the case of interior surfaces partly obscured by the frames or stringers.

For steel, there are several ways to clean the faces of the plates before you install them. Gritblasting or sandblasting is the easiest and best method, but in the case of steel, prime coating must follow immediately to protect the sandblasted surface. You can use a disk grinder, a power-driven wire brush, or one of any number of similar methods. These techniques are very noisy, and are only for tidying up the plate, rather than preparing it for painting.

You should remove mill scale and any other foreign matter so that the panel of plate has no imperfections before you install it. Before you paint the hull, you must bring the surface back to bare white metal. You must paint this within a very short time, minutes rather than hours, to ensure a rust-free surface in the future. Finishing techniques are discussed in chapter 10, Painting a Metal Boat.

The edges of the plate will need to be beveled before you install them. The amount of bevel will depend on the thickness of the plate and the metal you're using for plating. Note that aluminum and copper-nickel need to be prepared in a different manner to steel. Before hoisting the plate, you'll need to make provision for it to be supported while you're fitting it into position, and later welding it to the chines and stringers. One method is to tack-weld a few lengths of angle to a chine bar, frame, and stringer to support the bottom of the plate. Support the chine bar with another piece of angle that extends to the shop floor, thus transferring the load, so that the weight of the plate doesn't deform the fair line of the chine. The "plate holders" should be tilted inboard, so the plate will naturally slip into the correct location and not slip out of the holder as it's moved from side to side to get the exact alignment required.

You can use a selection of homemade C-clamps to draw the upper edge of the plate to the chine, the centerline bar, and the stem. As you tighten the clamps, you'll be drawing the steel plate into position in all planes. In a well-designed chine hull, you'll find that the plating will naturally conform to the shape provided by the framework of chine bars, frames, and stringers. Most plating is between $\frac{1}{8}$ and $\frac{3}{16}$ inch (3 and 5 mm) thick, so it will lie in place without your having to resort to extreme bending methods.

In cases where more pressure is required, several techniques will help you. A popular method is to tack-weld lengths of threaded rod in the area where you need assistance. You can judge the length of the pieces of rod needed for the job. Use ⅜-inch (8 mm) diameter rod that is tacked at a 90-degree angle to the inside of the plate, and use a prepared section of 2- by 2- by ¼-inch (50 by 50 by 6 mm) L-angle behind the stringers and chine bars to receive the inboard ends of the threaded rod. By tightening up on the rod, you'll be able to coax the plate into its correct location. Another method is to weld U-shaped eyes to the inside of the plate and then attach a "come-along" or other suitable device, such as a Spanish windlass, to pull the plate into position.

As you will have only tacked the stringers and chine bars into the slots, as we advised earlier, it's permissible and often desirable to "relieve" the stringers and even the chine bars by allowing them to come out of the slots to meet the plating. It takes some judgment to know when to let out the longitudinal, instead of pulling the plating in harder, to make the correct shape and fit. Do not hesitate to weld eyes, U-shaped round bar, and threaded rod to your plate, to help you get the result you want. You can knock off these temporary protrusions when you've fully welded the plate in position. Don't compromise on a good fit. Follow the welding guidelines given in chapter 5.

Butt joints (where two sections of plate meet end to end) can be drawn together with bolts and large washers. The butt joints must be in near perfect alignment to achieve a smooth hull surface, otherwise they'll show as bulges or uneven patches. Drill several holes in the beveled seams between the plates, and insert bolts fitted with large washers and nuts. When you take up on the nuts, you'll be exerting great pressure up and down the vertical butt joint and you'll even out any bulges or other irregularities in the joint. After you tack-weld the plates along the bevels, you can take out the bolts and close the holes with weld.

Once again, as you install the various plates, be sure to work from one side to the other and keep the plating evenly balanced. Be certain to achieve a good fit. A little grinding here and there can make all the difference in making the plates

fit as perfectly as possible. The plates may need to be slid back and forth to correctly position them. A "come-along," or a tap with a hammer (using a wooden block to protect the ends of the plate) can work wonders. The foregoing is another reason to ensure that you have the plate held securely, but with some freedom of movement, as you prepare to tack it into place.

Don't rush; you'll be looking at your hull for a long time. Don't fully weld any plate into position until you've installed all of the hull plating. Don't forget to work from side to side along your hull, never get more than one plate ahead on one side, and keep the plating balanced. Once you've tacked a few plates into position, you'll notice a considerable stiffening of the hull structure. Sight along the hull as each plate is installed to ensure that you are maintaining a fair curve and that no plate looks out of line. If you find you have incorrectly installed a plate, take it off and correct the problem before proceeding. The first plates will be the hardest to install, so make sure you get them right and you'll find that the plating process gets easier as you proceed. Most builders are able, after some practice, to pattern, fit, and install one or two plates a day. If you're achieving more than that, you may be working too fast at the expense of quality.

Any boat hull must look absolutely perfect *before* painting if it's to look reasonable *after* it's painted. If you're in doubt, splash some water on your hull to bring up a shine, and then judge how well you're doing. Another trick is to take a flashlight and examine your hull at night. When you shine the flashlight along the hull, all the imperfections become more apparent. Aim for perfection; you may not achieve it, but if you aim high, you should finish up with an attractive and fair hull.

RADIUS-CHINE HULLS

Here is what one builder had to say about plating a radius-chine section of the hull.

"Builders do not need to feel handicapped because they do not own several multi-ton rolling presses. Plate can be sent out for rolling to get the initial radius for $300 to $400 (£200 to £270) plus the price of transport. After that, all that you need are about three 'come-alongs,' a cutting torch, and a few dogs and wedges. The actual process of oxy-fuel torch cutting shrinks the perimeter of the radius sections, and with the help of the 'come-alongs' and wedges, the sections will develop a compound curve. With patience, skill, and time it is not difficult to build a radius-chine boat.

"I have built a radius-chine Roberts 53. The actual radius sections (24 sections, 12 on each side) took approximately four hours each to cut and fit into place. You spend additional time welding one extra horizontal seam each side and three vertical seams each side, for a total weld time of about 30 hours. After welding (100 percent X-ray quality) I spent another 40 or so hours grinding the outside weld profile flush with the hull. Yes, it takes longer than multi-chine, *but if it is properly done, it is hard to tell the difference between radius-chine steel and fiberglass out of a mold.*"

In the case of radius-chine hulls, we recommend that you plate the radius section first. Unless you have experience in rolling plate to an accurate radius, we suggest that you give this job to a local metal shop. Choose a metal shop that has the knowledge and the necessary equipment to undertake the work. A look in the telephone directory will provide many possibilities. Steel, aluminum, or copper-nickel are all easy to roll to a constant radius if you have the correct equipment and are used to this type of work. Perhaps the supplier of your metal plate will have these facilities; if not, he or she will certainly be able to point you in the right direction.

To ascertain the arc of radius you'll need for the largest (widest) plate, simply measure around this arc on your full-size patterns. Usually, the largest arc is at the stern or just ahead of the transom. It may be cheaper to have all the plates the same width, even though the arc (not the radius) will get smaller as the plating progresses toward the bow. You will simply trim off the excess and use the off-cuts for scrap. Needless to say, if you do measure each plate, make sure there's enough width to allow for trimming.

The radius plating should be ordered in about 10-foot (3 m) lengths. The center of the hull will almost always involve some compound curvature, and it will be necessary to split the center plate at least once, maybe twice, lengthwise. The plates on either side of the center one also may need splitting, but the plates near the bow and stern should fit in one piece. In a sailboat, with its greater beam-to-length ratio, you'll have more plates to split lengthwise to get a perfect fit. When the plates are split, the two halves are served up to the hull and allowed to overlap. The excess material is removed before tacking the radius panel into place. As with all plating, keep the ends of each plate exactly vertical, as this will assist in obtaining a good fit for the butt joints at the ends of each section of plate.

As we've already seen, you'll generally find that the

A rain shower shows up the fairness of this New York 65 radius-chine hull built by Howdy Bailey.

John Williams built this radius-chine Roberts 434. Note that he applied the radius panels first. We recommend that the radius panels be installed last.

The radius-chine hull form is one of the easiest to use if you want to achieve a professional-looking hull.

Interior of a Roberts 53 radius-chine hull, ready to receive bulkheads.

largest arc of radius is at, or near, the stern of the vessel. You should install the radius plates first, starting at the aft end of the hull and keeping the edges neat. Trim to a fair line, using a batten to strike a line where the radius panels meet the straight panels of the bottom and the topsides. You should previously have indicated clearly where the radius and straight sections meet on each frame.

Don't let the above explanation frighten you off the radius-chine technique. Hundreds of builders have used this method to build beautiful metal hulls. Many have taken the time to write, telephone, and seek me out at boat shows to report their entire satisfaction with this metal-building technique. The flat, or nonradiused, areas of a radius-chine boat are usually simpler to install than those on a regular chine hull. Simply lift on the bottom and or side plate, mark the join from underneath, and trim the plate to shape. Of course, all of the plating, including the radiused and straight sections, is only tack-welded at this stage.

ROUND-BILGE HULLS

Building a round-bilge metal hull is the most difficult hull-building method, and should not be undertaken lightly. You must know that you can produce a fair hull; if you're not sure you can, you should use either the chine or the radius-chine techniques. If you find a professional who can plate your hull to your entire satisfaction, then that can be the solution.

Some round-bilge hulls have been plated lengthwise using strips of varying widths, but allowing the strips to overlap. This technique is similar to that used to build timber lapstrake hulls. Although the famous Joshua class is built in this way—and these are proven boats—it's our contention that corrosion must occur where the plates overlap. Our advice is to avoid overlapping plates of other metal sections wherever possible. This applies especially to steel hulls. As for aluminum and copper-nickel, we are conducting research in this area. A copper-nickel lapstrake hull could be a possibility. Watch this space!

How you go about plating a round-bilge hull will depend on the shape of the hull. There are easy shapes, difficult shapes, and near-impossible shapes. Starting at the bottom of the keel, you'll find that the lower portion of the keel in a round-bilge hull will be similar in most, if not all, respects to one fitted to a similar style of multi-chine hull. If the hull features a "hollow heel," this will definitely be a job for a professional metal boat builder. If the hull and keel meet at right angles, or nearly, then plating the keel of the round-bilge hull won't present any undue problems.

Now you must examine the overall shape of the "canoe body." For instance, the traditional Spray design has a very full, golf-ball-shaped bow that makes it a difficult plating job even for an experienced metal boat builder. In our round-bilge versions of the Spray, and also in the chine hulls, we have drawn out the bow to make the hull easier to plate. In the case of the Spray, this also improves the performance and comfort of the vessel, as it cuts through short steep waves rather than pounding over them. Some metal hulls may have been designed with full-bodied, rounded sterns or other features that will make them difficult to plate. A careful study of the plans can give you some hints as to the "plate-ability" of the hull in question.

Once you're confident that your chosen design features a hull shape that's within your plating capabilities, consider the best technique for fitting the plate. There are three ways to lay plate on a round-bilge hull: longitudinally; in multi-shaped sections; and in diagonal strips. If the hull has a suitable shape, the diagonal method may suit the less experienced builder.

FINAL WELDING

Don't attempt any of the finish welding until all the hull plating is tack-welded into position. Before you start the final welding, give your hull a final check for irregularities. They will be easier to correct before the welding is completed. Bumps can be removed by any one of several metal-working techniques, including using a rubber mallet on one side while a helper holds a suitably shaped timber backing-piece on the other. Hollows on the hull are most unsightly, and must be removed. Small wrinkles along the chine can be removed from inside with the careful use of a large plastic-faced mallet and a person holding a suitable backing-piece from outside the hull.

Final welding consists of short welds laid down in the proper sequence for that particular plating. As mentioned in chapter 5, Welding, different techniques are required to weld steel, aluminum, and copper-nickel. You must be fully conversant with the method best suited to the plating of your hull.

Much of the work, up until the running of the finish welds, can be handled by a person with a minimum of welding experience, but the final welding of the plating is another matter. If you're not a fully experienced welder, this may be the time to hire a professional. If you plan to take this route, we recommend that you seek help *before* you start the project. Discuss with the professional how much you can do yourself, and when and where you will need his or her assistance.

If you're going to seek outside assistance, make sure the person understands the problems of welding a pleasure boat. Welding a boat is quite different to commercial welding. In commercial welding, strength is important but laying down a considerable amount of weld per hour also has a high priority. A commercial welder might not consider a fine finish to be so important. Explain your expectations to the professional before you enter into a firm agreement. If you find that the person you've chosen doesn't come up to your expectations, make other arrangements before the job gets out of hand.

When the welding of the plating is completed, you'll need to grind off some of your welds from the outside of the hull. If you have laid good-quality welds with good penetration, you'll have the minimum of chipping and grinding before repairing or rewelding any unsatisfactory joins in the plate. It's normal practice to grind only those welds above the waterline. Most classification societies insist that the welds below the waterline are left unground so they retain all the strength of the original weld. Do not over-grind the welded seams above the waterline, otherwise you may weaken them to such an extent that you compromise the strength of the vessel.

KEEL PLATING

If you've built your hull upside down, now will be the time to plate the keel. The keel's leading edge (usually pipe or split pipe), the webs, and the aft end of the keel will already be in place. Your plans will instruct you about the order in which to plate the sides and the bottom. In the past, we've usually specified ¼-inch (6 mm) material for the sides, and ½-inch (12 mm) for the bottom plate. Today, we'd be happy to have the whole structure built of ¼-inch (6 mm) plate; this means that at the intersections of the sides and the bottom, you'll be welding material of the same thickness. Also, in the case of boats built inverted, you'll not have to struggle with the heavier ½-inch (12 mm) plate at the bottom of the keel.

FORMING AND PLATING THE TRANSOM

If you're lucky, your plans will include an expanded pattern for the transom. If you don't have this pattern, it's a simple matter to make up some transom formers to the correct camber and then, using inexpensive plywood or hardboard, simply make up a pattern to fill in the transom cavity. Make sure you don't create a "fish-tail" effect at the aft end of your hull. This is caused by making the transom too large (usually, too wide), and preventing the side and bottom plating from taking up its fair line. Don't forget to allow for the deck or transom camber when you're making the pattern and cutting the plate for the transom.

Once you're convinced that the transom plate is the right size and shape, you can install it. It's usual to have a centerline bar extending from the bottom of the hull to the top of the transom, and you can hang the transom plate on this bar while you're positioning the plate. The remainder of the transom stiffeners, usually vertical and transverse stringers, can be installed from inside once the transom plate is fully welded from the outside.

RUBRAILS

You can make rubrails, rubbing strips, or rubbing strakes from the same metal as the hull, or from one of a variety of other materials. The selection includes, but is not restricted to, D-section rubber mounted on a suitable metal structure; timber bolted in place; and rope mounted in a channel or other similar arrangement.

If you're using timber for the rubrail, it should be hardwood. Timbers similar to teak, or softer timbers, can be satisfactory when fitted with a stainless protective strip. For the ultimate timber rubbing strake, Australian spotted gum

Chester Lemon fitting rubbing strip to his Roberts 44.

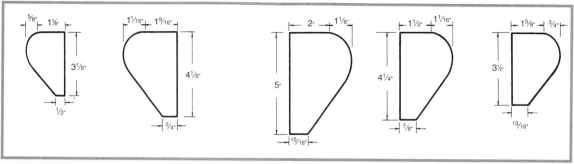

Here we see the correct proportions for a traditional timber rubbing strake.

has the advantage of being durable, flexible, and long-lasting without the need for any additional metal protective strip. In general, timber is easily replaced, can be attractive, and is kind to other boats and structures.

A metal half-round split pipe of suitable dimensions makes an ideal rubrail on a metal boat. We show it on all our metal sailboat designs. You simply take the correct length of pipe, split it lengthwise, and use one half for each side. The aft end can be sniped and plugged with an appropriately shaped piece of hull material. It will finish either at the transom or about 6 inches (150 mm) ahead of it. The other end is tapered so that it will

bend around the forward end of the hull, usually ending at or about station 0, or above the forward end of the waterline. Make sure that you give extra preparation and coating to the inside of the pipe and the hull where it will be installed. Placing underneath the rubrail a thicker hull plate that is 50 percent wider overall than the rubbing strip would provide extra insurance against corrosion and damage from contact with immovable objects.

The problem with this pipe rubrail is that you cannot repaint the inside. Even if you're very careful to give the inside a superior paint job before it's installed, the welding will undo at least

A half-round pipe, as described in the text, is fitted to a Waverunner 52.

part of your work. The pipe itself will have sufficient wall thickness to withstand many years of
interior corrosion, but the plating underneath
may not be so long-lasting. One solution would
be to have a thicker base plate under the pipe, say
three times wider than the pipe. It should be inserted into the hull plating, but not *over* the regular hull plating or you could have problems between the two plates. Skegs and other appendages
are covered in chapter 15. If there is a skeg involved in your hull design, you may prefer to install it after the turnover operation.

TURNING THE HULL

If you've built your hull upside down, now is the
time to consider the turnover. When the plating
is completed and all of the final outer welds have
been run, you can decide on the best method for
turning your hull and setting it in the upright
position. No matter if yours is a large or small
hull, give considerable thought to safety factors
when considering how you will turn it over. Plan
how to set up the hull and level it, ready for com-
pletion. The last thing you need at this stage is
an injury to yourself, a friend, or hired assistant,
so take care.

Several methods have been used successfully
to turn over large boat hulls. The method you

choose will be in some part decided by the size
of your boat, its location, and the accessibility of
your building site. Boats up to about 25 feet (7.62
m) long can be rolled over without the use of
mechanical assistance. For small hulls, you'll need
no more than a few willing friends and a few
bottles of cheer.

If you're building in a large, substantial
commercial building then you may have overhead
track fitted with chain blocks. It may be possible
to set up strong points in the building that are
capable of taking the load. You can arrange two
overhead chain blocks for two endless slings capable of lifting the hull. Now the structure can be
rolled over in its own width. The two slings are
placed about 20 percent in from each end of the
hull. You will need restraining lines to control the
hull during the turning-over operation.

It may be preferable to remove the hull from
the building and turn it over outside where there's
more room. Or you may already have built hoops
around your hull so that it can simply be rolled
over. The hoops will later be used to tilt the hull
to various angles, thus allowing easier access to the
job at all times. Or you may wish to build a
"turnover cradle," shaped something like a crate,
around your hull and turn it over one side at a time.

Our choice would be to hire a crane fitted
with a spreader bar and two endless slings. The
slings are placed in about 20
percent from the bow and
stern and the crane lifts the
hull sufficiently to allow it to
be rotated in the slings. Make
sure you determine the balance
fore and aft before the serious
lifting begins. You will need restraining lines attached to a
winch or other suitably strong
device, to control the hull as it
reaches the up and over stages.

*Many builders have fabricated
various turning-over devices.
These sophisticated turning
wheels are ideal if you're building
more than one boat.*

This Waverunner 44 built in Oman was turned over using one crane fitted with two spreader bars and slings.

When you have turned the hull, you'll need to set it up level in all directions. Use the waterline locations that you have previously marked on the outside of the hull as a guide. The simple type of water level with a clear tube will make it easy for you to set up the hull true and level in all planes.

MOVING THE HULL

You can move large, bulky, and heavy items such as boat hulls using the simplest of tools. You can use a few 2-inch (50 mm) diameter pipe rollers about 9 inches (230 mm) long to roll your hull. Simply lay down planks for the rollers to run on, and keep taking the rollers from the back and re-installing them at the front as the hull moves along the desired path. If you use either 4- by 2-inch (100 by 50 mm) timber, or 2 inch (50 mm) pipe levers, say 5 feet (1.50 m) long, you'll multiply your strength many times when it comes to lifting or shifting heavy weights. When you're lifting the hull or frame to insert the rollers, you'll find the levers are much quicker to use than a lifting jack.

Omani, *a radius-chine Roberts 434, was sailed around the world by Major Pat Garnett in only 218 days.*

9
DECKS AND SUPERSTRUCTURE

You'll want to give some thought to the sequence of the various steps needed to finish the deck and superstructure. You'll have to include gritblasting, insulating the hull, and fitting out the interior. You'll undertake some of these steps before you build the decks and superstructure, of course, so you'll need to plan your own work schedule. You must also be prepared to make minor changes as you proceed with the work. You may be considering building the decks, and/or the superstructure, in a different material from that of the hull. As most of you will be building the entire boat in one metal, however, we'll leave detailed discussion on alternative deck and superstructure materials until nearer the end of this chapter.

Before you start to build the decks and superstructure, you should consider installing all the bulky items that will need to be in the hull eventually, and which may be difficult, if not impossible, to install after the deck and cabin are in place. The engine, large tanks, bulkhead panels, the plywood sole, and similar items need to be in position before the hull is "closed up" by addition of the superstructure.

If your hull is large enough, say over 35 feet (10.67 m), you may plan to set up a small workshop inside the hull where you can manufacture much of the joinery. This is worthwhile if you can fit in a small bench, a table saw, and a band saw, otherwise it may be better to consider one of the alternatives. If your boat is smaller, or if you pre-

fer to work outside the hull, then consider setting up a work area at the sheer or deck level, then you'll only have to climb a few steps to saw, plane, rout, sand, or temporarily assemble a piece of joinery. This can save a great deal of time and effort. Getting up, and over, and out of the boat to make each cut can soon become very tiring, so a better plan is needed.

You may find that some of the cabinets and joinery can be set up inside the hull and then taken out to a nearby bench for sanding, painting, and so forth, before being reinstalled in the hull. It's better to undertake as much preparation as possible before the deck goes on.

GRITBLASTING AND PRIMING

This brings us to the gritblasting that's necessary in steel boats. When is the best time to undertake this work? In our opinion, the best time is before the boat is started—yes, this means pregritblasting and priming all of the materials. If you opt to work with untreated steel, you'll have some problems with working out the sequence of fitting out. You can't install the insulation, the engine, or other large items until after you've gritblasted and primed the inside of the hull. You certainly cannot gritblast the interior once these items are in place. You can see that if you work with untreated steel, you'll create scheduling difficulties. Builders who choose steel as their building material should avoid these problems by

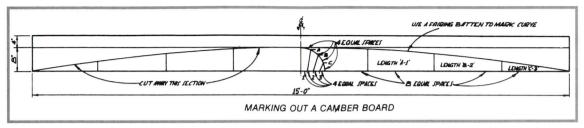

Laying out a camber pattern for deck or cabintop beams will be one of your first tasks before you start work on the decks and superstructure.

either purchasing the steel already preblasted and primed, or by doing the job themselves before they start construction. (See chapter 10, Painting a Metal Boat.)

CAMBER BOARDS

Your plans and patterns may include either the measurements or an actual full-size pattern for the deck and cabintop cambers. Using this pattern, it's a simple matter to cut a hard pattern from plywood or suitable timber. If you get the balance right, you can cut a male and female pattern from one plank. The pattern will be used to obtain the correct camber when you're bending the deck beams and cabin beams.

On sailboats, the cabintop and perhaps the pilothouse top will usually have more camber than the decks have. On powerboats, the opposite is sometimes the case, although quite often the same camber is used throughout. If your plans don't include full-size camber patterns, you can create patterns using the designer's recommended cambers, as shown below.

BULKHEADS

If you're building upright, you may have included some of the bulkheads as you were setting up the initial frames. It would also be possible to include bulkheads when you're setting up an inverted hull, but it may involve raising the whole structure so far off the floor that it would be impractical. Any setting-up method that makes you climb or walk more than is absolutely necessary is not

recommended. In all cases, my preference is to wait until the hull is plated and upright before considering the installation of any bulkheads. That gives you an overview of the hull, so you can take stock of the available space before making firm decisions about placing bulkheads that will affect the layout of the accommodation.

You'll need to decide which bulkheads will be metal and which will be plywood. The bulkheads that will be exposed to the elements should all be metal, including the aft bulkhead of the cabin and the bulkhead located at forward end of the aft cabin. If you have a pilothouse, the aft bulkhead should be metal. In Dutch powerboats, the aft end of the saloon or pilothouse is sometimes made partially of timber. This is acceptable if there is some awning or shelter over it to protect it from the elements. Bulkheads will usually be constructed from the same metal used for the decks. In boats under 40 feet (12.19 m), try to keep the number of metal bulkheads to a minimum, and use plywood where practical.

Metal Bulkheads

The bulkheads at the forward and aft ends of the engine room in both sailboats and powerboats should be constructed from the same metal as the decks. As was demonstrated in the Falklands War, aluminum can burn. For this reason, particular attention should be paid to insulating with fireproof material any aluminum bulkheads located where a fire may break out. The bulkheads that enclose the engine space, for example, will need special attention.

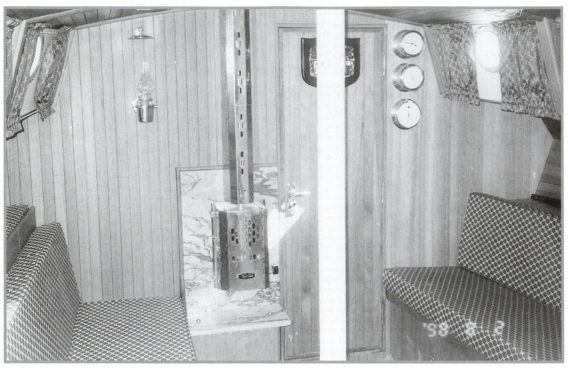

The interior of John and Joan McDermott's Spray 33, Donegal Breeze.

Steel bulkheads are usually placed each side of the engine room. In the case of a sailboat, they will often be at either end of the center cockpit, as shown here.

You will need to secure the lining material to the frames; installing timber "furring strips" is one method. Use a suitable wood preservative before installing the strips.

It's common practice to make the bulkhead adjacent to station 0 from the same metal as the hull. This "crash" bulkhead is usually at the forward end of the waterline. Some classification societies and authorities, including boats built to U.S. Coast Guard survey, require this first bulkhead to be located 5 percent of the load waterline (LWL) aft of the forward end of the waterline. This is a sensible rule, but it sometimes takes up valuable space. Boats built to the Coast Guard survey will need the accommodation moved farther aft than would otherwise be necessary.

Some bulkheads may need stiffeners, depending on the size of the vessel, the metal used in the bulkheads, and the size of the particular bulkhead. These vertical L-angle stiffeners are spaced about 12 to 18 inches (305 to 457 mm) apart and are installed with base of the L inward, thus making an excellent base for installing the cabin lining material. Some transverse stiffening also may be required. Check with the designer of your boat. The cavity formed by the L-angle can also be used to install the insulation.

Concerning those bulkheads that you're installing before the deck and superstructure are in place: make sure that the height above the sheer or deck will allow you to cut the correct cabin-top camber later. We always recommend that you don't try to cut the shape for the cambered decks, cabin sides, and top camber at this stage; simply allow the top of the bulkhead to stand up square from the sheer. This advice applies to all metal and plywood bulkheads. Later, you can mark out the deck camber, the lay-in of the cabin sides, and the cambers for the cabintop and/or wheelhouse top. These cuts may be more difficult to make with the bulkhead in an upright posi-

Timber "furring strips" installed on Roberts 34 built in Sweden.

John McDermott varnishes the meranti tongue-and-groove bulkheads in his Spray 33, Donegal Breeze.

line. One way to test the durability of plywood is to boil it. A widely used 8-hour boiling test will give you a clear indication of its quality. Plywood provides stiffening and strength in many directions and will keep the weight of the interior down. Plywood bulkheads should be installed with the tops left square, so the areas above the deck can be marked and shaped at the same time as the metal bulkheads. If your plans do not state the thickness for the plywood bulkheads, keep in mind that the adjacent furniture and joinery will add stiffness and strength.

The transverse plywood bulkheads will need to be bolted in place, either to existing metal frames or to short sections of framing material commonly known as "tags." The tags are 6 to 12 inches (150 to 300 mm) long and they're spaced at the same intervals as their length. They're welded to the hull to accept the bulkhead. The

tion, but they'll be much easier to mark out with all of the bulkheads in place, rather than one at a time before the bulkheads are erected. More experienced builders may prefer to mark and cut the bulkhead tops as they install each one.

If you're building upright, and if many of the bulkheads are on a frame location, then it may be worth your while to include the basic bulkheads as part of the frame construction. Our advice is still to leave the tops square, as mentioned above. If you prefer, you may carefully work out the measurements and cabin-side angles of each bulkhead, and cut them to shape before installation.

Plywood Bulkheads

Intermediate and partial bulkheads are best built from plywood. You can use any suitable grade that has a marine glue-

Plywood bulkheads can be attached to frames or to tags especially installed for the purpose.

tags become necessary if a transverse bulkhead is located between frames, or adjacent to a frame but not at its exact location. It may be possible to alter the bulkhead's location a small amount by bolting it to one side or other of the frame—but be careful not to create a space such as a berth that is too small or over-long. You'd do better to install tags at a location between the frames. These tags provide more than adequate strength for bulkhead attachment. Don't forget to predrill the tags at 4 to 6 inch (100 to 150 mm) centers to accept the bolts that will attach them to the bulkheads.

As you're unlikely to be able to purchase plywood sheets large enough to make the bulkheads in one piece, you'll need to join or laminate the sheets somehow. The thickness of the plywood bulkheads will vary, depending on the size of the vessel as well as the purpose and location of the bulkhead. Transverse plywood bulkheads are generally thicker than longitudinal ones. The designer of your boat may have specified the thickness required.

To form one complete bulkhead, you can use plywood of the specified total thickness and have this scarfed to the correct sheet size, or you can scarf or half-lap the sheets yourself. Our preferred method is to divide the thickness into two or more parts and then laminate two or more sheets face to face. For maximum strength, the joins can be widely staggered by alternating the joins in each layer. Plywood bulkheads, with the exception of those in the area of the mast in a sailboat, will not be exposed to great strains. The bulkhead adjacent to the mast can be strengthened by the addition of framing as required.

Cored Bulkheads

If you are weight-conscious, you can consider one or more cored bulkheads. They can be used to divide the accommodation longitudinally, or to construct half-bulkheads such as those that form one end of a hanging locker or similar piece of joinery. The core material can be structural sheet foam, a light timber framing, or other suitable material that is both light and fire-resistant. The

face plywood can be ³⁄₁₆-inch (4 to 5 mm) and can be veneered with teak or a similar surface. The fiberglass "bats" used in house insulation are unsuitable for core material as they will soon shake down into a floppy mess when exposed to marine conditions.

BENDING AND INSTALLING DECK BEAMS

The material for the deck beams can be flat bar, L-angle, or T-bar. It makes sense to use L-angle or T-bar, as either of these, when installed with the flange down, will provide an attachment point for the interior lining material. The insulation for the deck and cabin top will fit neatly in between the angle or T-beams.

The beams can be bent using the hydraulic-jack and steel-frame method, or you may prefer to have them bent by a professional metal shop. Your plan will at least give you a camber figure—for example, 6 inches in 13 feet (150 mm in 3.96 m). If you don't have a pattern, but you do have the numbers for the recommended camber, you'll have to make a pattern using the formula shown. If you have patterns for the various cambers, you should make a master pattern out of plywood or timber. You will use the pattern to check the beams as they're bent to the correct camber and also as a general pattern for cutting bulkhead tops.

In our designs, we recommend that you install the deck beams in one piece right across the hull. This method of installing the beams is much easier than trying to support short sidedeck beams while maintaining the correct sheer and curve of the deck/cabinside intersection. Later, you'll cut out the center of the beams and the section you remove will be re-bent for cabintop beams.

You may need fore-and-aft intercostal deck stringers, depending on the spacing of the beams and the size of your boat. The intercostals are best cut from flat bar and should be sniped in at the ends and welded in between the deck beams, as required. You could use a lighter angle for the intercostal and have the flange level with the

Cabintop beams and fore-and-aft intercostals tack-welded in position; see text.

inside to provide a base for the lining material. The depth of the intercostal should be the same as that of the deck beams as you may need to weld the underside of the deck plating to the intercostal as well as to the deck beams themselves.

Once all the deck beams are in place right across the hull, then you can mark the position where the cabin side intersects the deck, support the beams, and cut at the marked line on each beam. Next, install a carlin to accept the inner edge of the side-deck plating. The carlin will be a vertical length of flat bar running around the inner edges of the cut inner ends of the deck beams.

You can, at this stage, make provision for hatches in the fore and aft decks or you can cut them out later and install any extra deck framing at that time. Once you're satisfied with the framing for your deck, you can go ahead and plate the foredeck, side decks, and the aft deck area.

FORMING THE CABIN

Cabin Side Lay-In

At this stage, you'll need to consult your plans regarding the correct lay-in for the cabin and pilothouse sides. Lay-in of the cabin or pilothouse sides refers to the amount by which the sides are angled toward the centerline. In other words, the base (where the sides meet the deck) is slightly wider than the top (where the sides meet the cabin- or pilothouse top). Too much lay-in will be an invitation for leaky windows and may also interfere with your interior accommodation. Too little lay-in will make the superstructure on your boat look boxy and, at worst, can make it look as though it's actually leaning outward at the top. How much lay-in is correct? Never less than 5 degrees and usually no more than 20 degrees is

Quarter of pipe used at corners of pilothouse. This boat would have been better built from preprimed materials that were not so readily available at the time.

appropriate. When you cut the angle for the side lay-in, you may leave the tops square and cut the cambers after the cabin side is installed.

Setting up the Cabin Sides

Your plans should provide measurements for the cabin sides, so that you can make a pattern of the sides and then raise the pattern into position to check the accuracy before cutting metal and welding the sides in place. If your design includes a pilothouse, it may be part of the cabin side or installed as a separate item.

It's often preferable to have the sides of the pilothouse set slightly inboard of the line of the cabinside-cabintop intersection. This will break up the large pilothouse-cabinside area, and reduce the apparent height of the combined structure. Until you've installed the other parts of the superstructure, and to ensure that the sides remain at the correct angle and position when they are first installed, you'll need to use bracing from one side to the other, and to the bulkheads and other areas. Don't make any cut-outs for windows or portlights at this time. Cutting the cabinside plating before the whole structure is complete will cause the plate to buckle, and spoil the fair line of the sides. You may wish to mark out the windows and ports, as this will enable you to locate the correct position for any framing required in the sides.

Cabin-Side Stiffeners

Depending on the size and type of boat, you may need some form of stiffeners installed in the sides of the cabin or pilothouse. If possible, always line up the cabinside stiffeners with deck and cabin top beams, so you have, in effect, a "ring frame" that will always be stronger than a discontinuous framing system. You can use the same material for framing the sides of the cabin or pilothouse as you use for the deck and cabintop beams. Assuming you're using angle, the flange of the L or T will face inboard, and will assist in providing a ground to attach the lining. Don't forget to arrange some form of insulation in the cabin sides, otherwise you'll have condensation problems in the future.

Rounded Corners

Rounded corners where the cabin sides meet the top, and where the cabin front meets the top and sides, are a nice touch. You can use sections of suitably sized pipe, say 3-inch (75 mm) cut into quarters, or have some plate rolled to a suitable radius. We like beveled corners; they're easy to install and give an attractive appearance when used at the intersection of the cabintop and cabin sides, and in similar areas. The hull-sides-transom intersection may be fairly sharp without spoiling the appearance of the vessel. Sharp corners are hard to keep painted, though, so all corners should have at least a slight radius.

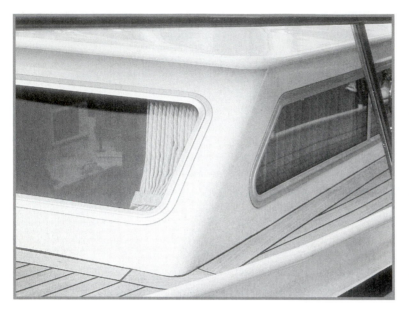

Rounded corners can enhance the exterior appearance of any metal boat.

Installing Cabintop Beams

Installing the cabintop beams will follow much the same procedure as you have used for the deck beams. Hatches can be framed in now or cut out later and framed from underneath. We recommend that you frame up the main hatchway at this stage, as you'll need access to the interior when you plate the cabintop. As the surface area of the tops of the cabin and pilothouse will most certainly be greater than that of the decks (except in a flush-deck boat), you'll need intercostal beams in the top. The intercostals can be installed before or after the top plating. If you install the intercostals from inside, after the plating is in place, you'll have more welding to do from underneath; however, installing the intercostals after the plating will ensure that you don't have any ridges in the cabintop caused by improperly aligned and installed intercostals. The intercostals can be installed in the same manner as those for the decks. Your cabintop may receive considerable traffic, so make sure the framing is adequate. A relatively light, closely framed cabintop will serve you better than a few, widely spaced, heavier beams. Follow your plans or consult the designer of your boat if you're unsure regarding the framing.

Installing the Cabin Front

The front of the cabin will most likely be curved; about the same amount of round as was used for the deck-beam camber will be about right. Cabin fronts on traditional craft can be flat. The problem with flat cabin fronts—or any part of a boat that is flat—is that they tend to look convex. For that reason, you should always have a slight amount of curvature in any flat area on your boat.

The cabin front will always have some layback. If a truly vertical cabin front were installed, it would look as though it were leaning outward (forward) at the top. Don't forget to allow for the camber when installing the cabin front. You are dealing with many angles in this area, and overlooking sufficient camber allowance in the front is not an unheard-of occurrence.

Plating the Cabin Top

By now, you should have the cabin sides, cabin front, and cabintop beams and intercostals all installed and checked for accuracy and fairness in all planes. You'll need to decide if you're going to let the top overhang the sides or front of the cabin. These overhangs have many advantages and are commonly seen. While overhangs on a fiberglass or timber boat may present a potential weak point in the construction, this doesn't apply on a metal boat.

Check your plans regarding overhangs and "eyebrows," as the forward cabin and pilothouse overhangs are sometimes called. Overhangs must have a trim to complete the edge; you can use pipe, solid round bar, or flat bar depending on the design of your superstructure. Side overhangs, especially on powerboats, can carry the rainwater or spray from the top out past the windows. You can see that a careful balance of cabin side lay-in and top overhangs can improve the appearance and practicality of the design. Installing the deck plate will follow the same procedure as used for the decks.

BULWARKS AND TOERAILS

If you plan to have bulwarks, you'll have fitted a deck stringer at the appropriate height. The lines plan and/or the full-size frame patterns may show exactly where this stringer is to be installed on each frame.

If this information isn't on your plans, you can scale off the relevant measurements and use a batten to fair in the deckline on each frame from stem to stern. Before or after the hull is plated, you can taper the inside of the frame between the deckline and the sheer. Taper the frame so that it is the right width on top to accept a flat or round bar to be installed as a caprail.

If your bulwarks are less than say 8 inches (200 mm) at the highest point, and your hull is $\frac{3}{16}$-inch (5 mm) plate, then the frames may finish under the deckline and it will not be necessary to have the frames extend from the deck to the

Steel decks and cabin on Roberts Spray, *built in England for Bruce Roberts U.K., Ltd.*

sheer. You should install a pipe or solid round of a minimum of ¾-inch (20 mm) diameter, or flat bar, to accept a wooden caprail on the top of the hull plating. In any case, you should stiffen up the cut-outs.

WATERWAYS AND FAIRLEADS

If your hull has bulwarks, you'll need to install waterways on the frames and freeing ports to allow water to flow between the frames as well as through the bulwarks and off the decks.

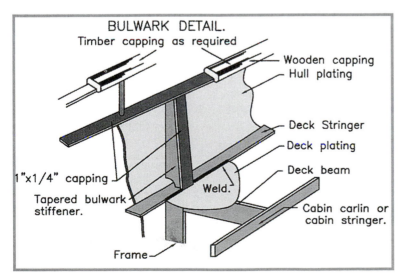

BULWARK DETAIL.
Timber capping as required
Wooden capping
Hull plating
Deck Stringer
Deck plating
Deck beam
1"x1/4" capping
Tapered bulwark stiffener.
Weld.
Cabin carlin or cabin stringer.
Frame

Drawing of bulwark detail.

A view of Bernhard Nentwig's Roberts 53.

The beveled cockpit coaming adds to the attractive appearance of this Roberts 53 built by A. Skodt, in Canada.

The Bevel

A beveled section makes an attractive intersection between the cabin or pilothouse sides and the top. There are other areas of the superstructure where a bevel can be an attractive alternative to a round edge or a plain right angle. The bevel is one of our favorite architectural features and we note that a few boat manufacturers are incorporating a bevel between the cabin sides and the top. The bevel can be of any size, but it's usually set at about 45 degrees to the vertical and could measure 3 to 6 inches (75 mm to 150 mm) depending on the size of the boat. The use of the bevel is also a good way to disguise cabin height. If your design calls for a high cabin structure, then consider the bevel. For the record, the bevel, when used in timber work, is often referred to as an *arras,* or small bevel taken off the corner of a post or other feature. The arras, or bevel, does soften the appearance of any area where it is used, and it's a great way to remove sharp edges from any object in your boat.

The bulk of the freeing ports must be situated at the lowest point of the deck/bulwark intersection, and the apertures must be large enough to let the water out without delay. Usually, several freeing-ports spread over the lowest area are better than one large hole. All openings made in the hull plating for freeing ports, fairleads, or any similar purpose must be reinforced with suitably sized solid round bar. If docking lines are used with fairleads, the reinforcing bar in a steel hull should be stainless steel. The movement of docking lines and the anchor rode would soon wear away any paint applied to mild steel reinforcing.

BUILDING OR ADDING A PILOTHOUSE

Consider a pilothouse if you want to improve the livability and comfort of your existing or future sailboat or powerboat. Pilothouses have gained in popularity over the past 30-odd years that we've been recommending these structures. Almost all of our sailboat designs feature at least one version that includes a pilothouse.

If you think your boat is a candidate for one, you'll need to consider the style and design carefully before starting the actual installation. We strongly recommend that you contact the original designers of your boat and request that they check the effect on stability and prepare plans for the structure. The addition of a pilothouse can not only provide more comfort aboard your boat, but it also can enhance its appearance and value. Conversely, a poorly designed appendage can totally destroy what you have set out to achieve.

One decision you'll need to make is whether you prefer forward- or reverse-sloping windows. Most fishing boats and workboats have reverse-sloping windows up forward; there is a good reason for this. When steering into the sun and under other difficult conditions, reverse-facing windows give you the best view. When the rain is light, the overhang at the top of the reverse-sloping windows will keep the windows clear. Reverse windows are practical, but their appearance is not to everyone's taste. Regular forward-sloping windows have a racier appearance and do enhance the appearance of your boat. For the best vision where you need it most, keep the slope

The low cabin on this Roberts 39 will receive adequate light and ventilation from the opening hatches and Dorade vents.

Flybridge decks need less camber than regular cabintops. Note our favorite trim angle, the beveled edge of the overhang.

of these windows to a reasonable angle; an extreme angle will cause vision problems.

Building a pilothouse follows a procedure similar to that used to build your regular cabin structure. You must make sure that supports of adequate proportions are placed between the generous-sized windows often associated with this structure. Additional strength by way of side framing may be required, and the windows should be divided up into reasonably sized areas. If your boat is capable of offshore work, then you should make provision for shuttering that could be fitted in the event of one or more of the windows being broken. In order to keep the weight of these rarely used storm covers to manageable proportions, you could consider building them of fiberglass sandwich, fiberglass-covered plywood, or aluminum.

HATCHES, COMPANIONWAYS, PORTLIGHTS, AND DOORS

If your vessel was designed for offshore use, your plans should indicate the size and location of the various hatches. If you're the builder, the details of strength and suitability will lie in your hands. In the interests of safety, all hatches and companionways are best located on the centerline of the vessel. This is especially important for passage-making vessels. In the event of a knockdown, an open hatch on or off the centerline can admit tons of water before it can be closed.

You should take some time in deciding where and when to fit hatches. Before you start making holes in your decks, you need to have a firm idea as to the exact layout of your accommodation. You can simply plate the entire decks and superstructure, leaving the main hatchway available for access, and lay out your hatches at a later stage. Always keep in mind, however, that these areas need to be carefully planned and strongly constructed, especially in long-distance

---

Adding a Flybridge

The main thing to consider when building a flybridge on any vessel is weight: keep it light. This structure is always high above the waterline, where weight is most undesirable. If you plan one of these items on your boat, be sure that the cabintop doesn't have excessive camber—usually the same camber as the decks is acceptable. No matter what material you used to build your hull, deck, and superstructure, you can use aluminum or fiberglass for the construction of the flybridge. Don't make the flybridge so large as to attract too many passengers. Keep in mind the stability of the vessel under all conditions. Some restriction on the number of seats available will help in this regard.

The pilothouse on the 28-foot Spray K*I*S*S has reverse-sloping windows up forward, and while they may not be to everyone's taste, they do have many advantages. Lack of glare and reflection and absence of moisture in light rain conditions are just two of the benefits of this arrangement.

sailboats and power cruisers. The hatches that cover the openings in your boat may be called upon to withstand tons of water being dumped on the deck. Don't treat them lightly; they need to be as strong as the hull.

About the only places in which a steel boat can leak are around the hatches and other openings. It's important to construct and fit these hatches so that they are absolutely watertight. Strong hinges and closing devices are a must. There are many cases where boats have been seriously damaged and lost through the fitting of inferior hatches. Combining safety with livability, it's best to fit hatches with hinges on both the forward and the after edges.

Readymade hatches can add a professional touch to any deck arrangement.

Commercially Made Hatches

Deciding whether you will make your own hatches or use commercially made ones may be a matter of economics. Careful shopping can often reduce the prices to an acceptable level. Professionally manufactured hatches may add a nice finishing touch to your otherwise self-built boat.

Most commercially made hatches will be manufactured from marine-grade aluminum.

Unless you have your decks and superstructure built out of the same material, you'll need to isolate the hatches from steel or copper-nickel. A good commercially made hatch will have a precision-cast body of high-tensile alloy that will not corrode in the harsh marine environment. Tinted glazing is preferred, and it must be capable of taking the weight of more than one person and able to withstand the force of a breaking wave without deforming. Larger hatches should have three hinges that have been cast as part of the body of the hatch. To ensure watertightness under adverse conditions, a hatch that uses a neoprene O-ring seal is preferable to one that uses soft rubber strips. The neoprene is far superior to the spongy type of rubber seal and it will not deteriorate as quickly; also the O-ring neoprene seals are more resistant to sunlight.

Making Your Own Hatches

If you decide to build your own hatches, you can save a considerable amount of money. It may be possible to construct them from materials you would otherwise throw away. We recommend that you build your hatches of steel, aluminum, copper-nickel, or fiberglass. Timber and plywood hatches require considerable maintenance and, if of insufficient strength, offer a weak link in the security of your boat. On the other hand, timber hatches and skylights can give a metal boat a touch of warmth, so if you're prepared for additional work, both during and after installation, then timber hatches may be worth considering.

Metal deck hatches can be built easily with inner and outer coamings. You can weld the coamings directly to the deck, making sure you've installed either deck beams or intercostals (or both) to reinforce the deck plating from below. You can install the reinforcing beams from underneath after you've cut the aperture for the hatchway.

Metal Hatches

Obviously, it's best to construct the hatches from the same material as the decks and superstructure. You're more likely to have these materials on hand, and there will be no additional corrosion problems caused by mismatched materials. Arranging rounded corners on your hatches shouldn't present you with any problems as all metals are capable of being formed into, say, a 3-inch (75 mm) radius. If you build your own hatches, some of the money you save can be invested in extra-thick acrylic-sheet glazing. Make sure it's set in a suitable sealant and bolted in place with an adequate number of fastenings.

Metal hatches can be built with inner and outer coamings; this arrangement is like a box made with a fitted lid. The inner box that acts as the coaming can be welded directly to the deck around the cut-out you've created in the deck or cabintop. The height of the inner coaming can be from 2 inches to 6 inches (50 mm to 150 mm), and higher in larger vessels. The hatch top can have sides of 2 to 3 inches (50 to 75 mm). The top will look best if it's cambered similar to the line of the deck. This will look more professional, but it's harder to build, especially if you plan to have acrylic, Lexan, or similar material included in the top of the hatch.

Hinges for metal hatches are simple and easy to construct. They are basically one set of square tangs welded on the hatch cover to face a set of lugs welded at a 90-degree angle from the deck. A suitably sized rod, usually ⅜- to ¾-inch (10 to 20 mm), depending on the size of the vessel and the hatch in question, is inserted through the tangs and lugs and the hatch cover will pivot on the rod. The rod will need a right-angle bend, a nut, or some similar stopper at one end, and a removable retaining device at the other end. If you install hinges on both the forward and after edges of the hatch, it will open either way. At sea, you should always have the hinges on the forward side, but in port or sheltered waters it may be useful to be able to open the hatch in more than one direction. On our current powerboat we have a hatch in the pilothouse top that can open straight

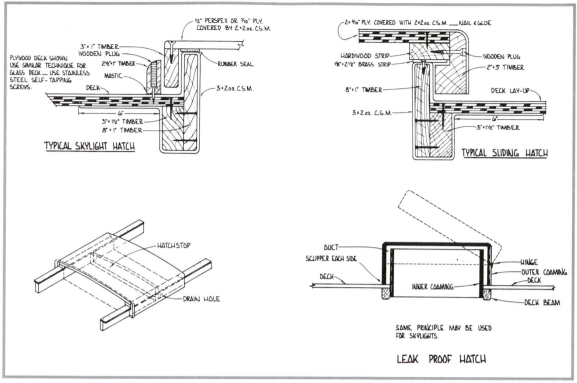

These plywood hatches can be used on timber or plywood decks and cabins, or adapted for use with a metal superstructure.

up or in any one of four directions—a wonderful arrangement when one is seeking relief from the heat and needs to catch some breeze.

Any one of a variety of locking devices can be arranged to work with a metal hatch. In serious offshore cruisers, both sail and power, it's important that the hatch can be screwed down tight to prevent pressurized seawater from forcing its way into the interior of the vessel.

The top of the inner coaming will need to be fitted with a sealing strip, as with other types of hatches. The round neoprene O-shaped material is the most long lasting and, properly installed, gives a superior seal. A proper hatch should have a separate raised coaming of sufficient height placed ahead of it and on the two sides of it, to deflect the spray and rainwater streaming across the decks and/or cabintop. Don't underestimate the power of water and its ability to force its way into any weak areas of your deck openings.

Wooden Hatches

Wooden hatches are relatively easy to construct but a perfect fit will take some woodworking skills. The best way to build these hatches is to build two boxes, one being the inner coaming and the other, the hatch itself. Obviously, one box will fit neatly over the other. The inner box should be made of 2-inch (50 mm) thick hardwood, and should be 4 to 9 inches (100 to 230 mm) in height. Usually, the larger the vessel, the higher the coaming. This box will be equal in size to the inner dimensions of the hatch opening. The minimum size to allow access by the average person is 20 inches (508 mm) square; however, you should decide what size hatches are most appropriate for you and likely crewmembers.

It's important the upper edge of this inner box (coaming) is perfectly square and level, as this is the edge that will contact the sealing material of the hatch itself. When you have constructed this basic square box for the inner coaming, you can cut a hole in the deck or cabintop to match the inner dimensions of the box. Next, add reinforcing intercostal and other beams underneath, around the perimeter of the hatchway.

Next, build the box that will be the hatch that will fit over the coaming. The hatch can be built out of 1½-inch (35 mm) timber, and 3 inches (75 mm) high is about right. This hatch will fit snugly around the coaming but will have sufficient clearance to allow the completed hinged hatch to be opened and closed. So far, you have no top to your hatch. You can use ¾-inch (20 mm) marine-grade plywood for the top, and screw and glue it to the frame. For a fancy finish you can glue and temporarily staple ⅛-inch (3 mm) mahogany or teak-faced plywood to the top of the hatch. In any case, the edges of the plywood top will need to have an outer timber strip to protect them.

You can have a Lexan or Plexiglas top instead of plywood, and you can have a combination of glazing and plywood for the top simply by fitting the ply top first, and then cutting out for the required amount of glazing. The glazed area should be of ½-inch Lexan or Plexiglas. When buying your glazing material, check the telephone directory and try to buy scrap material rather than specifying cut-to-size, for which you will pay a premium price.

You will need to take some special precautions when working with the plastic glazing fitted to your hatch tops and portlights. The holes you drill in the plastic must be slightly oversized. You must allow for the different expansion and contraction rate, as opposed to the timber framing. You will most likely use tinted plastic, and this will expand in hot weather; if the bolt holes or screw holes are too snug, the plastic will crack and need to be replaced. Usually, the next size up from the screw size is about right for the hole. The safest type of screw is round headed with a flat surface on the bottom of the head where it meets the plastic; self-tapping stainless-steel screws are ideal. Fancy screws, such as hexheaded, sheet-metal, stainless-steel screws will give you a good looking and strong fastener. Sheet-metal screws have larger threads than woodworking screws and therefore provide additional fastening surface.

The plastic should be bedded against the timber with as good a grade of silicone sealant as you can find. A small amount of the silicone sealant in each hole prior to screwing the glazing in place will ensure that the oversized holes remain watertight.

Hinges are fitted to the forward area of the outer coaming so that the hatch is aft-opening. The hinges should be heavy-duty and made of stainless steel or other noncorrosive metal. To secure the hatch from below, a number of catches and locking devices are available. One of the best is the type with screw-down devices, so you can dog the hatch down firmly onto its gaskets.

When fitting the wooden hatch, assemble it completely with gaskets and then lower it into position. The best way to make the fit between the coaming and the deck or cabintop is to first make sure the whole assembly is set up level. Next trace the shape of the cut required, allowing the coaming to make a good fit with the deck or cabintop. Now you can bolt or screw the coaming in place through the metal deck, working from underneath the deck. Make sure you bed the coaming in a suitable sealant.

Custom hatches can be made even more suitable for the rigors of cruising with a few simple additions. You can add an extra coaming on the deck or cabintop immediately adjacent to the hatch. This coaming should surround the forward edge and sides of the hatchway. It will be slightly lower than the entire hatch assembly and fit so as not to interfere with the operation of the hatch. The extra coaming will help keep water away from the hatch. The top of this extra coaming could be timber or metal. If you make it of timber, round off the top to give it the best appearance. In all cases, the sides can have holes in their bottom edges to allow for drainage.

Another improvement to any hatch is to install eyebolts close to either side of the hatch assembly. You can use them in extreme weather conditions to lash the hatch down even more securely. The eyes need to be close to the hatch so you don't stub your toes. Wood slats running fore and aft across the top of the hatch will strengthen Plexiglas tops and can improve the look of the hatch at the same time. These 1-by 1-inch (25 by 25 mm) timber slats can be screwed into the outer frame and then screwed to the acrylic from underneath. The slats will take some of the force and distribute the weight of persons standing on the hatch, or the weight of a heavy breaking wave. You can also make canvas covers for all of the hatches. Not only will you need these in hot climates, but they can also be a safety factor when included as part of the lashing-down arrangement.

Access Hatches

Access hatches, as opposed to hatches used only for ventilation, must be of a size sufficient to allow even a large person to enter and exit the boat in an emergency. The minimum size for an *average* person, as we've already seen, is 20 inches (508 mm) square, but don't make hatches unnecessarily large. They must be able to withstand all that the sea can offer. You should be able to open all your hatches from both outside and inside the vessel, and you should be able to lock them to deter unauthorized intruders. Hatches in accommodation areas should be built with some form of glazing to admit light and add a spacious feeling to the interior.

Companionway Hatches

The main access hatchway can be in the form of a sliding hatch, a hinged hatch, or a quadrant companionway type hatch, as illustrated. Sliding hatches should not be simply a sheet of plastic running in the simplest of aluminum tracks, even though this is sometimes seen on production powerboats. Build, or buy and install, a proper seagoing hatch as your main entry and exit point.

The companionway hatch consists of two main elements: the runners, which fit on the cabintop, and the hatch, which slides on or in the runners. The runners and the hatch may be constructed of timber or metal. If timber runners are used, you'll need 3-high by 2-inch wide (75 by 50 mm) timber. The timber runners could be deeper, and could be bolted directly to a set of intercostal beams situated around the perimeter of the hatchway. The runners will need to extend beyond the opening; the length is twice the hatch length plus 3 inches (75 mm). Where they extend over the cabintop, they'll need to be screwed from inside, through to the timber.

The tops of the runners are faced with heavy (say, ¼- by 2-inch, or 6 by 50 mm) brass strips that act as runners for the hatch top. The brass strips are set in silicone and screwed to the runners with flathead screws set flush with the surface. When it's properly set up, the hatch must run smoothly on the brass slider.

The sliding hatch is another box, with the frame built of 1½- by 2-inch (35 by 50 mm) hardwood. The corners can be half-jointed. Considerable care is needed to ensure that the frame is a true rectangle and sits perfectly flat on the runners. Around this inner frame, an outer frame is constructed from 1½- by 4-inch (35 by 100 mm) hardwood. The outer frame is glued and screwed

A garage, turtle, or seahood is an essential part of any sliding companionway hatch; this one is made of fiberglass.

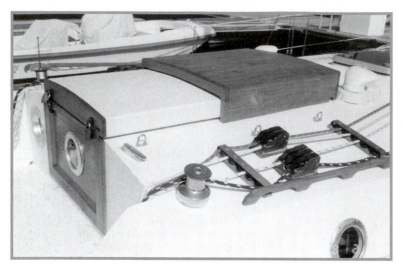

To soften the steel exterior, John McDermott added this timber "garage" and companionway door to his Spray 33.

to the inner frame, with the tops of both frames flush and the outer 4-inch-deep (100 mm) frame acting as a guide to allow the inner frame to slide on the runners. The whole arrangement must slide smoothly. A hatch that jams is in no way desirable aboard any boat. Now you need an arrangement to keep the hatch on the runners, and you can do this by gluing and screwing a ½-by ½-inch (12 by 12 mm) cleat inside the outer frame ⅛-inch (3 mm) underneath the brass runner. Now the hatch has to be slid onto the runners from the front.

The forward and after ends of the hatch are finished off with hardwood plates. The companionway end can have a handle or grip built into the top. The bottom of this facing board will need to be shaped to clear the cambered cabintop as it glides (we hope) forward to its fully open location.

If you have the recommended garage, then the front should be large enough to cover the aft end of this arrangement. Incidentally, the garage houses the hatch when it's open. The garage is particularly important in forward-facing sliding hatches, as it helps to divert water away from the open companionway. It also partly provides a neat cover for the runners and the open hatch, eliminating one area where lines can snag and toes can be stubbed.

The front facing of the hatch, with the handgrip built into the top, will also need to ac-commodate the hasp part of your hasp-and-staple locking arrangement. The top of the hatch can be finished with ⅛-inch (3 mm) teak plywood and the whole structure coated with epoxy and light fiberglass cloth for a long life.

The top of the hatch can be three layers of ¼-inch (6 mm) plywood, and if you've taken our advice and made the top match the cabintop camber, you'll find that the plywood will laminate into a strong and durable top. A trim strip will be required for the outer edges of the plywood top to seal them from the elements.

When you're building a timber or plywood sliding hatch above a metal cabin, the hatch opening can be finished off inside with a timber trim strip of suitable width. You'll also need washboards (vertical hatchboards or dropboards) that will fit in preinstalled metal channels to complete the closure of the main-access companionway.

It's worth noting here that any timber you attach to your steel hull or superstructure should be given at least three coats of epoxy resin, which will go a long way toward stabilizing and protecting the timber. All timber runners, hatch coamings, and the like must be set in silicone before they are either screwed or bolted in position. Space the screws or bolts at 3-inch (75 mm) intervals.

Deck Prisms

Another form of under-used light-admitting device is the deck prism. These wonderful devices admit much more light than their size would indicate, and they can be installed to be absolutely watertight and secure from the ravages of man and the sea. Check with your local hatch manufacturer and other equipment suppliers to see

Recessed ports and windows always add a professional finish to any metal hull; these are fitted to a Roberts 64 built in Canada.

what they have to offer in this area. If you fit prisms, make sure your crew is well protected from contact with the sharp inside edges.

Portlights and Windows

Portlights and windows can be opening or fixed, but it's a fact that the opening variety, no matter how well constructed and maintained, will always be a source of leaks and worry for the crew. It's often desirable to have one or more windows or ports that can be opened; however, it's wise to keep their number to an absolute minimum. The plans for your boat will no doubt give you some indication of the size and location of the ports and windows. Our advice is use only fixed portlights and rely on opening hatches to provide adequate ventilation.

If you're planning to use opening ports, they should be professionally made and of the highest quality you can afford. Most commercial ports are made from marine-grade aluminum, so if your boat is built of steel or copper-nickel you'll need to isolate the aluminum from the other metal. Neoprene is commonly used for this purpose. Don't forget to sleeve the boltholes where the ports are bolted to the hull or superstructure. Occasionally, you'll find steel-framed professionally made ports, but they're generally made for very large vessels so they may not be suitable for your boat.

There are many ways in which the windows can be fitted through the insulation. One popular way is to set the windows back into the cabin side or into the hull. To achieve the latter result, the window aperture is framed with an inward-facing, L-angle, shaped flange. The bottom of the L is where the window or fixed portlight will be set in sealant and bolted in place. With this arrangement, and the addition of suitable L-metal, angle, or timber furring strips as framing, we now have a cavity in which to fit our insulation and a framework on which to attach our interior lining.

As you will realize, this is a more complicated procedure than simply bolting the window into a hull or cabin-side cut-out; however, the results are worth the extra effort. Set-in ports and windows give a vessel that extra touch of quality that not only enhances pride of ownership, but one day will return dividends in a better resale value. Forward-facing wheelhouse windows that will be fitted with windshield wipers will need to be glazed with toughened glass instead of the usual acrylic favored for most other boat windows and ports.

If it's well made, the simplest portlight or window can have an appearance that belies its low cost. The design and method of installation is simple. You cut a hole 1 to 1½ inches (25 to 35 mm) smaller than the overall size of your port or window and fit and bolt a larger piece of Plexiglas or similar plastic over the aperture. The glazing is set in silicone, the holes for the bolts are drilled slightly oversized, and the corners of the hole for the portlight, and the covering Plexiglas, are all radiuses.

You can use clear silicone, but it's preferable to use silicone that matches the color of the area of the boat into which the port or window is being installed. If the bolts have hexagonal heads, and you line up the slots in the heads, you'll improve the appearance of the glazed area. If the ports or windows are located in a high-traffic area, such as adjacent to the side decks, then you should have bolt heads that fit flush with the glazing and thus avoid scratching crew members who brush by the window. Be careful when making countersunk holes to allow bolts to fit flush. Acrylic can be induced to crack if it's handled too roughly during the shaping and assembly stage.

Make sure the windows don't have an overlarge area without sufficient support in the underlying cabin or wheelhouse side. Plexiglas and similar acrylic materials come with a paper protective covering; never remove the bulk of this until the boat is completed and ready for launching. You'll need to remove a strip of the paper, of course, after you've drilled for the bolts but before you install the window or portlight. The thickness of the glazing will be between ⅜ and ¼-inch (10 and 20 mm), depending on the size and area of the aperture.

For most windows and ports, you can use Plexiglas or the harder and more scratch-resistant Lexan. You can dress up the outer edges of these bolt-on windows by using timber, stainless-steel, or other suitable metal frames that can be cut to, say, 1 or 2 inches (25 to 50 mm) wide and bolted in place at the same time as the window is installed. If you use metal, it can act as an outer washer for the fastenings and will generally enhance the appearance of the windows and ports on your boat.

With powerboats, where the boat is more-or-less always in an upright position, and where the boat is not designed or built for extended ocean voyaging, you can be more liberal with the expanse of glazed area. Most powerboats have at least one forward-facing opening window adjacent to the inside helm position. This opening window can admit copious quantities of fresh air, and when it's open it gives you better vision ahead in fog or poor visibility.

Even in powerboats, we find that opening windows, usually of the sliding variety, are a source of problems. Sooner, rather than later, the rubber or other material used in the bottom track for the glass will perish and allow water to enter. In some steel powerboats, it's common practice to have the large side windows fitted without any provision for insulation. Perhaps the designers and builders feel that the expanse of glass takes up so much of the available area that it is not worth insulating the remainder. The problem is that when plywood lining is attached directly to the steel cabin side, the resulting condensation can cause problems. In one case, it was natural (though wrong) to blame a leaky window for causing discoloration of the teak plywood lining. It took some time before the culprit was diagnosed as lack of insulation in the cabin side, which caused condensation. It would have been too expensive to remedy the situation, but luckily it was discovered that a dehumidifier would solve the problem. Lesson: always insulate all areas of your accommodation.

Outer Doors

As a rule, outer doors are seen in powerboats. If you wish to have a door opening in the side of the accommodation, usually near the helm location, make sure it's properly designed, fitted, and suitable for marine use. Marine doors are usually of a more robust construction than sliding windows and are therefore easier to maintain and keep watertight.

Side doors in a trawler yacht's cabin can be built of timber and may be arranged to slide; or, if you have a very large yacht and wide side decks, then it may be possible to have the door hinged at the forward edge, or perhaps open inward. On smaller boats, a half-height, side-access door adjacent to the inside helm position may be found useful. All doors, especially sliders that are either outside or inside the accommodation, should have a means to secure them in the open position, as well as when closed.

A recent report told of a boatowner receiving severe injuries to his neck from an unsecured alu-

This neat Roberts 34 cockpit was built in Sweden about 25 years ago.

minum sliding door. Patio-style aluminum doors at the aft end of a powerboat's main saloon? *Ugh!* The sliding variety, especially, are famous for lopping off fingers. And the large glass area is vulnerable to being broken in a variety of ways.

If your powerboat is of the aft-cockpit variety, then you'll most likely have a metal aft bulkhead in which you can fit a pair of timber doors. The top one-third of the doors can be glazed, and you'll have all the light you need. As the cockpit and after deck is usually well protected, the timber doors will need little maintenance.

On a similar subject, you may wish to lock some of the interior doors; this may slow down an intruder. If you're interested in learning more about additional security arrangements, please consider the relevant books listed in appendix 1.

COCKPITS

Not all boats have cockpits but most sailboats have, or should have. Most of us prefer the security, real or perceived, offered by a well-designed, self-draining cockpit. They work particularly well when combined with protective coamings and comfortable seating.

The dimensions of this arrangement are most important and can influence the safety and comfort of the boat in many ways. It's desirable, but not always possible, to have the cockpit seats measure 6 feet, 6 inches (2 m) in length to allow a person to lie full-length. The width of the cockpit is best arranged so a person can rest one or both feet on the seat opposite; this usually results in a well that is 2 feet, 3 inches (686 mm) wide. The

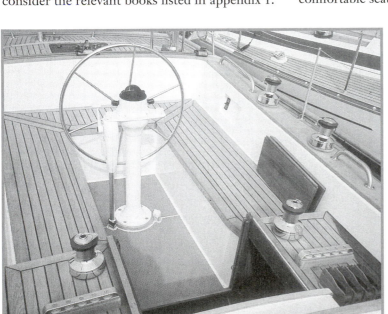

This teak-trimmed cockpit is installed in a radius-chine Roberts 432 that sold in the U.K. for a handsome price.

depth is best at 1 foot, 6 inches (457 mm). Seats should be between 1 foot, 3 inches (381 mm) and 1 foot, 6 inches (457 mm) wide. For comfort behind your knees, the inboard edge of the cockpit seat should be rounded.

The height of the seat back (usually part of the coaming) will vary depending on the design; however, about 2 feet (610 mm) seems to work out well for most people. All cockpits should be self-draining, with two separate outlets of generous size, a minimum of 2 inches (50 mm) in diameter. The cockpit drains should be fitted with seacocks that can be closed when required. Finally, you should have a reasonable view forward when you're seated in the cockpit. This is easier said than achieved, especially if there is a pilothouse ahead of your cockpit.

The choice between center cockpit and aft cockpit is usually governed by your choice of interior layout. This choice has become blurred with the advent of staterooms fitted beneath and around an aft cockpit.

Metal cockpits can be framed up using L-angle or flat bar, depending on the size of the vessel. Boats under, say, 30 feet (9.14 m) can use flat bar, and larger boats can use L-angle placed flange-down. Provided the transverse framing is

Cockpit and coamings on a Spray 33.

spaced the same as the hull's, a minimum of fore-and-aft reinforcing should be required. Most boats today have cockpit cushions, so these need to be considered when laying out the area. Self-draining arrangements for the well are obvious, but don't forget to drain the seats. Wet seats and continuously wet cushions make for very uncomfortable sitting, so consider how you can best drain these areas. A teak grating in the well adds a nice finishing touch to any cockpit.

DECK COVERINGS

Your metal deck will need some form of treatment to provide a nonslip footing as you

This attractive cockpit is devoid of timber trim, but it can be dressed up with cushions and still retain its maintenance-free concept.

move about the boat. The least expensive treatment is to apply a special paint that contains grit. Many metal boats use this paint/grit combination, and provided it's installed in a proper manner it can look attractive and it does work well in practice. When you're installing a painted nonskid surface, you should leave small borders around various fittings and alongside the cabin and inside the bulwark and so forth—places that do not have grit added. Be careful how you lay out these ungritted areas, though, as you don't want to leave skid-inducing shiny spaces in high-traffic areas. If the ungritted areas are no more than 1¼ inches (320 mm) wide around any feature, you shouldn't have a problem. You can always fill in any problem spaces with gritted paint.

The next step up in cost and appearance is to use a deck covering like Treadmaster or a similar product. These coverings are composite materials formed in patterned sheets suitable for gluing to your deck. When laying out this covering, you should use a similar pattern as suggested for painting decks with gritted material. Available in a range of attractive colors, these products are bonded to your deck with special glue.

The diamond pattern on some of these sheet products can be hard on your bottom and other areas that may come into contact with the deck. So don't use it on cockpit seats or similar locations. There are alternative, less harsh patterns that can be used where a user-friendly, nonslip surface is required.

Of course, some of you will settle for nothing but a laid wood deck. You may be surprised to learn that there are species of timber other than teak that are suitable for laid-plank decks. In Australia, beech is widely used, and in the U.S. quarter-sawn Douglas fir has been used for the same purpose. Nonetheless, teak is the premier material and the one you are most likely to be using to finish the decks of your metal boat in style.

After you decide that a laid deck is for you, the next step is to determine if you're going to have a "wannabee" teak deck or the real thing.

The steel deck on this Roberts 64 is now ready to receive a laid wooden deck or one of many other alternative treatments.

Reinforced chainplates and deck fittings. Note that the Treadmaster deck covering is kept clear of the fittings to allow the free flow of water off the decks.

The "wannabe" type is usually ½ inch (12 mm) or less thick, and in most cases it will not do justice to your boat or to the craftsmanship needed to install any laid deck. A "proper" laid deck should have planks of at least ⅝ inch (15 mm) and preferably ¾ inch (20 mm) minimum thickness.

There are many ways to install this deck on a metal boat but all will involve setting the planks in some form of bedding compound. Again, we can take a lead from Dutch builders who have been successfully installing laid decks on steel and other metal boats for a long time. The outer planks will need to be fastened to the steel deck itself. The inner planks may simply be set in the bedding compound and caulked.

The regular planks should be about 1¼ inches (42 mm) in

width. The outer and inner covering boards, king plank, and other featured planks around hatches and vents will be wider, usually 4 to 6 inches (100 to 150 mm), depending on the size of the boat and the way the deck is installed. The outer covering board is a misnomer in this case, as there should be a space between the edge of the teak covering board and the edge of the deck to create a channel for water to run alongside the outer teak plank and on out through the scuppers.

The bulk of the fore-and-aft planking can be laid in several ways. It can follow the outer shape of the hull, it can follow the line of the cabin sides, or it can split the difference. The main effect of these various methods is the way the

This 1-inch (25 mm) teak deck has been in place for 9 years; some recaulking will be necessary soon. Note the low bulwark, ably supported by a pipe caprail.

Deck and cabin of a very attractively finished Roberts 434 built in the U.K. Note the recessed ports.

planks need to be "nibbed" into the outer and inner covering boards and king plank. It's also possible to lay the deck in a herringbone pattern; this has been done on more than one of our designs, but we prefer longitudinal planking that splits the difference. (Naturally, this is the most expensive form of planking.)

ALTERNATIVE DECKS AND SUPERSTRUCTURES

Although there are arguments for building a boat using all steel, all aluminum, and perhaps all copper-nickel, there are many reasons why some of you may prefer to take a different approach. In the case of copper-nickel, as this material is somewhat more expensive than either steel or aluminum, it would make sense to have the hull built from copper-nickel; the hull is where the material is most beneficial; the decks and superstructure could then be built from an alternative, less-expensive material. If your metal-working skills are limited, and you have more experience with working in timber, you may consider a timber deck and superstructure. As you can see, there are a considerable number of options and you have to weigh up the benefits and disadvantages for yourself.

Plywood and Timber Decks and Superstructure

A good reason to install a plywood deck and superstructure on a small steel boat is to keep weight down. If you take the timber-and-plywood deck option, you'll need to select a point where you make the transition from metal to timber. The choices are to have the hull built in metal and install a "margin plate" welded to the inside or sheerline of the hull, where the deck will join the hull. The margin plate will take the place of, and be installed in the same location as, the deck stringer in an all-metal boat. Another alternative is to have the hull and complete decks built from metal and include an "up-stand" in metal to accept the timber superstructure, located all around the inner edge where the cabin sides will be installed. In both cases, the timber and/or plywood would overlap the metal so that surface water or other moisture would be less likely to get between the metal and timber to cause corrosion.

If you're planning a laid teak deck, it may influence your decision. A teak deck is much easier to install over a timber and plywood deck than it is over a metal one. There's no doubt that a timber deck and superstructure is a beautiful sight from both without and within. You pay a price, though, at least for the beauty of the exterior. The maintenance requirements of external tim-

Teak decks require a lot of maintenance; with any luck, your partner will be as willing to assist with the more onerous tasks as is mine.

ber and plywood will be far greater than if the items were constructed from metal. This applies not only to large items, as in a pilothouse or cabin structure, but extends to timber hatches, handrails, caprails, and rubbing strips. These items, when built in timber and finished "natural," do improve the appearance of any boat, but the maintenance requirements can be horrific.

After you've installed either the metal margin plate to the hull, or the metal up-stand to the inner edge of the metal decks, then you should install a timber carlin to allow you to carry on the remainder of the construction in timber. You should rebate this timber in such a way as to discourage any water from becoming trapped in the joint and later causing rot in the timber. It's imperative that you make a watertight join between the timber and the metal.

Deck beams may be of timber or metal. In the case of a metal deck, then L- or T-metal deck beams will be used; however, in the case of an all-timber-and-plywood deck and superstructure, you may choose either metal or timber beams. If you use metal beams with a plywood deck, make sure you place the flange upwards. This is opposite to what you would do for metal decks. The flange will provide a ground and will allow you to screw the plywood to the beams from underneath. Timber beams can be laminated or sawn, but laminated beams are recommended.

This is a good time to mention that you should use epoxy-based adhesives throughout the construction of any plywood decks and/or superstructure. Where the plywood is attached to the metal margin plate or up-stand, a suitable bedding compound will be used rather than an epoxy adhesive. An epoxy system such as the West System should be used to saturate all of the timber and plywood parts used to build your decks and superstructure, but not on teak decks.

It's usually preferable to laminate the decks and cabintops from more than one layer of plywood. If your deck calls for ½-inch (12 mm) plywood, then use two layers of ¼-inch (6 mm) each. If the recommended thickness is ¾-inch (20 mm) plywood, then use two layers of ⅜-inch (10 mm) or, better still, three layers of ¼-inch (6 mm). Use either bronze nails or staples to apply pressure to the glue lines until the adhesive has cured.

If you're installing plywood decks, one labor-saving tip is to paint the underside of the first sheet before you install it. Make sure you don't paint the strips where the plywood will be glued to the beams. Fit the panels first, and, from underneath, mark where the beams will fall and where the plywood rests on the other timber supports. Now mask off those areas on the plywood and paint the rest.

There are several methods of finishing off your plywood decks and cabin structure but no matter how you do it, we recommend that you give the entire area a coat of fiberglass cloth in epoxy resin. Don't use polyester resin for fiberglassing over plywood or timber, always use epoxy resins. The only place for polyester resins is in the building of an all-fiberglass boat.

When you're using epoxy resins and adhesives, make sure that you follow all of the safety precautions recommended by the manufacturers. When handling these materials, always wear protective gloves and use protective skin creams. Keep in mind that epoxy stays toxic for several days while it's curing. When you're building timber and plywood decks and superstructures, you'll find the Gougeon brothers' West System book a good source of information. See appendix 1 for more details.

This attractive skylight is an example of what can be achieved by a dedicated metalworker.

Aluminum Decks and Superstructure

When you build an aluminum hull, you'll almost certainly install decks and superstructure of the same material. The benefits of installing an aluminum deck and superstructure on any metal boat include less weight up high, where it's detrimental. Aluminum is easier to form into small-radius sections such as those used on the corners of cabins, pilothouse fronts, coamings, and similar areas. A little forethought and a considerable amount of welding can be saved by combining seats to backs and so forth.

The aluminum decks and superstructure are somewhat more removed from the seawater elements than the hull is, and it's easier to avoid some of the electrolytic problems suffered by boats built completely from this material. The practice of installing aluminum decks and superstructures on steel hulls has been well proven over the past 30 to 40 years, so you can consider it an acceptable boatbuilding practice.

Aluminum decks and superstructures fitted to steel or copper-nickel hulls will need to have the different metals isolated from one another to prevent electrolysis. There are a number of methods you can use to achieve this isolation. The first that comes to mind is to insert a neoprene strip between the two different metals and bolt them together with bolts housed in nylon sleeves and nuts that are isolated with nylon washers.

The superior way to join aluminum and steel is to use the specially manufactured strip that has aluminum on one side and steel on the other. The two metals on this strip are explosively fused together so that when you weld the steel to the steel side and the aluminum to the aluminum side, no contact occurs between the two metals, and the possibility of electrolysis is eliminated, or at least reduced. Careful planning will be required so that the intersection of the two dissimilar metals is located in such an area as to reduce the chance of prolonged contact through salt water.

Transoms can be customized to suit the owner's needs. Boarding from the dingy was a major concern for the owner of this Voyager 495, which we overcame with transom steps.

10
PAINTING A METAL BOAT

COLOR

This subject will probably be the first thing that comes to mind when you, or at least the family, are considering the paint job for your new or used metal boat. Even a simple matter like choosing the colors has its technical side.

In metal boats, a darker color for the hull makes good sense. The darker color will absorb sunlight and drive off both the dew and some internal condensation. If the decks are painted, then you may choose a two-tone scheme of light beige for the larger areas and cream for the trim or unsanded areas. This arrangement will look smart and it will be easy on the eyes. You should never paint decks white, as the reflected light will cause too much glare. Except in the coolest climate, dark-colored decks will be too hot for bare feet and will also make the interior of the cabin unbearably hot.

GRITBLASTING AND PRIMING STEEL

This process is variously referred to as sandblasting and gritblasting. It's the only way you can provide a satisfactory base on which to apply your prime coating and subsequent layers of protective paint. Blasting is necessary to remove all contaminants and corrosion from the surface of the metal; and as this process slightly roughens the

This Roberts 370 built in Finland shows one reason good protective coatings are essential.

surface, it also provides an excellent "tooth" for the paint. For reasons that will become clear, we believe the best way to build a steel boat is to use preshotblasted and primed material, and to build under some form of cover. Nonetheless, some builders do blast their own steel.

The exact roughness of the surface will depend, for the most part, on the particular metal, the type and grade of grit used, and the force with which it's applied during the blasting process. The result is commonly referred to as the "anchor pattern," and will vary between 1.5 mils (thousandths of one inch) and 4 mils (0.038 mm and 0.1 mm) in depth. Four thousandths (0.1 mm) is considered a heavy and deep blast, and may be satisfactory for tar-epoxy finishes. For most paints, however, you should aim for a 1½-mil to 3-mil (0.038 mm to 0.076 mm) anchor pattern. Your paint manufacturer may have special recommendations in this area. Make sure you choose a warm and dry day with low humidity when you are blasting your boat.

For blasting, you'll need a powerful compressor; for instance, one that can deliver something over 350 feet (107 m) per minute would be perfect. You need manpower: two or three people plus yourself would be adequate. There are various specifications for the blasting of steel. For our purposes, "near white" blast-cleaning will deliver a successful, corrosion-free, and long-lasting paint job. "Near white" blast-cleaning produces a surface in steel that, when viewed without magnification, is free of all visible oil, grease, dirt, dust, mill scale, rust, and paint. Generally, evenly dispersed, very light shadows, streaks, and discoloration caused by stain of rust, stains of mill scale, and stains of previously applied paints may remain on no more than 5 percent of the surface.

Sand is the least expensive abrasive, but because of its high silica content and the health hazard presented by silica, you may find that your local contractor is not willing to use this material. If you're doing the job yourself, and you wear the correct protective face mask, then blasting one boat with this material should not represent an undue health hazard. It's your responsibility to decide on using sand as opposed to the more expensive alternatives. Sand can't be reused, so you'd need more sand than slag or grit.

Grit is a little more expensive than sand but contains none of the silica that, when used over a period, can cause respiratory and lung problems, among other things. In the U.S., these products are marketed as Copper Blast, Copper Slag, Green Diamond and Garnet. Similar products are available in Britain, Australia, and elsewhere.

Crushed-steel shot is more expensive than either sand or grit, but as it can be reused many times you may consider it to be worth the additional expense. It's formed from crushed iron or steel, and has irregular shapes with very sharp edges. It's one of the better blasting materials.

You'll need to consider matching the type and roughness of the blasted surface with the paint you plan to apply. A surface that's too rough will show through your paint finish, and a surface that's too smooth won't provide a good grip for that most important element in your paint job, the primer.

Many builders have found that it takes a lot of effort to undertake this job, and it saves very little in cost. By the time you hire the equipment, purchase the grit, and arrange for the help needed, it can cost nearly as much as a professional job. You need three people for this operation; one to operate the blasting gun, one to feed the material, and one to apply the primer. If you don't have three people, the job will take much longer. For instance, if the blaster has to feed his own abrasive, he has to remove and replace his bulky helmet each time more grit is needed: a time-wasting exercise.

In the case of steel hulls, the prime coating must be applied immediately after the blasting. This means that the painter has to follow the blaster as closely as is practical. Rust can form in a surprisingly short time; the actual time depends on the weather and humidity prevailing when the blasting takes place. It's usual for the owner or his employee, as opposed to one of the contractor's employees, to undertake the painting. If you

Careful masking of the various parts of the boat will play an important part in ending up with a professional-looking paint job.

control this critical job yourself, you'll be assured of its success. Make sure the paint is being applied to a perfectly clean and dry surface at a minimum temperature of 50°F (10°C). The paint is best applied within 30 minutes of the blasting. That way, as well as avoiding rust, you'll have the extra advantage that the steel should still be warm from the blasting. Finally, three to four hours is the absolute maximum time lag between blasting and prime coating. This is definitely not a one-person operation.

Estimating the time it takes to blast and prime coat is difficult, given all of the variables involved. However, about 50 square feet (4.65 square meters) per hour seems about average. No grit operator or painter can operate flat-out for extended periods. It's wise to divide the hull, deck, and superstructure into reasonably sized segments; say, quarters on a small- to medium-sized hull, and smaller proportions on larger craft. Keeping the blasting and the painting apart will take some organizing, but you will need to do it to ensure a clean and long-lasting priming job.

When you purchase preblasted and primed steel from a specialist supplier, then these materials have most likely been "blasted" by a wheel rather than blasted in the regular way. This process is most effective in plate of ⅛-inch (3 mm), or 10-gauge, and larger thicknesses, but lighter plates may distort when exposed to wheel "blasting."

Wet blasting involves using water mixed with the grit or sand. This process keeps down dust, but afterward it leaves a great deal of heavy, wet grit or sand to be cleaned up. A rust inhibitor is used in the water, but you have to blow the hull dry and apply the paint before the effects of the inhibitor disappear.

The interior of the hull, under the decks, and inside the superstructure will all need to be gritblasted: a difficult and messy job. Don't forget to have all of the cut-outs and openings for windows, ports, and hatches already completed before you gritblast and apply the prime coat. It will probably be best to blast the outside first; that way, you won't have any worry about grit coming through openings into an already prime-coated hull interior.

We have now come full circle. We've considered the alternatives and you can see that my advice to use preshotblasted and primed material makes more sense. Even if you are building in the open, depending on the climate and the amount of care you take in covering the hull, you may find that the preblasted and primed materials are worth the extra cost and effort. Even so, covering your hull during nonwork periods will pay off. Of course, you could consider the excellent alternative of installing an aluminum deck and superstructure on your steel hull and thus eliminate many of the problems of blasting above the sheerline.

If you use preprime-coated steel, then you'll need to clean up only in the area of the welds. You'll recoat these areas before proceeding with another prime coat of the entire hull, deck, and superstructure. The welds can be cleaned with a grinder, a wire brush, or a similar device to expose a clean surface that's ready to be touched up with matching prime coat.

Be careful when you're using solvents and other liquids to clean metal; be aware of the deposits they leave behind, so that you're not faced with a never-ending circle of cleaning and re-cleaning a particular area. Acids can sometimes be used to advantage to remove surface contaminates, including rust. Acids tend to etch the surface and thus improve the adhesion of the paints you apply afterward. Generally, acids are only used as cleaning agents in smaller areas such as those where welding has spoilt an otherwise prepared and primed hull.

FILLING AND FAIRING

For a perfect or near-perfect finish, almost all metal boats need some filling and fairing, but it's important that you do not rely on the filling compound to cover sloppy workmanship. The following advice will probably be ignored by the sloppy builder and resented as unnecessary by the perfectionist. It's to the greater proportion of you occupying the middle ground that we address this advice. Your aim should be to make every step of the building process produce a fair and smooth hull, deck, and superstructure. You should strive to build a boat that will require the minimum of filler.

Now, having established that all hulls and

This Roberts 434 shows that a stripe can enhance the appearance of most hulls.

Spraying Hot Metal

This method of applying a protective coating is included here because we're still occasionally asked about its merits for a steel hull. Metal spraying was at one time popular with some steel builders. During the 1970s, when it was most popular, there were many who decried its use on the grounds that if it chipped or otherwise failed, water would creep underneath and cause considerable invisible corrosion problems. Time has proven these critics correct, in fact, and the method is infrequently used today. Another drawback was that the materials used for these coatings were notoriously averse to holding paints as intended. The development of modern epoxy and urethane protective coatings has allowed "flame spraying" (or "metalizing" as it was popularly known), to fade from the scene. In the interests of thoroughness, however, here are the details.

Hot-metal spraying is accomplished by melting either zinc or aluminum metal wire in a special gun that drives it at high speed onto the bare steel in the form of molten droplets. Like a surface prepared for painting, the steel surface must be prepared by gritblasting down to white metal.

Without this etched surface, the hot metal spray will either roll off or flake off after cooling.

Many advocates of this method claim a chemical bond forms between the aluminum or zinc and the steel; they claim that the metals are "fused" together. Actually, the hot-metal spray forms a mechanical bond only. It depends on the correct spraying techniques, as well as a grit-blasted surface, to maintain its grip on the steel. If you plan to metal-spray your hull, don't use sand as the blasting agent. Commercially manufactured grit is necessary to give the correct key for the metalization process.

If you use a hot spray involving aluminum or zinc, then you should apply a special wash to the aluminum coating before applying any paints. An example of such a wash is Interlux Viny-Lux Primewash, which is specially formulated to adhere to bare aluminum and is a good primer for the other coats that will follow. If you are considering one of the hot-metal spays for your boat, you should seek out the latest information on the subject. My advice is stick to the well-proven regular painting procedures for metal hulls.

most superstructures need some filler to produce the near-perfect appearance, it's simply a matter of choosing and correctly applying the right material. Automotive body putty is not the correct filler for your boat. It won't withstand the rigors of marine use.

Incidentally, please let the recommendations of your paint manufacturer overrule any advice we give here. You must choose one manufacturer and use its products exclusively. If you mix brands, you'll have no protection if the product fails. Each manufacturer will blame the competitor's product as the cause of the problem.

The correct filler for your metal boat should be epoxy, not polyester based (as is usual) with automotive fillers. Your fairing compound should contain inert fillers such as microballoons. Many paint manufacturers have their own fairing compounds as part of the overall paint system. Make sure you choose a manufacturer who will give you local advice and technical assistance. This is not just a case of visiting your local marine store and taking what's on offer. You'll need to undertake considerable research to ensure you end up with a long-lasting and attractive paint finish on your metal boat. To quote our own experience; our 38-foot (11.58 m) steel powerboat was originally painted

The long-lasting paint job on this early version of the Waverunner 34 has proven the benefits of using preprime-coated steel.

in 1991, and today the superstructure looks as good as new. Due to mishandling and neglect by the previous owner, the hull recently needed a "blow-coat" to cover scuff marks.

PAINTING

In the process of selecting the paint, you'll have to consider how it will be applied. Certain finishes lend themselves better to one application method than another. Some paints can be applied in many ways, so this may influence your choice of paint as well as what equipment you either purchase or hire for the job. No matter what method you choose for applying the various paints, you'll need a selection of brushes, rollers, paint trays, scrapers, sandpaper, and all the usual tools one associates with painting any structure. We've seen many fine metal hulls painted with hand tools, including a combination of rolled and brushed finishes.

Airless, or air-assisted spray equipment is favored by those experienced in painting hulls, and it's possible to lay on high-build paints in a way that could not be achieved by hand. If you elect to blast your boat, it's well worth considering using a professional team to at least apply the prime coating on your hull immediately after blasting. A team of, say, three or four professionals can blast and prime your boat in just a few hours and thereby ensure that you get the best cover for the blasted steel before it starts to rust.

The success of your paint job will depend on the care and attention you lavish on the preparation of your vessel before the first finish coat is applied. You must identify individual items that will be more prone to rust, and then give them additional attention. One way to identify potential problem areas is by studying other older steel boats. If you've followed our advice on layout and construction, then you will already have avoided most of these potential problems. Now, all you have to do is carefully check your own boat before you start to paint.

Usually, rust doesn't form on smooth areas of the hull. Irregular and sharp surfaces are often the culprits. For instance, we have always recommended that you avoid sharp corners on your hull or superstructure. To avoid creating rust traps and areas where paint is easily damaged, liberal use should be made of split pipe and/or rolled plate. When you eliminate the potential problem areas, you will also eliminate the corrosion problems that, at best, ruin the appearance of any metal boat, and at worst endanger its security. Therefore, no sharp edges, sharp corners, water traps, overlapping plates, or other bad practices that we have already covered in earlier chapters.

Don't attempt to paint areas of high wear, such as anchor fairleads, cleats, and similar fittings. They must have a stainless-steel liner welded in place to accept the wear, and thus avoid any corrosion problems. All welds in areas above the waterline must be ground smooth and filled. This will ensure that no jagged edges or high spots are present. Sharp corners and jagged welds prevent the layers of paint from covering evenly, and thereby diminish protection.

As we've said already, we don't recommend that you grind smooth the welds below the waterline. This is a safety factor, and it means that these welds should be most carefully executed to give maximum strength and maximum smoothness, to enable them to accept a full quota of paint.

Aluminum

Many aluminum workboats are left unpainted and this is not a problem when the correct grade of marine aluminum has been used to build the vessel. The metal forms an oxide on the surface and further protection is unnecessary. But even these unpainted aluminum vessels need some protection below the waterline, so the underwater hull must be coated with a suitable antifouling paint. In France, we've seen many aluminum-hulled sailboats and powerboats with unpainted topsides, and quite frankly, they look unfinished. Unless you want your boat to look like an untidy workboat, you should accept the fact that you will be painting your aluminum vessel.

You'll need to abrade the surface of your aluminum hull by sanding it, or by using abrasive pads to roughen the surface of the metal. Next, thoroughly clean the surface with the chemical preparation recommended by your particular paint manufacturer. Now etch the surface. This is usually done with a phosphoric acid solution that changes the chemical properties of the surface of the aluminum, allowing better adhesion for the first coat of paint. Your paint manufacturer will recommend an etch primer or a wash. A primer coat will follow this. Needless to say, this primer coat is one of the most important of the whole system; if it fails, then the whole system will break down.

After you have applied the primer coat, follow it with two or more high-build barrier undercoats above the waterline. The finish coats will be applied above the waterline. A special tin-based antifouling is normally applied below the waterline. In some areas, a license is required to purchase and use toxic tin-based antifouling. Check locally to see if you require a permit to use this material. Because of galvanic corrosion problems, you must never use copper-based antifouling paint on an aluminum boat.

Copper-Nickel

Preparation for painting copper-nickel should include good-quality gritblasting or sandblasting followed by a high-build epoxy filler/primer or epoxy mastic. For final coatings, polyurethane-based coatings are recommended. As with the painting of all metal boats, advice and assistance should be sought from a local paint manufacturer, or at least one who has a readily accessible and knowledgeable technical department.

This beautifully painted radius-chine steel Roberts 434 shows the excellent finish that can be achieved on a well-built steel boat. This hull has no filler.

Finish Painting All Metals

Most paint manufacturers have their own specifications for painting the various metals. Many of the procedures are similar, and consist of roughening the hull surface, and/or using chemical preparations to thoroughly clean off any impurities. Next comes the application of prime coats, and more than one barrier coat. The process is completed with several finish coats to the hull topsides as well as to the decks and superstructure.

The bottom paint requires a thicker application. Paint located on and below the waterline must not only protect against corrosion, but also must prevent excessive marine growth. Nature helps out; the area under the water has less exposure to oxygen, which is one of the agents needed to promote rust, and other corrosive elements. Your metal boat should be hauled at least once a year and the bottom should be given a thorough scrub.

The bottom paint must be checked for flaws and a new coat of antifouling applied. Make sure it's applied according to the paint manufacturer's specifications. Even if your boat is continuously moored in freshwater, you'll still need to antifoul the hull regularly. Details on the installation and replacement of anodes, together with other actions you should take to protect the underwater areas of your hull, are covered in chapter 12, Preventing Corrosion.

Decks and Superstructure

In general terms, you'll use the same paint on the decks and superstructure as you have used on the hull topsides. The cabin sides and ends will al-

most certainly be painted in the same way as the hull. With a few exceptions, the preparation methods for the decks, cockpit and cabintops will follow a similar routine. Don't have too many colored strips, and don't chop up the area into many small sections or you may end up with a pattern that looks fussy. It takes careful thought and some experience to lay out a successful two-color paint scheme for the decks and cabintops. The designer of your boat may give you some advice and assistance in this area.

If you're planning to install one of the composite patterned deck-covering materials such as Treadmaster, then obtain it in advance and carefully study the installation instructions. You must ensure that the adhesive used to install the decking will be compatible with the paint used on the deck. Having the decking material on hand will also allow you to make a better choice of color for the painted areas of the deck, that is, those areas that will remain exposed after the patterned material is in place. If you're planning a timber-laid deck, you'll need to make sure that the preparation is in keeping with the materials you'll be using.

No matter what arrangement you decide on for your decks and superstructure, make sure you give the area adequate coats of paint. Our steel power cruiser has five hand-applied finish coats; a

Fine signwriting puts the finishing touches to any well-painted metal boat; Sea Pea II is a Spray 38 built in the U.K.

perfect finish after many years of constant exposure to the elements proves the worth of a good paint job. Always carry a supply of primer, undercoat, and finish paints to touch up the dings and scratches that one gets from time to time.

Antifouling

The technology behind antifouling paints is constantly changing. On boats with copper-nickel hulls you won't have to worry; they don't need antifouling. The natural action of the metal keeps most marine growth at bay. But steel and aluminum boats need a preventive coating for the areas below the waterline.

Just when we believe we've found the answer to the antifouling problem, along comes an environmentalist to point out the toxic problems caused by the use of certain protective bottom paints. For this reason, it's hard to make specific recommendations. As is the case with the entire paint job, my advice is to select one manufacturer and use their system from the first etch primer through to the final coat of antifouling. When you're applying antifouling, you will need to estimate the load waterline and make sure your antifouling is carried to about 2½ inches (60 mm) above this line. The reason for painting the antifouling above the true waterline is that the water is never static, and if you finish the antifouling right at the waterline, you'll soon have an ugly growth of weed at, and just above, the true waterline.

Boottops

You shouldn't paint the boottop until after the boat has been launched and trimmed. After you've conducted trials, loaded stores and water, and determined the exact load waterline, only then should you consider painting the boottop. Incidentally, they're not just a straight, parallel line; they need to be applied so the line, when viewed from the side, appears parallel, or appears to have slightly more width at the ends. These lines are difficult to get right, especially on sailboats where the aft sections sweep underneath the hull and require quite a wide line to give the correct appearance. Avoid excessive upward sweeps of boottop at the bow.

If you start with a level line parallel to the load waterline, it can represent the bottom of your boottop; next, using a level, strike a second line above and parallel to the first, you will see how this line widens out at the stern. Study other boats that are out of the water, and you'll get the idea. Don't copy the ones that don't look right. Powerboats will not present the same problems, because the hull sides are more-or-less parallel. A boottop made of a tape of constant width can work with a powerboat, but it would look totally wrong on a sailboat hull.

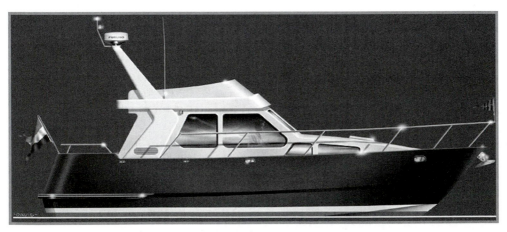

This Almarine 950 at 31ft / 9.5 m, available as a kit, is one of the smaller powerboats suitable for steel construction.

11
ENGINES AND ACCESSORIES

In our opinion, engines powered by gasoline (petrol) have no place in any metal boat—or in any other cruising boat, for that matter. Those who build or buy metal boats are usually thoughtful individuals, and safety is one of the reasons they choose metal. Petrol or gasoline engines do not fit this profile. We recommend diesel engines.

ENGINE COMPARTMENT

When you're choosing your engine, make sure that there's sufficient room to install it (or retrofit it). It isn't just a matter of shoehorning the engine into a given space; you'll also need room for insulation and servicing. The engine must be accessible. If access is difficult, then there is always the chance you'll neglect essential maintenance work.

Out of the several boats we've owned, we have never been totally satisfied with the accessibility of all of the items that need servicing on a regular basis. Unfortunately, total accessibility, although aimed for, is seldom achieved. For example, batteries need regular inspection, testing with a multimeter and/or hydrometer, and topping up with distilled water. These inspections are likely to be far less frequent if the batteries are in some difficult-to-reach location. The oil dipstick and the water filters should be inspected every day that the boat is in service. Primary fuel filters fitted with water traps need to be drained

on a regular basis. Water impellers need to be changed occasionally, sometimes in a hurry. Main fuel taps should be easily accessible; and the list goes on. Can you easily reach the injectors, stuffing box, and fuel-tank inspection hatches?

Some single-engined, semidisplacement powerboats have insulated engine boxes in addition to an insulated engine room. This makes for very quiet running but it does restrict accessibility to some items on and around the engine. In sailboats, the engine often intrudes into the accommodation, where it is inaccessible and almost impossible to service. If you're building a new custom-designed boat, or rebuilding an older

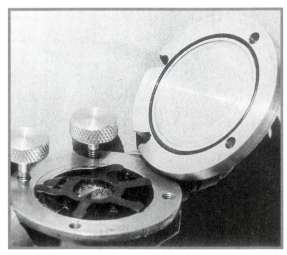

This Speedseal makes changing the impeller a little easier and much faster; a handy addition to any engine installation.

one, here's your chance to do yourself a huge favor: consider accessibility a number-one priority.

Engine room insulation in one form or another is essential if you want to keep noise down. In a sailboat, the engine box is usually a fairly close-fitting affair and the problem is also one of accessibility.

You can use several combinations of materials to insulate and quieten your engine, but however you do it, make sure the insulation won't give off toxic gases in the event of fire.

Here are some suggestions: aluminum-covered Styrofoam; fiberglass insulation with a lead insert; fiberglass and foam; and layers of lead, foam, and aluminum (or vinyl foam) sheeting. Most boatowners have found that a material that incorporates a layer of lead is usually the most effective in reducing noise. The classified pages of your local boating magazine or the advertising pages of your telephone directory will reveal many sources for these products.

Insulating the engine room in powerboats is relatively easy, as there is usually more room to lay out the insulation without interfering with access to the engine's vital organs. In some powerboats with relatively cavernous engine compartments, it's necessary to insulate the engine separately by having a separate, insulated box around the motor. In a single-engined powerboat, while an insulated sound box reduces the noise to almost a whisper, it does make access to the engine more difficult and it certainly earns its share of rude comments, especially during service checks.

ENGINE BEARERS

The engine bearers, or beds, should be made as long as possible to spread adequately the various loads imposed by the engine. We recommend beds that are two or more times the length of the engine. Space restrictions may defeat this ideal, but make them as long as possible. In our powerboat designs, we always try to mate up the engine bearers with fore-and-aft webs that run almost the full length of the boat. These webs also add strength throughout the hull and have the secondary use of helping to support the sole.

The engine bearers should be made of plate that is two to two-and-a-half times the thickness of the hull plating. Naturally, the exact thickness should be specified in your plans. The size and horsepower of the engine, and its size compared with the hull, will also have to be considered when designing the beds and their supports.

The transverse web supports in our designs are part of the regular frame web construction sequence, with additional webs added as required by the spacing of the frames. For example, if the frames of the hull are spaced, say, 10 to the waterline length, then additional webs will be required between the stations.

It's difficult to match the height of the beds with the line of the shaft and the stern bearing. If you don't already have the engine on site, then using a three-dimensional plywood mock-up of the engine can help.

These engine beds embody many of the features described in the text.

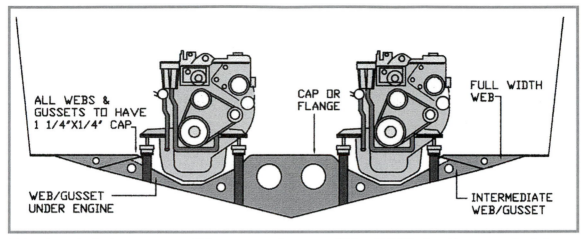

ALL WEBS &
GUSSETS TO HAVE
1 1/4"X1/4" CAP

CAP OR
FLANGE

FULL WIDTH
WEB

WEB/GUSSET
UNDER ENGINE

INTERMEDIATE
WEB/GUSSET

This twin engine-bed arrangement will fit most powerboats over 35 feet (10.67 m) and leave room for fuel tanks outboard of each engine.

THE DRIVE TRAIN

You must consider the drive train of your engine, from transmission to propeller, to be a single, integrated unit. Most engines have flexible mountings and feature a suitable coupling, such as an Aqua Drive unit to complete the vibration-free installation. The Aqua Drive and similar units allow for slight misalignment between the shaft and the engine transmission. This is a necessary feature because when the engine is mounted on flexible mountings, there will be some movement between the engine coupling and the propeller shaft.

Stuffing Box

You'll need some form of gland to prevent the water entering your boat where the propeller shaft passes through the hull. Your main choices will be between a traditional stuffing box and one of the newer devices,

such as a Deep Sea Seal. If you choose a stuffing box, it may have an external grease-lubrication system or depend on the natural oils of the stuffing and the water for lubrication. Grease-fed stuffing boxes usually employ a remote cylinder that you have to pack with waterproof grease. One or two turns on the plunger each day forces enough grease through the line to the bearing; this helps to keep the water at bay. All stuffing boxes (also known as packing glands) will drip twice or so per minute and produce about a cupful of water per day. If they're overtightened, and don't drip, then the bearing and the shaft will probably suffer from excessive wear.

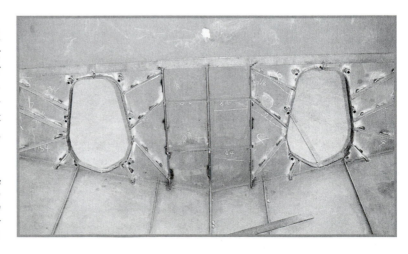

This stiffener arrangement was used to beef up the transom when fitting a pair of diesel Volvo stern drives to a steel Wave-runner 342 built in Europe.

The engine bearers in the Almarine-built powerboat kit are precut and only need the tops added to complete the beds.

Patented Stern Bearings

Stern bearings, such as the unit marketed as the Deep Sea Seal, have long been used on large ships, but only in the past few years have they been installed in pleasure boats and workboats of all types. The Deep Sea Seal has an excellent reputation and has been fitted to many thousands of boats around the world. The basic DSS has been improved with the addition of an additional red clamp that allows the unit to be serviced while the boat is still afloat The basis of the Deep Sea Seal is a rubber bellows that is fitted with a bearing steel ring that runs on a bearing surface in such a way as to prevent water from entering the hull through the stern tube. The rubber bellows is adjusted to maintain constant pressure on the bearing surface. The unit is lubricated by some of the engine-cooling water being introduced through a spigot on the bearing surface.

The main advantage of installing a Deep Sea Seal–type stern bearing is that it doesn't drip, hence there's one less way for salt water to enter the hull and promote corrosion. Another advantage is that the unit needs only an occasional check to ensure that it's doing its job, as opposed to the constant attention required by the conventional stuffing box bearing.

There are other manufacturers of these devices, and you should investigate the various types, before making your choice. See supplier's addresses in appendix 2.

Either a Y-bracket or a P-bracket is required to support the shaft between the hull and the propeller.

If your boat has twin engines, it's a sure thing that on many occasions you will want to run on one engine. If your engines are equipped with Deep Sea Seals or similar water-lubricated stern bearings, you should consider the need to supplying water to the bearing of the shut-down engine. The Pedro 41 *Van Hoff*, a custom-built, steel trawler yacht with aluminum decks and superstructure, owned by our friends Mike and Caroline Hofman, is fitted with a crossover water supply to both Deep Sea Seals. We confess we showed only moderate interest when Mike explained this system. The twin water supply was necessary, because, as with most twin-engined vessels, *Van Hoff* is often operated on one engine for the sake of fuel economy. In light of subsequent events not fully detailed here, we should have taken more notice! There follows a clue!

Even if you have only one engine, consider the possibility of engine failure. Then, when your vessel is towed, do you let the shaft rotate? If so, how do you provide water to the bearing? If the situation persists for more than a short time, unlubricated stern bearings can be damaged. It may even be wise to consider installing shaft-locking devices that are available to suit most size engine-shaft combinations.

Aft Shaft Bearings

Your boat will require a bearing where the propeller shaft leaves the outer end of the tube. The choice is between a fiber bearing, a Tufnol bearing, and a Cutless rubber bearing. Cutless bearings are well proven and when properly set up with two small water scoops at the fore end of the tube to introduce lubricating water, they will give long and trouble-free service.

If the distance between the inboard stuffing box (or seal) and the outboard end of the tube is over say 6 feet, 6 inches (2 m), you may require an intermediate bearing generally known as a plummer block. This may be another Cutless bearing that has been slid down the tube to the midpoint location.

If your shaft protrudes from the tube by more than a few inches, you may need a Y-bracket bearing to support the outer end immediately ahead of the propeller. Decisions as to whether you need an intermediate bearing and similar questions are best addressed to the designer of your boat or a qualified marine engineer.

EXHAUST SYSTEMS

Most diesel engines do not come completely equipped with a suitable exhaust system. In the past, one exception was the range of diesel auxiliaries supplied by Vetus den Ouden. Unfortunately, the engines and equipment are now sold separately. Vetus does have a good range of exhaust systems that are available all over the world. (See appendix 2 for addresses.)

Diesel engines fitted to sailboats or powerboats will need a properly engineered exhaust system. Engines mounted below the waterline—and most are—will need special antisiphon devices. There are two basic ways to cool an engine and both have a bearing on the type of exhaust system required. Most air-cooled (noisy) engines have a dry-exhaust system, which means that no water is added to the necessarily heavily insulated (lagged) exhaust. In the confines of a sailboat, dry exhausts are hot and noisy but this type of exhaust can be used to good effect in some types of traditional powerboats. Dry exhausts, combined with a vertical stack, are often seen on fishing boats and workboats.

A wet-exhaust system cools the exhaust gases with water soon after they leave the engine. The water and gases are expelled together. This system is necessarily interrelated with the cooling system of your engine. A stainless steel "water-lift" muffler is a nice addition to any exhaust system and will dampen noise.

Stern-drive engines and outboards have the exhaust systems built in. Outboard engines are beyond the scope of this book, but you may be considering a diesel powered stern drive for your metal powerboat. Stern-drive exhausts usually exit via the center of the propeller, no doubt adding a minuscule amount of thrust in the process.

COOLING SYSTEMS

Heat Exchanger Cooling

Most modern diesel engines feature freshwater, heat exchanger cooling. This method uses a special tank of freshwater that runs through the engine's cooling system. The freshwater tank contains internal piping and is, in turn, cooled by seawater pumped through the pipes. This method prevents the internal cooling system of the engine coming into contact with salt water. Most modern diesel engines are cooled in this manner. One problem with this method is that if the outside intake for the cooling water becomes clogged, then the whole system overheats. A sensor in the system can warn you about this condition, before your engine overheats. Make sure each engine is equipped with this warning device.

Raw-water cooling is usually found on older diesels. The method is to pump outside water (seawater or freshwater) through the engine cas-

ing and then out through the exhaust, thus cooling the engine in the process.

Engine Water Pump

Most cooling systems include a water pump that draws water from outside the hull and forces it through the cooling system. The pump will include an impeller that will need replacing from time to time. Most water pumps, unfortunately, are located in inaccessible places. Make sure you know where yours is, and check that you have a spare impeller. Also, check the difficulty of removing the impeller and its cover plate. You can buy a special Speedseal cover plate that's attached with only two knurled screws. Because it can be removed and replaced quickly with one hand, you might want to replace your regular water pump cover with one.

Engine Water Filter

If your engine uses water drawn from outside, either directly as raw-water cooling or by way of a heat exchanger, you'll require a water filter to remove any foreign matter that could damage the water-pump impeller or otherwise clog the cooling system, and, in turn, cause the engine to overheat. The usual arrangement is to place the water filter immediately after the seacock where the outside water enters the system.

The filter should be easily accessible, as it should be checked daily—even more often if you're motoring in weed-infested waters. It's often made of clear plastic so you can see what's going on inside, but don't let this discourage you from removing the top for regular inspections. Plastic bags are one of the most common foreign bodies lurking in our waterways and they're not always visible without removing the top of the filter. Most filters have a rubber sealing ring, and you may find that a light coating of Vaseline will prevent the unit from sucking air. In any case, the rings will need replacement every two years or so. If you have a diesel-powered generating set, you should have a separate water filter for it. If possible, place the two filters close together so you can check both at the same time.

Keel Cooling and Similar Methods

There is a third method of cooling that requires no external water to be drawn into the boat. The most common of the self-contained cooling systems involves outside pipes that are usually tucked into the keel-hull intersection. Hot engine water flowing through them is cooled by the surrounding seawater. The most interesting version of this method is only possible with boats that have a hollow metal keel. It involves boxing off a section of the keel to store a 50/50 mixture of antifreeze coolant and freshwater. This mixture is run through the engines' cooling system, and provided that the surface area of the selected portion of the keel is adequate, the system works extremely well. This arrangement employs two header tanks, and works in a manner similar to the way your car's engine cooling system works.

There's another advantage to these engine cooling systems. You can incorporate an insulated hot-water tank, or calorifier. This tank has an internal pipe coil through which hot water from the engine cooling system is circulated. This pipe, in turn, heats the domestic hot water. In the sailboat we owned previously, *K*I*S*S*, we found that running the engine for about 20 minutes every other day was sufficient to provide hot water for two days of showers, plus other daily hot-water requirements.

Any internal cooling system that doesn't import raw water requires a lagged, dry exhaust. Considerable care is required in routing any exhaust line, especially the dry variety, which can get hot despite the lagging. If you have a dry exhaust, pay particular attention to the ventilation of your engine space and the surrounding area. The main negative feature of this arrangement is that dry exhausts are usually noisier than the water-cooled systems.

Mufflers

Many exhaust systems involve the use of a water-lift muffler. The engine cooling water is fed into the exhaust pipe just aft of where it leaves the en-gine, and then into the muffler, where the pressure of the incoming exhaust gases forces the water out of the boat. This system can be one of the quietest, and quietness in your exhaust system is a very desirable feature.

If you are purchasing a ready-built new or used metal boat, the engine cooling and exhaust systems will already be in place, and usually it's an expensive proposition to change from one system to another. If you're building your own boat, however, you should choose carefully. Check other boats; weigh up the advantages and disadvantages of each system before you make your final decision.

Raw-water cooling (no heat exchanger) is the least desirable because the innards of your engine are constantly exposed to the ravages of salt water or outside water containing all sorts of pollutants. Your choice should be between a system with a regular heat exchanger (using outside water to cool it) and a system that has outside piping to allow keel cooling. Alternatively, you can choose the fully internal system. The fully internal system is similar to keel cooling using external pipes, the difference being that a reservoir of coolant is arranged in a section of the keel instead

Alternative Power

Hydraulic drives, electric drives, jet drives, and the like have no place in a sailboat. Over the past 30-odd years, we've been asked to design every imaginable type of "alternative" power arrangement. After completing many, sometimes longwinded, investigations, we've reached the conclusion that diesel power is the way to go. If you have a particular hobby, such as steam engineering, and you wish to combine this with your boating activity, then there may be an argument for installing an engine that allows you to indulge in your pet interest. But it's worth noting that you'll probably need to remove this unique installation before you sell the boat.

Understanding Horsepower

When you're considering horsepower, be aware that there are several terms used to describe the power generated by the engine at certain revolutions. One term you'll encounter is brake horsepower (BHP). This is the power produced by the engine without regard to the power loss caused by the transmission gearbox, or other losses from such items as the alternator, water pump, and general friction in the transmission system. Shaft horsepower (SHP), on the other hand, represents the power available at the propeller.

Usually, more than one rating is shown. For instance, there's *maximum* power. This is the power you could get for a very short time before you burn up the engine. Then there's *intermittent* power, which is the power the engine can deliver for a limited period—usually 30 to 60 minutes—without problems. *Continuous* power is the rating at which the engine can operate for long periods without damage. *Continuous* is the rating that will be of primary interest when you decide what horsepower you need to move your boat at the desired speed. Increasingly, you will find that the power ratings are given in kilowatts (kW). The Système International d'Unités, overseeing body of the official metric system, gives the conversion as 1 kW = 1.341 hp and the reciprocal = 0.746; 746 Watts = 1 hp.

of outside pipes. This system is not recommended for engines over about 120 hp or for the tropics, where the ousted water temperature would not have enough cooling effect.

No matter which system you choose, remember the advantages of having your hot-water tank (calorifier) as part of the engine cooling system.

SAILBOAT AUXILIARY POWER

You'll want to know whether your cruising boat has sufficient power to do the job. The auxiliary is often undervalued until you need it most. There are many formulas used to ensure it is up to the task; for preliminary calculations, we use a power-versus-weight ratio. This calculation will reveal if your sailboat has enough power to propel it in the direction you want to go when, for one reason or another, the sails can't do the job.

We can start with a ballpark calculation and estimate that for any sailboat, 2 hp per 1,000 pounds (454 kg) displacement is a reasonable requirement. The addition or reduction of horsepower from the above calculation will depend on your philosophy. In general, American sailors prefer more power than their European counterparts.

Most inboard engines fitted to sailboats require gearing down by way of a transmission gearbox to produce the power required to drive the vessel in anything but a flat calm. We usually recommend a 2:1 reduction, thus halving the rotation rate of the propeller versus the engine revolutions. You'll find that most manufacturers have a range of reduction options between 1.9:1 and 2.15:1; any one of these can be considered to fall within the 2:1 recommendation. Generally speaking, the larger the reduction, the larger the propeller diameter required. For this reason, it's not practical to install a very small engine that is geared down to say 3:1 or 4:1. The large propeller required would destroy the sailing performance.

Single or twin engines? Unless your sailboat is over 55 feet (16.76 m) long, this is hardly worth discussing. And by over 55 feet, we mean considerably over!

METAL POWERBOAT ENGINES

Because of the variables involved, this is a much more complex subject than powering a sailboat. For want of space, we can only give a brief overview of this subject, but if you're interested in

Table 11-1. Brake horsepower for sailboat auxiliary engines.

This chart reflects data collected by the John Thornycroft Company (U.K.). The figures represent the various brake horsepower (BHP) requirements for auxiliary engines installed in sailboats. The calculations assume a three-bladed propeller. The BHP quoted is at the engine and allows 15 percent for engine and shafting losses.

Waterline Length	Tons Displ.	5 Knots	6 Knots	7 Knots	8 Knots	9 Knots
25 ft. (7.62 m)	2	5.0	5.0			
	3	6.5	6.5			
	4	8.7	8.7			
	5	12.0	12.0			
30 ft. (9.14 m)	2	1.9	3.6	6.4		
	3	2.5	5.0	9.7		
	4	2.9	6.4	13.0		
	5	3.3	7.7	16.0		
	6	3.5	8.8	19.0		
	8	4.0	11.0	26.0		
40 ft. (12.2 m)	4	2.8	5.2	8.5	13.0	
	6	3.5	7.0	12.0	25.0	
	8	4.0	8.4	15.0	26.0	
	10	4.4	9.9	18.0	33.0	
	12	4.6	11.0	21.0	40.0	
	14	5.0	12.0	24.0	46.0	
	16	5.2	13.0	27.0	53.0	
	18	5.6	14.0	30.0	59.0	
	20	5.9	15.0	33.0	66.0	
50 ft. (15.2 m)	8	4.1	7.2	13.0	19.0	28.0
	10	4.6	7.9	15.0	23.0	35.0
	12	5	8.8	17.0	27.0	42.0
	14	5.3	9.6	20.0	30.0	49.0
	16	5.6	10.0	11.0	34.0	56.0
	18	5.8	11.0	23.0	38.0	63.0
	20	6.0	12.0	25.0	41.0	70.0
	25	6.5	13.0	30.0	50.0	87.0
	30	7.0	14.0	34.0	57.0	105.0

learning more, check out the recommended reading in appendix 1.

Powering a Displacement Hull

Powering a displacement-hulled motor vessel follows much the same rules as those used to calculate the requirements for sailboats. The exception is that while the sailboat has its sails to use in an emergency, the displacement powerboat relies to-tally on its engine. Most displacement powerboats are fitted with only one main powerplant, so you should select yours with care. To estimate the horsepower requirements, start with an estimate of 2 hp per 1,000 pounds (454 kg) of displacement. This should be taken as the minimum requirement.

You can gear down your engine to give maximum performance at lower speeds and reduce the amount of power required to drive your vessel. This option results in a larger-diameter propeller, and there may not be room for it. There are also other disadvantages to taking this minimum-power route; one day you may need extra power to get out of a sticky situation, or tow another vessel. Conversely, a diesel engine likes to be worked moderately hard, so it's not advisable to have an installation where only 50 percent or less of the power can be used without driving the stern down to an unacceptable level. If you want more power, you may wish to consider a semidisplacement hull that can make better use of it.

Powering a Semidisplacement Hull

A fact you must consider is that it takes excessive power to drive a semidisplacement hull faster than 1.5 times the square root of its waterline length. For example, a semidisplacement hull measuring 36 feet (10.97 m) on the waterline would have a square root of 6. So 6 times 1.5 equals 9 knots. A broad definition of "planing" is when a boat reaches a speed in knots of twice the square root of the waterline length in feet.

Taking the 36 foot (10.97 m) example shown above, the square root of 36, times 2, gives us a 12-knot planing speed; at this speed, the necessary horsepower and fuel requirements will turn a comfortable, economical cruising boat into an expensive proposition. Please note that the formula given is only for the *start* of planing, and to make a semidisplacement hull reach a full (near-level) planing attitude will take considerably more power, and use more fuel than consumed by a similar-sized true planing hull. The point is that it makes no sense to grossly overpower any semidisplacement hull—you'll be just spinning your wheels or, in this case, your propellers. This whole subject will be fully covered in my forthcoming book, *Choosing a Cruising Powerboat/ Motorboat*. See appendix 1 for details.

Next, we have to consider the weight of our vessel. Weight in this instance means *loaded* displacement. This includes not only the weight of

the finished boat but also fuel, water, stores, and the crew. In addition, there are all of those items that are brought aboard for a particular use or occasion and then never leave the boat.

Now, there are many kinds of semidisplacement hulls, ranging from a full displacement vessel through to almost a full planing hull. The degree of rise in the chine or buttock lines aft will determine how fast the hull may be driven. Simply put, the more stern there is in the water at rest, the faster the hull may be driven. Overpowering a hull will cause the stern to drop and create a large stern wave. In certain instances, this wave can overwhelm the vessel.

Powering a Planing Hull

Only a few years ago, it was thought impossible to build a successful small-to-medium-sized steel planing hull. Fortunately, modern building techniques and technical advances in design have not only made this possible, but practical as well. As mentioned above, planing occurs when the boat reaches a speed in knots equal to twice the square root of the waterline length in feet. A planing hull will then make the transition from "just about planing" to "full planing" with less fuss, less extra horsepower and less extra fuel than a similarly sized and equipped semidisplacement hull or semiplaning hull.

Aluminum has been used to build hundreds of thousands of small, medium, and large planing hulls. Although at first glance this material may appear to be the ideal metal for a fast hull, we have reservations about this material when used in any type of hull, preferring to recommend it for decks and superstructures. You'll find our thoughts on this material scattered through this book, so it's not necessary to repeat them here.

Now, for those who prefer aluminum: you'll find that the performance of planing hulls relates to *weight* and *power*. Unlike displacement hulls and (to a lesser extent) semidisplacement boats, waterline length plays a smaller part in the performance of a planing hull.

So, in simple terms, the more power and the

less weight you have in your planing hull, the faster it will go. Fortunately for designers like us, however, it's not that simple. A well-designed planing hull with modest power will outperform an overpowered, poorly designed vessel.

"Get-You-Home" Engines

Before we consider the subject of single or twin engines, we should touch on the possibility of installing a "wing" engine, or using the diesel that powers the generating set as an emergency arrangement to get you home. Most owners prefer a separate "wing" engine consisting of a smaller diesel engine set off to one side and equipped with its own shaft and propeller. This engine is generally only required in the case of failure of the main engine, but of course it will need to be run from time to time for maintenance and testing purposes. For obvious reasons, the wing engine is only needed in boats with a single main engine. The wing engine and similar arrangements are often referred to as "take-home" engines. Some owners have installed an electric drive powered by the gen-set, and have used this as emergency propulsion.

Circumstances have caused us to give this matter considerable thought. In the near future, we will be designing a range of long-distance power cruisers. These vessels are generally referred to as passagemakers and, to be successful, they need a minimum range of 3,000 miles. Some vessels in the 50-foot plus range (more than 15.25 m) can be built to cover up to 6,000 miles without refueling. For various reasons, most of these long-distance vessels are fitted with a single engine, hence the interest in alternative propulsion methods. As a safety factor, both for medium-distance and local cruising, my choice would be for a wing engine.

One or Two Engines?

As mentioned earlier, most displacement-hulled vessels are traditionally fitted with a single engine. But many owners have twin installations, and the bulk of them quote safety as the prime reason for taking this route.

We've always maintained that when you install twin engines, as opposed to a single engine of the same total horsepower, you'll lose 20 percent in total output. More recently, we've decided that the effective loss of power may be even higher. Other examples show that the additional fuel consumption of the second engine is not justified by the small increase in performance when the two engines are used.

If you're considering a new boat, and you're considering twin engines in the interests of safety, you should be aware that in the interests of economy you might be operating only one engine for much of the time. You would be well advised to lay out your engines and systems with the above facts in mind. Owners who regularly take this course use each engine alternately on a four-hourly or daily basis.

PROPELLERS

It would be convenient if we could buy a propeller to match our hull material. Builders using copper-nickel are fortunate; the bronze propellers that are readily available are a close relative to the hull material, so the interaction between different metals that causes corrosion is at least reduced. Steel, or cast-steel, propellers are very difficult to obtain, so steel boat owners are forced to use the bronze versions, or to join their aluminum-boat-owning friends and opt for an expensive stainless-steel "wheel." So there you have it: steel boat, bronze propeller; copper-nickel boat, nickel-aluminum-bronze propeller (must be more noble than the copper-nickel hull); aluminum boat, stainless-steel propeller.

Propeller nomenclature is simple, but choosing the correct size and pitch of the wheel is somewhat more difficult. The *diameter* refers to the size of the circle scribed by the tips of the propeller blades. The *pitch* is the distance the propeller would travel in one full revolution if it were rotating in a solid. *RPM* refers to the revolutions that the shaft achieves in one minute; this figure is usually a factor of the engine RPM, but due to the transmission reduction (1.5:1, 2:1 and so forth) the shaft RPM will be different to the engine RPM. When calculating propeller sizes, it's the shaft RPM that is important. The *slip* refers to the loss of forward motion due to the fact that the propeller is rotating in a liquid, not a solid. Slip is the theoretical difference between what a propeller of a given pitch would travel, and what it actually is expected to achieve, usually expressed as a percentage. The *pitch ratio* is figured by dividing the pitch by the diameter. Fast powerboats sometimes have a diameter and pitch of the same number; this is referred to as a "square wheel."

Propellers for Powerboats

In powerboats, you'll want to install the most efficient propellers that will allow the engine to reach its operating and top RPM when required. In some designs, the propeller aperture is not sufficiently large enough to allow the correct propeller to be installed, and in this case a change from a three-bladed to a four-bladed wheel may prove successful. If you're experiencing cavitation because the tip clearance is too small, or because of the shape of your particular hull, then a change to four blades may remedy the situation.

The design and matching of a propeller to the hull, engine, and reduction ratio is something of an occult art. As designers, we do our best, but even the most detailed calculations can result in a propeller match that can be improved during trials conducted over a variety of conditions. You can also contact one of the many well-known propeller manufacturers in the U.S., Australia, U.K., and elsewhere. They will usually be most helpful. If you have a propeller problem, don't disregard it; seek assistance as required.

Propellers for Sailboats

The most efficient propeller from a sailing point of view is the two-blade *folding* variety. Two blades mean a larger diameter, and this can cause problems where space is restricted. These may be considered if you're building a high-performance metal sailboat. Some of these two-bladed folding propellers are inefficient and others have a reputation for not always opening on demand, which could be disastrous. If you do decide to choose a two-bladed type, make sure you are able to get a first-hand recommendation from another person who has already had experience with the brand you favor.

The elimination of drag is the aim of every sailboat owner. One way around the problem is to use a *feathering* propeller. These units are complex and expensive. Finely engineered feathering propellers may be suitable for larger yachts, where the owners have the resources to cover the initial expense and possible high maintenance costs. Unless you have very deep pockets, you're best advised to accept a small loss of speed under sail and select a *fixed* three-bladed wheel.

Rope Cutters

These devices are mentioned here because they may require a slightly longer shaft to be fitted. Suitable for both sailboats and powerboats, rope cutters are designed to be clamped on your shaft just ahead of the propeller. They can be very effective in cutting rope or a similar obstruction that would otherwise foul your propeller.

FUEL FILTERS

Does your engine have a separate primary fuel filter? Not all boat manufacturers fit these essential items as standard. The fuel filter that comes with the engine is basically a secondary filter, so a good primary fuel filter that incorporates a water trap is needed between the fuel tank and the engine. The filter should have the capacity to handle a considerable amount of dirt and water. Twin primary filters can be arranged so one can continue while the other is unclogged or changed. The installation of primary fuel filters should be a serious consideration in single-engined craft.

Filters with glass bowls have pros and cons. The sealed-filter units have expensive cartridges that need to be replaced completely, rather than simply replacing the internal filter. A major advantage of glass is that one can quickly observe if water is present. However, the glass-bowl filters are now outlawed in Europe for all boats and in the U.S. in gas-powered vessels, the argument being that in case of fire they present an additional danger.

Recently, we met the owner of a motor cruiser, a Dutch-built steel vessel of 34 feet (10.36 m), who got into trouble because of the glass bowl. This fellow, an experienced boater, was alone off the Spanish coast, near Barcelona, motoring along in heavy seas, when his single engine stopped. Upon investigation, he found that the glass bowl on the primary fuel filter had shattered. This had allowed diesel fuel to spray in all directions—and of course the engine stopped for lack of fuel. Fortunately, there was no fire. No replacement bowl was available and the engine was too hot, and the motion too violent, to allow the owner to deal with the situation. He was forced to swallow his pride and call out the Spanish Coast Guard, who responded promptly. Within an hour, the disabled vessel was safely in port. The owner believes he overtightened the glass bowl on the filter and when it expanded, due to the heat from the engine, it shattered. There are two lessons here: reconsider the use of glass-bowled filters, and don't overtighten them.

You'll need to change the filters at regular intervals. In the case of a fuel blockage, you'll need to change them as required. This is a very messy job and is one area of boat maintenance that you must understand. You should practice preventive maintenance wherever possible. When you're reassembling filter units, make sure you have the sealing O-rings in the correct order and position; sometimes the top and bottom rings look similar but are different enough to allow fuel or oil to leak out when the engine is fired up. Start the engine with caution after servicing these items.

VENTILATION

In all boats, ventilation of the engine space is an important feature. Your engine needs a considerable amount of fresh air. Install two vents of adequate size, one ducted below the engine to bring the fresh air in, and the other ducted high up in the engine space to take the hot air out. Generally, a blower is not required in northern latitudes. In hot climates, however, you may need one to turn the air over at the correct rate. An engine-space blower is simply a ducted fan that is designed to either import or export larger quantities of air than would circulate naturally.

INSTRUMENT PANELS

Your engine will usually be equipped with an instrument panel, but you may want to add to the instruments supplied in the standard package. The minimum engine instrumentation should include a tachometer (revolution counter), an engine-hour meter, a fuel gauge (notoriously inaccurate in boat installations; have a dipstick handy), and a volt/ampere meter. You'll require an instrument light switch, including a dimmer control for night use, an audible alarm to indicate if you fail to switch off the ignition after the engine has been stopped, an engine stop control, and a water-temperature gauge. Warning lights and or buzzers may indicate some potential problems; in our opinion, warning lights are not as effective as proper gauges. Audible alarms are recommended for water temperature, alternator output, and the other "vital life signs." Your electrical panel, complete with fuses, is usually located in a separate box; however, in some boats with inside steering, it may be incorporated in the main panel.

BILGE PUMPS

Take some time planning and laying out your bilge-pumping systems. Bilge pumps can be driven manually, electrically, or mechanically. Usually, the first line of defense is the automatic, electrically powered unit situated in the lowest point of the bilge. This bilge pump should be fitted with a strum box. This is a special perforated box, or strainer, fitted over the end of the bilge pump hose that is installed low in the bilge. If you have an automatic shower pump-out system, this can double as another bilge pump. The shower and toilet pumps will often be located in a different compartment to the main unit.

You'll need at least one, preferably two, hand-operated bilge pumps and one of these should be a large-capacity, portable unit mounted on a board, thus allowing it to be operated in any part of the vessel. The Edson 18 and the Whale Titan are both excellent hand-operated pumps.

You'll also need to arrange a sump or suitable collection point for bilge water. This sump is usually under, or nearly under, the engine so that any spilt diesel fuel and other unwanted liquids can be pumped or sponged out. A hand-operated bilge pump with a hose attached is useful in this area so that you can pump any contaminated water into a separate container for proper disposal ashore. U.S. federal law prohibits the pumping of oily bilgewater directly into the surrounding water. For instance, in Florida a heavy fine can

be the result of pumping even the smallest amounts of polluted water into the local canals. Any bilge pumps located in the sump or elsewhere should be fitted with a strainer. In the event of any large particles being present, you need to ensure that they will not find their way into, and totally block, the pump.

FUEL TANKS

Aluminum is often used for fuel tanks, but there have been many problems. Aluminum tanks are susceptible to vibration and can fracture along the weld lines where baffles are attached inside. If you do use aluminum for tanks, make sure they are made from a high-magnesium alloy such as 5083 or 5086 specification. It may be better to consider tanks made of, or molded from, polypropylene.

Aluminum and steel tanks are sometimes built with the hull acting as one side of the tank. It's preferable to have the tanks built as a separate unit and tested before installation in the boat, because this will ensure that there are no leaks. Air pressure of about 3 pounds per square inch (psi) can be used to test the tanks. *On no account simply connect the tanks to a high-pressure air hose.*

These tanks were fabricated and tested outside the hull and then installed as shown. As it is usually impossible to remove tanks without destroying interior joinery, you must make sure that your tanks are thoroughly tested before installation.

Tanks can be neatly arranged under the sole. Note the inspection and cleaning hatches in tank tops.

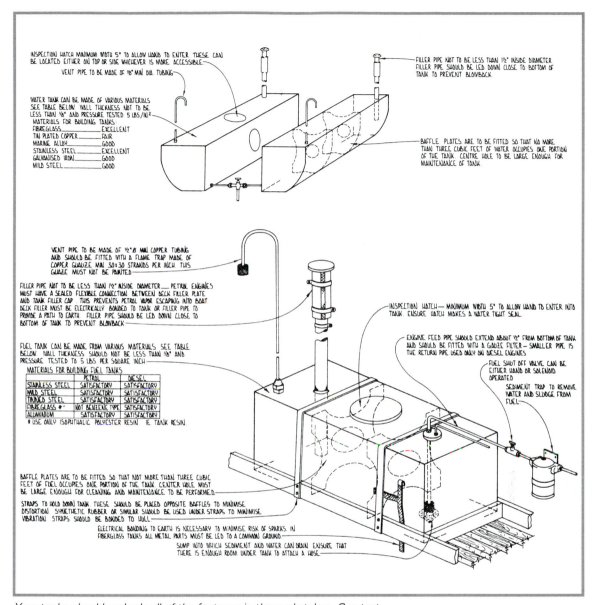

Your tanks should embody all of the features in these sketches. See text.

You may cause the tank to explode. Because of the risk of explosion, some experts recommend hydrostatic testing rather than the air test mentioned above.

Diesel fuel tanks may be built from a variety of materials, including high-density polyethylene, stainless steel, aluminum, or mild steel. Most builders choose regular mild steel. This material has the advantage of low cost, ease of fabrication, and low maintenance. The diesel fuel inside the tank prevents interior corrosion, and provided you keep the outside well painted, your steel fuel tanks should give you long service.

Tank capacity is a contentious subject. Most designers specify small, easy-to-remove tanks. The builder wants large tanks so he can offer a cruising range greater than the competition. The owner often requests an *enormous* cruising range under power.

All tanks should be fitted with inspection hatches and be capable of being cleaned through these openings. Fuel is drawn off by way of a pipe that enters the tank from the top and extends to within 1 inch (25 mm) of the bottom. Arrange the tank and fuel line so that any sludge will collect below the drawing-off line. A drain cock from the bottom of the tanks will allow you to flush out the tank. In the U.S., these drains are not legal. Outside the U.S., check local regulations before fitting the bottom drain. All tanks will need breather pipes—see the sketch on page 139 for these and other details. If you are purchasing a used or new production boat, your tanks may not meet all the criteria outlined in this chapter, and they may need attention in one or more areas that we have already mentioned.

If you're installing new tanks, or replacing old ones, choose tanks that give you a sensible cruising range. If you plan to have a diesel-powered generating set, a diesel cooking stove, and/or a diesel-powered heating system, take the usage of these items into your calculations. Remember that to avoid condensation and to minimize the chance of bugs infecting your fuel, you should keep your fuel tanks topped up whenever possible. In any case, it doesn't make sense to be carrying excessive weight in the form of too much diesel fuel. So the size of your fuel tanks is important. Large is not always the answer.

Sailboat owners should make careful calculations of their requirements. Armed with the knowledge that you will need to use the engine for a percentage of the time, allow for this and then add the other uses, such as diesel heating. Now decide on the size of your fuel tanks.

No matter what type of material you choose for the fuel tanks (or any other tanks), make sure they're firmly anchored in place. The thought of a loose tank, full or otherwise, charging about the boat in a rough seaway, should be enough to make you check all tank supports and containment arrangements very carefully.

MICROORGANISM CONTAMINATION

All diesel fuel systems can be contaminated by microorganisms. Neglected or unprepared fuel systems will continue to provide life support to these pests once they are introduced into the system. Problems show up in shortened fuel life, clogged fuel lines, and increasingly corroded fuel-system components, including the tanks.

The degree to which microorganisms grow and prosper in the fuel system is relative to how fast the fuel is used up. Boats with small fuel tanks or with high-horsepower engines are less likely to have this problem. For several reasons already covered, cruising sailboats tend to have larger tanks and keep the fuel longer.

If you leave your boat for extended periods without making sure that the fuel tanks are totally full, then you run the risk of allowing microorganisms, or "fuel bugs," to breed in the tank. Partially empty tanks allow water to condense there, and the least effect of this is that your water trap and fuel filter will be working overtime. These bugs—in the form of algae, bacteria, yeast, mold, and fungi—all thrive when water is present. All owners and operators of diesel engines face this problem, no matter where the engines are located or what type of transport the engines are installed in. Boats used and laid up in warmer climates are most susceptible to the bug but many cases have occurred in the U.K. and colder parts of the U.S., so this problem is not confined to tropical areas.

To eliminate bugs from your fuel, you need to understand how they breed. The various microorganisms need water to survive, since they live at the interface between the water and the diesel fuel, and they use the fuel as a food source. Diesel contains carbon, hydrogen, and dissolved oxygen, so it's a good source of nutrition for the bugs.

Once you've removed water from the system, you still need to take preventive measures against microbial growth. In a marine environment moisture is always present, and diesel bugs can grow quite rapidly. They can be present in

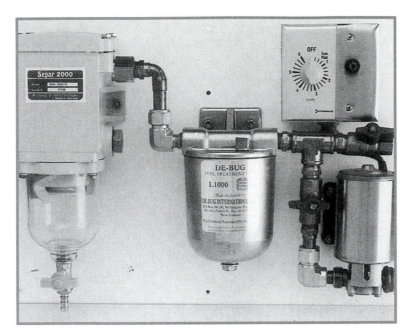

A fuel recirculation system is an effective solution to maintaining onboard fuel. The unit pictured is the ESI-Clean Fuel System.

the air, or in fuel taken aboard after you thought you had cured the problem. Some bacteria can grow into a mass many times their original size in just 24 hours. Other types can corrode fuel systems without being so obvious. They may show up as black grit, resembling coffee grounds, either in the filter, or, if you still have one, in the water-separator sight bowl.

Biocides

If you purchase a boat that hasn't been used for some time, you'd be wise to remove all the existing fuel from the tanks and have them flushed out and filled with fresh fuel. If you're in doubt about the cleanliness of the existing fuel, or if you're refilling after flushing out the tanks, you should add a biocide to your fuel. This will ensure that any remaining bugs are destroyed before they multiply and clog your fuel system at some inappropriate moment.

There are many brands of biocides available and they have one major factor in common. They are all expensive, usually costing around $20 (£12) for an amount sufficient to treat a 150-gallon (680 L) fuel tank. Another shared feature

is that they are all composed of highly toxic chemicals; so highly concentrated, in fact, that they need to be handled with utmost care. It's as well to keep in mind that over time biocides lose their effectiveness and have to be replenished. If you have a bad case of the bug, don't be afraid to give your fuel tank a double dose of biocides. Select a safe storage method and wear disposable rubber gloves when handling biocides. Needless to say, keep these chemicals well away from children.

Water Dispersants

These additives are only successful when you use them as a preventive, rather than as a cure. The biocides should be used if your tank is already infected with the bug. Water dispersants are designed to absorb water into the fuel and in this way remove it before the fuel reaches the filters. Before using these additives, you must first drain off as much water as possible. There are other benefits claimed for these products, including the fact that they inhibit separation of the waxes and gums that are present in diesel fuels. Only use dispersants if you have minor water problems or as a preventive method.

Enzyme Treatments

Having tried several methods to cure the chronic attack of "diesel bug" that attacked the diesel fuel in one of my own steel boats, I finally tried an additive called Soltron. This product was developed in Japan, but my supplies came from the U.K. After three treatments, my diesel fuel system was finally free of the bug that had clogged my filters on several occasions. Soltron is a clear, enzyme-based liquid, and about half a pint treats 660 gallons. A trip on the World Wide Web should locate a source near you (www.soltron.co.uk in the U.K. and www.solpower.com in the U.S.).

Microorganism Fuel Filters

The system as described here is best used as part of your overall fuel-scrubbing system. Since not all diesel fuel sold at the various waterside filling stations is equal, it's possible to introduce unwanted additives to your fuel tanks just by filling up at an unknown fuel dock. This can be especially troublesome overseas. The best solution to this problem is to have a system in which all the fuel is cleaned before it reaches the main engine filters.

The De-Bug filter is part of an overall fuel-filtering and scrubbing system marketed by the manufacturer. The De-Bug filter doesn't only kill the diesel bug, it also gets rid of the bodies. Those of you who plan to operate your boats under conditions where the fuel bug is likely to be an ongoing problem may want to consider a more positive solution to microorganism growth. Developed over 10 years ago in New Zealand, the De-Bug Fuel Decontamination unit uses patented and unique "multi magnet" technology to kill microorganisms. When it's correctly sized to the fuel flow of the particular engine installation, this unit kills 97 percent of the bugs in a single pass.

The De-Bug filter produces magnetic fields from ceramic-coated magnets. They destroy the microorganisms as they flow through the filter. This unit is a one-time installation; it has no moving parts and no electrical power is required. Replacement filters are not necessary and the only maintenance required is an occasional cleaning. Unlike the chemical biocides, the dead bacteria cells are destroyed in a way that does not result in a messy residue that will clog filters.

The De-Bug filter comes in various sizes and has been used in all types of diesel-powered applications, both ashore and afloat. The smaller unit is capable of handling up to 35 gallons (160 L) per hour. Larger sizes of this unit can handle amounts ranging from 265 gallons (1 kL) to 5,000 gallons (18.925 kL) per hour, and remembering that a 97 percent bug kill is claimed, this is one of the most efficient pieces of equipment you could add to your boat. Do you need it? We do, after the experience of losing engine power in a rather embarrassing situation—and all due to "the bug." Our boat is now fitted with this device.

SPARE PARTS, TOOLS, AND MATERIALS

The field of spares alone covers a multitude of possible items. Add some construction materials, and you can see that a large number of items could be assembled under this heading. Perhaps this is a good time to review those items that you have already decided to install, and to decide if you really need them. Now consider how likely they are to need spare parts in order to remain in service.

You'll need to carry an adequate number of spares for your engine, of course. For instance, you must have at least two replacement sets for each filter installed on your boat. If you have more than one type of filter, then you need two spare filters for each one. Filters clog up at the most inopportune moments. Usually, one set of spares is just not enough. Don't forget the spare oil filters. While they're not needed as often as fuel filters are, they're required at regular intervals.

Hoses, cooling-fan belts, alternator belts, impellers; the list goes on. Ask your engine supplier to suggest a complete list covering your expected requirements. Most manufacturers have recommended lists for local, coastal, and offshore cruising. Look over these lists and choose the one most appropriate for your needs.

On the subject of marine engine "manufacturers," the word manufacturer is misleading. Most marine engines are "assembled" or "marinized" from another manufacturers' basic engines. Many of the filters, fan belts, and other consumable spare parts are available at less cost when some other manufacturer supplies them. The engine manufacturers naturally discourage you from obtaining these outside-sourced spares. You'll need to decide for yourself whether to buy and use these less expensive, "unofficial" spare parts.

12
PREVENTING CORROSION

You'll find various references to corrosion throughout this book, but I feel the subject is sufficiently important to warrant a chapter of its own. In seawater, corrosion is electrochemical in nature, and it's important that every boatbuilder who works with metal is familiar with the causes and effects of the more common types of corrosion. You should know how to avoid corrosion problems.

Corrosion is not confined to metal boats, nor to modern boats. Corrosion can damage every type of vessel, including those built of timber, fiberglass, and ferrocement. It is because of corrosion that keels and rudders fall off, that stainless-steel tangs break, and that rigging fails. Corrosion is often the cause of fastening disease, an age-old problem with wooden boats. The results of corrosion can be severe, to the point of failure for rudderstocks, through-hull fittings, propellers, and seacocks. There have been instances where the seacocks have been caught in the final stages of disintegration just before they crumbled away and let in the outside water.

When a metal is immersed in seawater, it will achieve a certain electrochemical potential. Different metals have different potentials. Different potentials can also occur locally—from area to area in a single metal surface, for example, or near a weld area, or between areas exposed to different levels of oxygen. It's the potential difference between metals in contact with each other,

or areas on the same metal surface, that acts as the driving force for corrosion under certain circumstances.

GALVANIC CORROSION

When two different metals are immersed in such a good electrolyte as seawater and connected through a metal path, an electric current will flow, causing corrosion of the metal with the lower potential. The metal that corrodes is called the *anode* and the metal that has the higher potential (the nobler metal) is called the *cathode*. When this type of corrosion occurs it is termed galvanic or bimetallic corrosion.

Although the less noble metal in the galvanic couple will corrode at a higher rate than it might otherwise have done, the more noble metal will corrode at a lower rate. You can use this to your own advantage; in fact, it's the basis for cathodic protection. The accompanying table shows the Galvanic Series, and will help you predict which alloy in a metallic couple is more likely to corrode.

The metals and alloys lower in the Galvanic Series have lower potentials and will be corroded by those higher in the list. The degree of corrosion that occurs depends not only on how far apart they are in the galvanic series (and thus the size of the potential difference), but also on the relative surface areas of the cathode and anode. Alloys close together in the series, such as cop-

Table 12-1. Galvanic series of metals in seawater. The position of the metals on the scale may vary slightly depending on the exact composition of the particular metal.

Cathodic or most noble

Platinum
Gold
Graphite
Silver
Titanium
Hastelloy C
Stainless steel (304 and 316 passive)
Nickel
Monel (400, K-500)
Silicon bronze
Copper
Red brass
Aluminum bronze
Admiralty brass
Yellow brass
Nickel (active)
Naval brass
Manganese bronze
Muntz metal
Tin
Lead
Stainless steel (types 304 and 316 active)
$^{50}/_{50}$ lead tin solder
Cast iron
Wrought iron
Mild steel
Cadmium
Aluminum alloys
Galvanized steel
Zinc
Magnesium
Anodic or least noble

Source: Copper-Nickel Association, 1998.

per and bronze, will be less prone to galvanic corrosion than those further apart, like copper and steel. Corrosion can be expected to be greater if the exposed surface area of the more noble metal is large compared to that of the less noble alloy. An example of this is that steel bolts in a Monel structure will corrode very quickly, whereas Monel bolts would corrode insignificantly in a steel structure, unit for unit.

There are various ways of controlling galvanic corrosion. Choosing metals close together in the galvanic series can be a good way of reducing galvanic problems. If possible, you should use only similar metals throughout the vessel. In this way, no galvanic current will flow.

It's not always possible or desirable, of course, to use one metal throughout the hull, deck, and superstructure. Luckily, galvanic current can be avoided by electrically insulating the two metals from each other. Insulating washers and sleeves can be used on bolts; nonconductive gaskets can be used on flanges.

Paint coatings can also be used as protection against galvanic corrosion. In this case, the temptation is just to coat the alloy that is likely to corrode in the metal couple. But coatings may have imperfections or "holidays" in them, or can be damaged, so the current can pass through in very localized areas. The large area of the uncoated cathode produces high rates of corrosion in the small areas exposed through the coating. Always apply coatings to the more noble metal, or to both metals, rather than to the anode alone.

Nonmetal fittings are another possibility; however, some classification authorities are reluctant to accept this solution. They suggest that fire and degradation from sunlight could be a problem. We have seen examples of the latter, where plastic (presumably nylon) skin fittings were wiped off when the vessel rubbed against a piling. This vessel had spent a considerable time in a sunny climate and the sun had affected the fittings to such an extent that they had very little strength. There are some plastic seacocks, skin fittings, and the like, that are said to be unaffected by the sun and ultraviolet rays. You should check these out for yourself before purchasing them and fitting them to your boat.

Again, the best overall protection is to stay with one metal, especially in the hull, where you have a good chance of maintaining all-steel, all-aluminum or all-copper-nickel structure. In practice, the solution is to use a combination of the above methods to minimize chances of galvanic corrosion.

In the interior of your metal boat, you can choose the closest compatible metal to attach the interior joinery to the metal hull. There is no point in using regular steel screws, as they would soon rust in the marine environment. You can use stainless-steel screws or Monel screws and bolts (expensive), or you can plan your interior to avoid as much contact of dissimilar metals as is possible.

Galvanic corrosion can also occur in the same metal. For example, type 303 free-machining grades of stainless steel suffer extraordinarily severe corrosion in salt water. These metals contain high densities of manganese sulfide, or selenium inclusions, which create many, built-in metal-to-inclusion galvanic cells. These grades should never be used in salt water.

SELECTIVE CORROSION

Selective corrosion can occur in certain alloys when one component of the alloy corrodes away more quickly than another. We've seen this with brass seacocks, which contain copper and zinc. The zinc dissolves in seawater and leaves behind a weak and spongy mass of copper. This is called dezincification. Bronze seacocks prevent this.

Cast iron also can exhibit a form of selective corrosion called graphitization. The matrix of cast iron contains flakes or spheroids of graphite. The iron can corrode, leaving a weak, brittle network shell of graphite. The external appearance remains unchanged, which can make the condition difficult to detect. A further consequence is that the graphite shell is galvanically very noble and can then cause galvanic corrosion of adjacent parts.

Stainless steels can undergo selective attack in heat-affected weld zones. You can avoid this completely if you weld with carbon-L grades, or titanium- or niobium-stabilized grades, of stainless steel.

CREVICE CORROSION

In seawater, stainless steels have very low general corrosion rates. If they corrode, it's normally in localized areas under hard fouling or tight, man-made crevices such as gaskets. When the oxygen in the crevice is used up, an oxygen-concentration cell forms with the oxygenated metal outside the crevice. This can lead to corrosion reactions within the crevice. The 316 alloy has better resistance to this than the 302 or 304 alloys. Cathodic protection by anodes or galvanic contact with other less noble alloys can also help.

STRAY-CURRENT CORROSION

This is another type of corrosion that can be prevented. Unlike galvanic corrosion, which is caused by two different metals in water, stray-current corrosion results from an outside electrical source, such as direct current from the ship itself or alternating current from a shore electrical hook-up. You will find additional information on the cause and remedy for this situation elsewhere, including Del Kahan's essay in chapter 14.

In most cases, the villain is one of these sources: a current leak in the wiring from frayed or broken wires; improper or crossed grounds; electrical leaks from loose, broken, or poorly insulated terminal connections; or bad marina shore-power equipment.

When you're connected to shore power, you should always use heavy-duty extension cords. The length should be sufficient only to transfer the current from the power source to your boat. Power tools often generate stray currents and on-board radios can also cause problems in this area.

Unfortunately, while galvanic corrosion occurs relatively slowly and over a period of time, electrolytic corrosion can occur rapidly, depending on the strength of the stray current. The stray current can be a mere trickle of direct current from an area that is damp, to a blue-sparking short circuit on board from a marina's 220/110-volt system. Stray current can also give shocks to the crew and can cause fire or explosion.

Warning signs can range from blue sparks and a crackling noise from a shorted-out power cable to heavy static on radio speakers because of voltage drop. If you have electrical equipment that doesn't function up to expectations, suspect a stray-current flow that ends up somewhere other than where you want it. Voltage can be traced with a multimeter. Metal damage in the grounded area, resulting from electrical leakage, shows up as massive rusting and scaling on steel parts, abnormal brightness on bronze, and the total disintegration of aluminum parts.

Stray currents, like galvanic corrosion, can be eliminated when electronic devices are installed on the vessel. A custom builder should take the approach that both types of corrosion are predictable problems that not only can be built in, but can equally be "built out" of the boat and totally eliminated.

You should use high-quality wiring, fittings, and switches designed for the marine environment by a reputable marine manufacturer, to protect yourself against most of the potential problems described in this chapter and elsewhere. Shore power needs particular attention since it has the greatest potential for danger. You'll want to use heavy-duty cord that is moisture-resistant and specifically made for marine use. Use watertight marine connectors at both ends and, if possible, use a "molded-cord set," which is the last word in connecting shore power to your vessel.

Install a ground-fault circuit interrupter in the vessel's panel or fuse box. It will help prevent electrical accidents, especially those that result from current flowing from a hot wire to a ground. It will also reduce your chances of getting a shock.

CATHODIC PROTECTION

Many people are under the false impression that boats that cruise exclusively in freshwater do not require any special form of cathodic protection. The most commonly used method of protection is to install anodes to various underwater locations on the outside of the hull. M. G. Duff, the British experts on this subject, have produced two excellent pamphlets. One is for boats operating mostly in salt water and the other covers the freshwater environment. These publications explain the special requirements needed to protect your stern gear, rudder, and associated underwater equipment from the ravages of mysterious gremlins that can damage them and even the hull itself.

Most metals are extracted from ores by various processes, and they are prone to return to their natural state under the action of oxygen and water. We have all seen unprotected metals react in this way. Marine aluminum is one exception, it can be left unpainted and still not deteriorate even in a saltwater environment. The French build aluminum sailboats and leave them totally unpainted above the waterline; the Canadians do the same with fishing boats built in British Columbia. Pity about the appearance of the unpainted boats!

Cathodic protection is a means of transferring the corrosion electrochemically to another less noble metal. The concept is not new. For instance, Samuel Pepys, back in 1681, noted in one of his diaries that the removal of lead sheathing on ships of the line reduced the corrosion on the iron rudderposts. Over 100 years ago, the Italian physicist Luigi Galvini conducted experiments in this field and proved that when two metals were electrically connected and immersed in water, the resulting corrosion of one of the metals was speeded up, while the other received some level of protection. Once we understand this concept, the method of controlling hull corrosion and protecting immersed fittings becomes relatively simple. Sacrificial anodes of reactive metals can be applied to a metal to protect it.

A word of caution: cathodic protection of a copper-nickel hull is unnecessary because the alloy already possesses good resistance to corrosion by seawater. The use of cathodic protection will also reduce the effectiveness of the antifouling of the material. Hull attachments below the waterline should, if possible, be copper-nickel, or if not, the fittings should be made of a slightly more noble metal.

SACRIFICIAL ANODES

Sacrificial anodes are usually made of magnesium, aluminum, or zinc. For metal boats, anodes are either zinc or magnesium, and come in various shapes and sizes. These protective devices are relatively inexpensive and a complete spare set should be carried at all times. An unexpected haul-out could reveal the necessity to replace the anodes, so a set should always be on hand. For freshwater, use magnesium anodes and for salt water or heavily polluted water, use zinc anodes.

If you're building a new boat, the designer will be able to recommend the type, number, and placement of the anodes, and they can be either welded or bolted to the hull. We recommend the bolt-on method, as the replacement of this type will not cause the paintwork or inside foam to be damaged by additional welding. Bolting on replacement anodes is a much simpler process than removing and replacing old spent ones that have been welded in place.

When you're setting up your anodes for the first time, simply use the anode attachment straps and bolt holes to mark the position of the threaded studs to be welded to the hull skin. The fact that

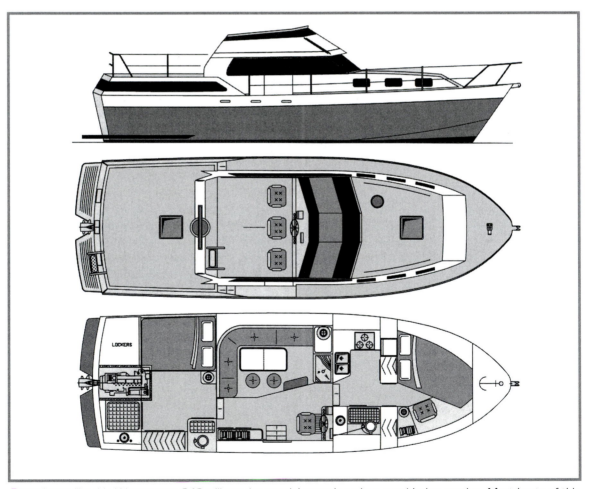

Powerboats like this Waverunner 342 will require special attention when considering anodes. Most boats of this type have a considerable amount of electrical equipment that can give rise to all types of corrosion problems if not correctly wired and suitably protected.

you're going to reuse the same locations and bolting arrangements, is another good reason to have more than one spare set on hand. On one occasion, we had to redrill several anode straps to match existing studs when we were unable to buy the same brand with matching holes. The studs and surrounding area should be painted after the studs are installed. Under no circumstances paint the anodes: this stops them from working.

The position and placement of the anodes depends on the size and displacement of your boat. The anode manufacturers have special charts showing the relationship between the size of boat, the number of anodes required, and where they should be located. It's common practice to have one anode on each side of metal boats up to 25 feet (7.62 m) long; they're placed below the waterline about 25 percent forward of the stern. Boats up to 35 feet (10.67 m) long require four anodes, two per side, one 25 percent and one 50 percent forward of the transom. Boats up to 44 feet (13.41 m) in length can use the same numbers and positions, but larger anodes. For larger boats, it's normal to have three anodes per side.

In addition to anodes already mentioned, every boat should have a small anode placed around the propeller shaft, another on the rudder, and a third in the area of the bow thruster, if fitted. When placing the anodes, either make sure that they're adjacent to the seacocks (if they're made of dissimilar metal) or fit additional anodes as required. For a foil-shaped rudder, the anode can be fitted with threaded studs about 25 percent below the waterline. On a powerboat's single-plate rudder, the anode can be through-bolted in position, using a bolt of the same metal as the rudder.

If you fit a bronze seacock on a steel or aluminum hull, make sure you insert a heavier metal section in the hull skin in the area where the metal standpipe is located. We recommended that the standpipe be carried inboard until the bronze seacock can be fitted clear of the waterline. The seacock will be isolated from the standpipe by liberal bedding compound installed between these two items.

Please note that the installation of anodes for a metal hull differs from that of a wooden or fiberglass boat in that the metal hull and metal fittings inside conduct galvanic current to the anodes. You don't have to run wires from the engine, engine shaft, or other similar items to the anodes. The reason is that the engine and other fittings are already grounded to the metal hull and carry the galvanic current to the anodes.

If you keep the hull of your steel or aluminum boat well painted, especially the area below the waterline, this alone will contribute to your maintenance of the boat and reduce the demand on the anodes. Anodes will need replacing before they are totally used up. Deterioration of the anodes shows that they are working. As mentioned elsewhere, the underwater sections of a copper-nickel hull will not need any painting or antifouling protection.

When laying out your anodes, don't forget the rudder.

13
METAL BOAT INTERIORS

INSULATION

All cruising boats need some form of insulation. Even fiberglass boats need insulation, as they "sweat" in the same manner as metal and wood boats. Now is the time to select and install the insulation. If you are planning spray-in-place foam insulation, then this should be installed after the deck and superstructure are in place, but before you start work on the interior joinery. An alternative is to install "bats"—sheets of foam glued or held in place by the "ceiling." (See Lining Materials, opposite, for details on installing the ceiling planking.)

My choice for foam insulation is the type of urethane foam that is fire-resistant and nontoxic, and is sprayed in place. In steel boats, the interior of the hull should first be gritblasted and

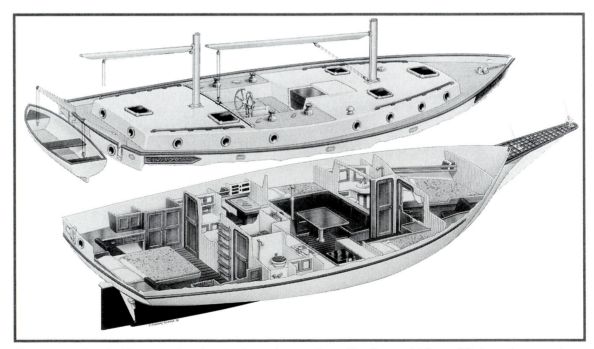

First you need to decide on the best interior layout for your boat. The Centennial Spray 38 shown here can be laid out in several different ways.

The supplier of the foam usually has all the equipment needed to install the material, and charges by the cubic foot (cubic meter) or by the pound (kilogram). Make sure you obtain an estimate of the cost for the boat to be sprayed to the desired thickness. Be very careful that you get what you pay for. Measure the depth of the foam and check that it's a reasonably constant thickness throughout the boat.

LINING MATERIALS

There are a variety of materials that can be used to line the interior of your metal boat. This is one area where the wrong choice can damn your boat and scream "Amateur!" If you want a decent re-sale value, then you'd better get it right.

If you're building a traditional-style metal boat, such as a Spray replica, or if you like the warmth of an all-timber interior, then ceiling planking can go a long way to achieving the right effect. Ceiling material should be 1 by ⅝ inch (25 by 15 mm), light-colored, fine-grained timber that is rounded or beveled on the outer edges. Install the planks longitudinally and space them at about ¼ inch (6 mm) apart. You can plank only those areas that are visible after the joinery is complete, or you can plank the entire accommodation area and use the material as the lining for the various lockers. If you take this latter course, then you'd better reduce the spacing to say ⅛ inch

Foam sprayed in place offers the best insulation, and has another benefit: it can protect the interior metal. Install it in the hull (above the sole line) and in the deck and superstructure areas as well. Make sure you have adequate thickness and that you get what you pay for. See text.

primed (if it's not built of preprimed materials). The foam will now be sprayed to a depth between 1 and 2 inches (25 to 50 mm); the thicker the better. It's a good idea to cover the stringers, and they will most likely be about 1¼ to 2 inches (30 to 50 mm) deep. The foam should be of a type that forms a skin on the surface that is impervious to water. Make sure you choose a variety that won't give off toxic fumes in the event of fire. You'll also need to make sure that the foam is of the self-extinguishing type.

The overhead areas will need insulation, too; again spray-in-place foam is hard to beat.

Ceiling (timber planking) is a popular way to line the interior of the boat. Correctly installed, this material will allow air to circulate behind the planking and help keep the boat free of condensation.

(3 mm) so you will not lose small items through the gaps in the planking. If you use ceiling only where there are no lockers, you may have a problem getting a fair curve where there's no frame to which to attach one end of the planks.

The lockers can be lined with plywood. Leave the bottoms loose with a neat fit but not tight; you'll often want to get under and behind the locker to have access to cables and the inner hull. Don't forget to put finger holes in the lining.

Lining the entire interior of the accommodation with light, plain, painted or veneered fancy plywood can produce a pleasing result when combined with solid timber trim. Too much varnish, or areas of paintwork that are too large, can spoil the interior appearance, so you will need a balance between the two finishes. If you are unsure of this balance, use as much varnish as you like; you can always paint over it at a later stage. The reverse is obviously not so simple.

For overheads and the interiors of the cabintop, you can use painted plywood. Use some timber trim to relieve and break up the area. Timber planks, similar to that used for ceiling, but say 2 inches (50 mm) wide, can also be used to line overheads and cabintops. There are several alternative vinyl products that have a light foam backing and are ideally suited to overheads and certain bulkheads. Be careful when you use this material for bulkheads

One builder used inexpensive cardboard to mock up his joinery; if you want to try out a piece of furniture, this looks like a great idea.

in the main living areas, however, as it can cheapen the look of your interior. The foam-backed vinyl can look acceptable in some parts of sleeping cabins. The use of vinyl is fine for overheads in any part of the boat. Use timber trim as needed to break up any large expanses of lining material.

In the past, some builders, both professional and amateur, used carpet and carpet-like materials for lining the hull and overheads. These materials are inexpensive and easy to install but can look cheap. We don't recommend this route; besides the interior would look dated.

CABIN SOLES

The sole framing will need considerable planning. Usually, L-angle is used for the main framing and some timber can be used where it would be attached to vertical plywood surfaces such as bunk fronts and dinette ends. The size of the angle will vary depending on the span and spacing of the framing. Your plans should give you a guide. If you change the accommodation layout, you may have to use your judgment. There are few things more annoying than a springy or squeaky sole.

Plywood is universally accepted as the material to use for cabin soles. The thickness will vary between ½ inch and ¾ inch (12 mm and 20 mm), depending on the spacing of the under-sole framing. Usually, ⅝ inch (15 mm) is sufficient, and the thickness can be less if you plan to add teak or another timber surface. This is such an important area that you should try a sample before deciding on an overall thickness. A spongy sole is most undesirable, but you don't want to add unnecessary weight.

While you're still constructing the interior, you should only fit and lay the plywood in position; don't screw it down until the all of the joinery work is completed. It's advisable to arrange the sole so you can remove all parts of it, including those areas that form the bottoms of lockers and closets. This may mean additional under-sole framing to provide a base at the edge of the particular area of the sole. Under no account build in

These light companionway steps are practical and reasonably easy to construct.

areas of the sole so they are impossible to remove. The plywood can be screwed down with self-tapping stainless-steel screws.

Make sure you have carefully planned hatches to those areas of the sole that will need frequent (or even infrequent) access. The hatches should be laid out in an orderly manner and have aluminum or similar trim around the edges and be provided with flush ring-pulls. Hatches in unseen areas such as inside lockers, may have finger holes in lieu of more expensive hardware. Where carpet is installed, aluminum edge trim is an important feature around the sole hatches.

Carpet-covered soles are fine in most powerboats and also in well-maintained and dry sailboats. If your cruising habits mean that you will be bringing a considerable amount of water into the cabin, then carpet is not a sensible option. I personally like carpet; it offers a good footing under most conditions, is warm and attractive and—considering the small area of a boat interior—it can be replaced at very little cost.

Don't finish a teak-and-holly sole to a high gloss. Rather use a matte finish that will give you some chance of remaining upright in adverse conditions. A slippery surface can be deadly in anything of a seaway.

BUNKS

Your first consideration will be how many permanent berths to build into your interior. Fewer is better! Our idea of the perfect number of berths is a spacious double for use in port and in suitable weather; two single berths, suitable for watchkeeping and for use in adverse weather conditions; and additional single berths for the permanent crew. The number of berths should not exceed four, plus those required for the permanent crew. Boats under, say, 38 feet (11.60 m) should not have more than one double and two single berths, otherwise too much of the interior space is used up.

All boats are compromises. You may have to be creative to provide the necessary sleeping accommodation without turning the boat into one large dormitory. Avoid berths that are too narrow. Singles should be a minimum of 2 feet (610 mm) wide and preferably just a little wider. Doubles should not bear that title unless they have a minimum width of 4 feet (1.22 m) and preferably more. You will find 4 feet, 6 inches (1.37 m) is ideal, and up to 5 feet (1.52 m) in width is fine in a larger boat. For designers and builders, achieving adequate berth length is always a problem. It's a fact that as each generation becomes taller, they require longer berths for a good night's sleep. In new designs, we use 6 feet, 6 inches (1.98 m) as a reasonable length. It's hard to include longer berths than this without encroaching into other areas of the accommodation.

Berths can be framed up in 2- by 1½-inch (50 by 30 mm) timber, or 2- by 1- by ¼-inch (50 by 25 by 6 mm) L-angle. Depending on which metal you use to build your hull, framing in the same material may give satisfactory results. In steel boats, in the interests of saving weight, you may prefer to use timber framing throughout the interior. Plywood of ⅝-inch (15 mm) thickness will be adequate for all berths, and if you have adequate framing then ½-inch (12 mm) may be sufficient. Berths should have hatches in the top to allow access for stowage and inspection of the boxed-in areas of the hull. The plywood tops of the berth should also have a few 1-inch (25 mm) diameter holes bored at random to allow the air to circulate in the area under the mattress.

Face the berths with a timber board of around 6 by 1 inch (150 by 25 mm) and round off

Forward V-berths are often too cramped for two adults, but they are useful for sleeping the younger members of the crew. They're sometimes used for general stowage.

the top and bottom of this face plank to remove any sharp corners. This facing will hold the mattress in position and give a finished look to the berth.

The mattresses should be of good-quality foam, between 4 and 6 inches (100 to 150 mm) in thickness and covered with a light cotton or other suitable fabric. Hooray for the duvet! Duvets make the best bedding arrangement; they're easy to make up, especially where a berth doesn't have access from all sides. A fitted undersheet, combined with a duvet that's equipped with a slip-on cover, makes for perfect sleeping. This arrangement also provides easy bed-making in the morning. Duvets used on settee berths have the additional advantage of being easy to stow.

HEAD AND SHOWER COMPARTMENTS

If space permits, a separate shower compartment is very desirable, especially on any boat intended as a liveaboard. The shower can be totally separate, with its own entrance, or simply a shower stall entered through the main head. On boats where the regular crew is four, we prefer two medium-sized heads and one separate shower compartment. Choices in this area are a personal matter, so you should discuss the options with your partner and family members who will be crewing regularly on the boat.

The floor of the shower/head can be formed from fiberglass and laminated as a one-piece unit. Don't forget to include a nonskid surface. The actual shower pan can be slightly lowered and fitted with teak slats. This arrangement may allow a wider sole, even if some areas include a slight slope. Separate shower stalls can have a tiled sole, a nice touch if your boat can accommodate the additional weight. The walls or bulkheads in the shower/head area should all be lined with a plastic finish such as Laminex or Formica. The entire floor area, as well as the bulkheads and cabinets, should be designed for easy cleaning.

If you're building, or own, a small or minimal boat, then you may be happy with a solar shower bag. These plastic bags are wonderfully efficient. Provided you have a reasonable amount of sunshine each day, one bag can provide hot showers for two. Shower bags are great water savers and recommended on vessels where replenishment of water tanks is infrequent. Shower bags can be a great backup device, and even if you only use them infrequently they'll pay handsomely for the small amount of stowage space they require.

Drainage for the shower can take many forms. In our sailboat the 28-foot (8.53 m) steel Spray *K*I*S*S*, the builder had fitted a fiberglass shower tray in the head and drained this into the main sump in the keel. The sump was emptied by way of a manual bilge pump in the cockpit. This pump also served as the emergency bilge pump—that arrangement was fine, except that you had to pump out the water soon after your shower, otherwise the sump would generate sufficient gas to set off the alarm intended to service the gas stove rather than the shower sump. A better arrangement would have been to have a separate gray-water tank to temporarily store the shower water, or an automatic pump. In our present boat we have a plastic sump about 1 foot (300 mm) square, fitted with a lid and an automatic Rule shower/bilge pump. The 800-gallon per hour (3 kL per hour) unit, has the same physical dimensions as those of smaller capacity and this unit provides a backup to the regular bilge-pumping arrangements. Shower pumps need regular cleaning, usually about once every week or more often if the facility is used by more than two persons.

Manual or vacuum toilets are a must. The electric varieties, while they do reduce the solids to a fine mist, are incredibly noisy. Unless you can find a quiet version, don't consider these devices. To those traditionalists who wonder, "What is this fellow doing talking about electric toilets?" please remember that not all metal boats are built as basic cruisers. Make sure, especially in a sailboat, that the plumbing for your toilet is such that it cannot back-siphon and sink the ship.

Sailboats often have the galley located just inside the companionway, like this.

You should fit a reasonably sized hand basin. If freshwater is at a premium, then the smaller variety saves water. One with a diameter of about 9 inches (228 mm) is the smallest that can be called a basin. On smaller boats, and boats with medium-sized head/shower combinations, a convenient arrangement is to have an economical shower rose serve as both the faucet for the basin and as a shower head. The flexible supply hose leads through the countertop and stows itself under the basin. You can then draw the rose out when you need a shower. When you're using this system, and if hot water is available, then a mixer faucet can serve both shower and basin. On all boats, the basin or sink should have a shut-off valve or seacock fitted, and its location should be familiar to all crewmembers. This advice applies to all inlets, outlets, and seacocks.

THE GALLEY

This is an important area of your boat and if you want to keep the cook happy, then you'd better get it right! In *Choosing for Cruising* and *Choosing a Cruising Powerboat* (see appendix 1), we've covered the subject of designing a galley in considerable detail. These books have much more information on all aspects of design than space allows here.

You can arrange the galley benches to suit the available space. We've found that a U- or L-shaped arrangement usually works best. In a sailboat, the stove is best placed outboard, facing inboard. For easiest drainage, the sink on a sailboat should be as close to the centerline as practical. You can build galley benches from ¾-inch (20 mm) plywood and cover it with Formica, Laminex, or other laminated plastic. If saving weight isn't critical, then tiled bench tops add a nice touch to any galley. Make sure that you round off any corners, otherwise the cook will soon be covered in bruises.

Framing for the galley can be 2- by 1½-inch (50 by 40 mm) timber. The framework will generally be arranged to accommodate standard-sized doors and drawers. Unless you're fitting out a Dutch barge or some other vessel mainly intended for use in inland waters, we don't advise you to install the standard kitchen units available at the local home improvement store or lumberyard.

There are many suppliers of ready-made teak and mahogany door and drawer fronts that you can incorporate into your galley and elsewhere. They may be more expensive than those you construct yourself, but unless you can produce fine cabinet and joinery work, you're advised to investigate this option, at least. The resale value of your boat will be considerably affected by the quality of the interior finish of your vessel. Three-ply sliding galley doors with finger holes as openers may be inexpensive and easy to construct, but they'll add little to the resale value of your boat.

Your galley stove will get considerable use. First, you must decide which fuel you'll use. The choices include liquid petroleum gas (LPG), compressed natural gas (CNG, available only in certain areas), diesel fuel, alcohol, and kerosene (paraffin). Most galley stoves on sailboats are gimbaled, but powerboats and stiff sailboats like the Spray types may not require gimbaled stoves. Discuss this option with the stove manufacturer.

Today, many if not most, new sailboats and powerboats are fitted with LPG. You can get it in two main types called butane and propane. They're similar in usage, and each has its advocates. If you choose gas, then you'll probably choose the one that is more readily available in your area. Most appliances will burn either type; some may need minor adjustments to the burners to get the best results. If you choose gas as a cooking and/or heating fuel, you must have a certified technician install the system. Also check it over on a regular basis. LPG is a wonderful aid on any boat, but it's heavier than air and can lie in the bilge. Even a small amount of stray of gas, when ignited in the confines of a boat, can cause a catastrophic explosion. You must locate the bottles in their own self-draining locker; fortunately this is easily arranged in most metal boats. Usually, two bottles are carried, thus ensuring continuity of supply; when one bottle runs out, you switch to the next, and refill the first one at the first available opportunity. We've had gas in our own boats, having followed our own advice regarding installation and servicing of the installation and the individual appliances. If you have gas aboard, then you must install a reliable gas detector with one or more sensors. One sensor is required for each gas appliance you have aboard. If your gas appliances are grouped in one area then a sensor may be arranged to suit the group.

Paraffin or kerosene stoves, once the mainstay of any galley, have largely given way to LPG.

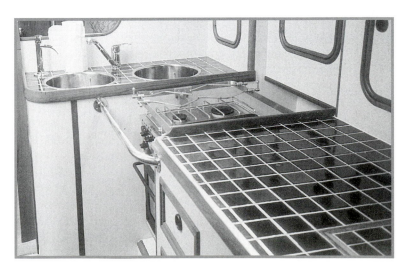

A rail protects and steadies the cook in front of this stove.

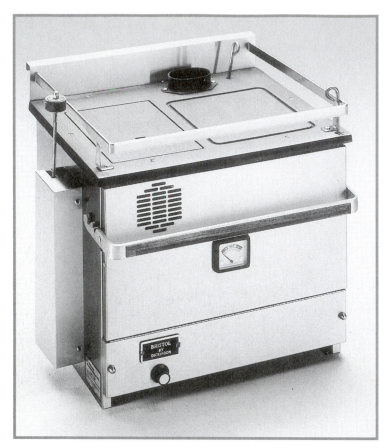

Diesel galley stoves can supply hot water as well as performing the normal cooking functions. See text.

or galley cupboards should be arranged to make best use of the available space. The plates, mugs, and eating utensils should be always at hand. Regularly used food such as condiments that do not need refrigeration should all be at eye level, more or less. Pots and pans will normally be stored in lower cupboards, and cleaning and dishwashing fluids may be under the sink or in nearby lockers. If you have steps nearby, they make excellent stowage areas if you give them hinged tops. If you lay out your galley along the lines of the kitchen of a regular house, taking into account the obvious space restrictions and with the necessary changes to suit a boat, you'll go a long way toward keeping the cook happy.

Under-sole stowage for canned goods and other nonperishable foods is a great idea. Try to arrange these lockers so that the cook is able to reach them without having to disrupt the area around the galley. Properly fitted hatches in the sole and drop-in plastic bins are most useful. You can store most general foodstuffs, except items that need refrigerating, in under-sole lockers. You should equip all hatches in the sole with ring-pulls or finger holes.

You should also ventilate lockers in the galley and elsewhere. You'll need louvered doors, or doors with built-in vents or other arrangements, to encourage air to circulate freely in these areas. You'll need a garbage locker, too, and one can often be fitted on the end of one of the lower galley benches. The bin can be hinged at the bottom to open outward, and designed to accept a medium-sized garbage bag. Most cruising folks and liveaboards use supermarket bags as liners for garbage and trash bins.

If you can stand the smell (although some fuels are now supposedly odor-free) and you don't mind the fiddly lighting procedure, then you may find kerosene an ideal fuel for the galley stove.

Galley stoves fired with diesel fuel would seem the obvious alternative. Diesel fuel does work well in a properly set up appliance. The drawback is that it takes these stoves some time to reach operating temperature. Perhaps diesel fuel stoves are more suited for use in colder climates. To be practical, you should be able to leave the stove on low heat between meal times.

STOWAGE FOR FOOD AND STORES

This is another area where the person who will actually be working in the galley should be consulted at the planning stage. The storage lockers

Another attractive galley. This one is situated partially in the walk-through on a Roberts 434 built in the U.K.

This owner-built icebox, or built-in refrigerator, would be a welcome addition to any boat.

In my opinion, a diesel-powered heater is an essential part of any boat, sail or power. These stoves work well and they give out an incredible amount of heat for a small fuel cost.

REFRIGERATORS AND ICEBOXES

This is another subject too complex to be covered in detail in this text; however, there are a few comments we'd like to make. Firstly, avoid most ready-built refrigerators powered only by 12-volt DC power. They can consume large quantities of your valuable battery storage capacity. In powerboats, you can use gas refrigeration, and this is generally very efficient. It does generate a considerable amount of heat, though, so make sure it's properly ventilated. For more information on this important and complex subject, please see recommended reading in appendix 1.

Iceboxes are useful but need to be very well insulated to be of any value. The most practical arrangement is an icebox that can accept one of

the freezer-conversion kits. A freezer compressor powered by a take-off from the main engine can be a good alternative in cruising or liveaboard vessels.

HEATING THE CABIN

On traditional boats you may want to consider a wood-burning stove. For this type you will need a good supply of fuel, that in turn requires adequate stowage space. For cabin heating, the diesel-fueled heater has no peer. A drip-feed version is ideal for installation in any boat; one per cabin, if you have a large cruiser. These heaters are trouble-free and throw out great quantities of heat for a miserly usage of diesel fuel. Dickinson (Canada and U.S.) and Taylor (U.K.) are two popular makes, but there are several others available in various parts of the world. All fuel-consuming appliances require good ventilation, so keep this in mind when installing your heaters and similar items.

This attractive heating stove was made by the builder of a steel Roberts 53.

Vetus produces a range of molded plastic water tanks in a range of shapes and sizes.

Diesel-powered, forced-air heating can be a troublesome partner aboard any boat. While forced-air heating with multiple outlets is a great convenience, the Eberspacher and similar units need lots of tender loving care to keep them operating.

FRESHWATER TANKS

This is another area where modern technology has made inroads into our cruising lifestyle. Watermakers have removed the need for large water tanks on the modern sailboat or power cruiser. Powerboats and sailboats that cruise locally need to carry only about three to five days' worth of freshwater. Watering points are now available in all marinas and other havens, so replenishing supplies presents few problems.

That said, those with long-distance cruising in mind will still need to give this subject considerable thought. The choices lie between modest tankage with severe economy, and large-capacity tanks with a better lifestyle. The best solution may be a combination of reasonable tankage, backed up by replenishment techniques, including rain collection and the use of a watermaker.

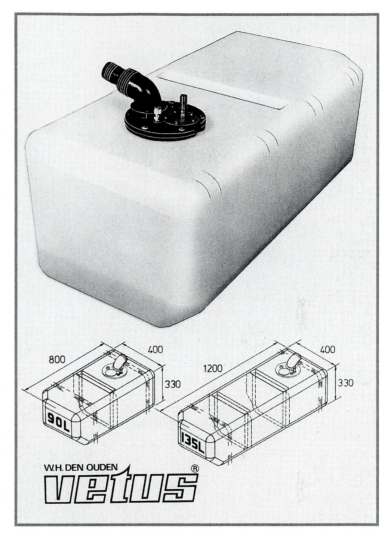

Although it's possible to build water tanks from mild steel, they do need to be coated inside, and we don't recommend this combination for storing freshwater. Aluminum tanks can have various problems, so this leaves stainless steel, sheet or molded plastic, fiberglass, or inflatable tanks.

Our choice is either stainless steel or molded plastic with fiberglass as a last alternative. Our experience is that tanks fabricated from sheet plastic have not proven successful. All tanks should be fabricated outside the hull and tested against leaks with air pressure of 3 pounds per square inch. Take care when testing tanks. We once heard of a builder simply connecting a compressor to the steel tanks; goodness knows how he managed to avoid an almighty explosion. Tanks need only modest air pressure to reveal leaks. Vetus Den Ouden manufactures a fine line of plastic tanks in several shapes and many sizes; they're available with matching hardware and could well suit all but the largest metal boats.

FRESHWATER PUMPS

The type of pump you select to dispense your fresh water, will have a great influence on the amount of tankage required. Serious offshore sailboats are usually fitted with hand- or foot-operated pumps. These manual pumps may be in addition to a more convenient electrical pumping system. You can turn the latter off during long passages; then everyone uses the manual pumps. If your boat is fitted with a gas-fired, on-demand, hot-water system, then you'll have to install an automatic electric pressure water pump. At least one saltwater (or outside freshwater) manual pump should be installed in every boat.

Most powerboats are fitted with automatic electric water pumps as standard equipment. Rarely will a manual backup, or alternative hand-operated system be installed. Electrically operated pressure water pumps are a great convenience, but you should install at least one hand-operated backup pump in your boat. Some of you may prefer to carry extensive spares for your electric unit. The "outside" water should be available through a hand-operated pump; in a powerboat, this is often arranged via an electrically powered, deck-wash unit.

SEATING

It's surprising how many boats don't have even one really comfortable seat. When you're planning your accommodation, give this matter considerable thought, and provide a comfortable seat for each member of the crew. In the case of a couple, two really comfortable lounge-type chairs are required and the remainder can be normal dinette or settee seating. On all but the smallest metal boats it's possible to arrange two really comfortable seats.

Seats can be too wide as well as too narrow. This may be a problem when designing and building settee berth arrangements. A settee berth that is wide enough to make a comfortable single berth is too wide as a seat. These problems can be overcome by arranging the back cushions to sit on top of the settee berth, the cushions can be stowed when the area is used as a berth.

When designing a boat for myself, two comfortable chairs similar to the ones shown here would be the first items to be placed in the interior layout.

Dinettes come in all shapes and sizes. Some convert to double berths.

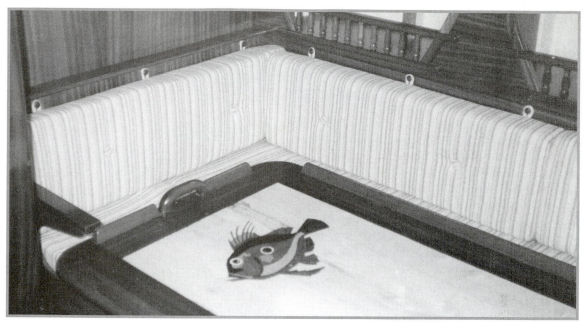

Some builders spend a considerable amount of time on adding attractive finishing touches to their boatbuilding projects, as evidenced in this Roberts 36 built by Don Reynolds.

Note the comfortable forward-facing navigation station tucked out of the traffic in the walk-through on this Roberts 434. A selection of repeater instruments is yet to be added to this area.

CHART TABLE AND NAVIGATION STATION

Thanks to advances in electronic navigational aids, especially global positioning systems (GPS) and GPS-linked plotters, the need for a large chart table has been reduced. The chart table is still an important part of any cruising boat, and in all but the smallest cruisers it should be possible to arrange a permanent, purpose-built navigation area. A satisfactory arrangement is to use the inboard end of a quarter berth as a seat, and build the chart table just ahead of it. Not only does this utilize some of the space for two purposes (very important in any but the largest boat) but also it locates the chart table athwartships and places the navigator facing forward; the ideal arrangement.

In most powerboats, the "chart table" is an area immediately adjacent to the helmsman where the navigational aids are visible. The layout is quite different to that required in a slower-moving sailboat (if you'll excuse the generalization). Persons who are moving from sail to power may have a problem in giving up a purpose-built navigation station located well away from the helm.

You'll appreciate space at or near the chart table for folded or rolled charts and electronic equipment such as radio(s), GPS, and other navigational aids. Even if your boat carries mainly portable navigational equipment, it should have a regular stowage area.

Some navigators prefer to work standing up. Others prefer to allocate any spare space to another priority and use the main saloon table for laying out the charts. Given the option, unless you're prepared to have your chartwork disturbed by a variety of other activities, you'd be better served with a dedicated navigation area, no matter how it's arranged.

SAIL STOWAGE

In the not-so-distant past, the sail locker was one of the more important areas of the vessel and considerable space was provided for this purpose. Today, many sails are stowed on, or adjacent to, the areas where they're used. Mainsails are stowed on the boom, in the boom, or inside the mast. Headsails are fewer in number, and are left rolled in place on the headsail furler. Depending on the layout of the rig and what systems are chosen for reefing and stowage, it's important to provide covers for the sails when you're not using them. On sailboats that are used seasonally, you should remove the sails (and other selected gear) during the off-season and stow them ashore.

There will still be some sails that will need to be stowed aboard when they're not in use, including spinnakers, light-weather genoas, and special storm sails. On most sailboats, these sails represent a small percentage of the sail wardrobe, but you still need space for them. The sail stowage area can be combined with one of several other areas, including the chain locker or workshop area. Or, as is often the case, they can be stowed in the forward cabin, or on (or preferably under) the V-berths.

14
ELECTRICAL SYSTEMS FOR METAL BOATS

There are two simple equations that you should write in your log and learn by heart:

VOLTS x AMPS = WATTS

and

WATTS ÷ VOLTS = AMPS

OHM'S LAW

As you become more involved in studying your boat's electrical system, you may wish to refer to these formulas:

voltage	$E = I \times R$ or $E = P/I$
current	$I = E/R$ or $I = P/E$
resistance	$R = E/I$ or $R = E2/P$ or $R = P/12$
power	$P = E \times I$ or $P = 12 \times R$ or $E2/R$

E = VOLTAGE in volts
I = CURRENT in Amps
R = RESISTANCE in ohms
P = POWER in watts

Because electrics will play a large part in owning and operating your metal boat, you must learn all you can about this subject. Unless you become well versed in marine electrics, you will need to seek professional help in either fitting or surveying your boat's electrical installations. Whenever you're required to seek professional assistance, look over the shoulder of the technician so that you can learn to make a similar installation or repair yourself. To increase your understanding of all of these items, make sure you're around when the experts are working on your electrical system. You can gain as much from asking questions and absorbing knowledge as you can from having the work performed on your boat. This advice extends to any area where you need to employ outside labor.

Make an early decision regarding how many electrical items you're going to install. If your cruising is local or coastal in nature, and your boat is large enough, you'll most likely want to consider having all the same goodies on board that you use at home. Metal boats intended for long-distance voyaging may benefit from an electrical system that's simpler and easier to maintain.

Before you decide on how you are going to satisfy your metal boat's electrical requirements, you must decide how many appliances and other electrically driven devices you're going to install. Take the worst-case power requirements and make estimates from the literature or the nameplates of the appliances. Estimate how many of these items will be running at one time. Now select the power sources you plan to install, such as alternators, generating sets, solar panels, wind generators, or other alternatives that will supply the total load. You should be aware that generating sets prefer to be run with loads of at least

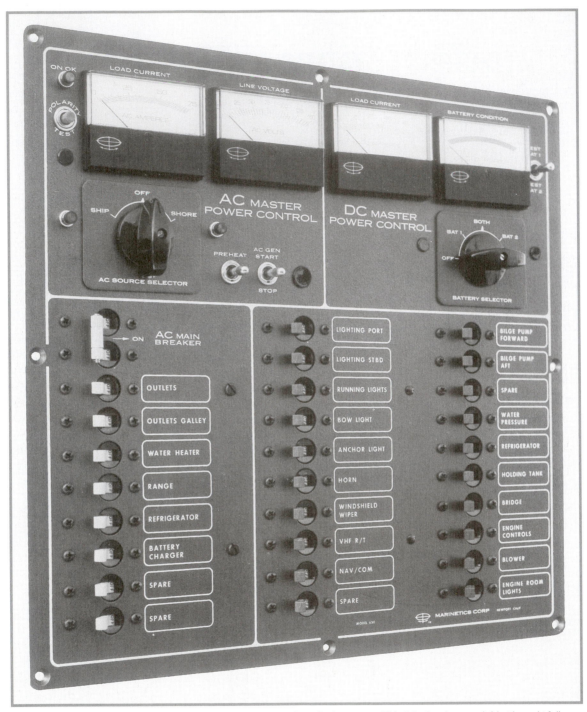

A suitable main panel is required when laying out your electrical system. This Marinetics model is thoughtfully arranged and would suit many builders.

40 percent (and up to 75 percent) of their capacity, so you may be forced to actually waste electricity if you overestimate your requirements.

BATTERIES

We're referring here to lead-acid, wet-cell batteries. Later in this section, we outline some of the claims made for gel-cell batteries. You can choose either type with the knowledge that 50 percent of the battery "experts" will agree with your choice.

In Europe, batteries are sized by quoting amp-hours and in the U.S. the size may be quoted as a "group" or a "D" followed by a number. As the numbers are not always consistent between manufacturers, you should inquire further to establish the actual storage capacity of the particular battery in amp-hours.

A few examples of the U.S. system of denoting capacity are as follows:

Group 24 = 70 to 85 amp-hours; Group 27 = 85 to 105 amp-hours; 4D = 160 to 180 amp-hours; 8D = 210 to 225 amp-hours. A 6-volt golf cart battery is usually 180 to 215 amp-hours.

It's sometimes hard to remember in what order to connect and disconnect the battery terminals. The negative terminal is removed first and connected last.

Traditionally, the batteries have been divided into two or more banks, one for starting the engine and one or more for everything else. As batteries have become more reliable, there are some battery "experts" who argue that it's no longer necessary to divide the battery banks into domestic and starting units. If you have a generating set with its own starting battery, you can fire it up to charge batteries and start the main engine. In a worst-case scenario, you may be able to use a set of jumper cables to connect the generating set's battery to start the main engine. Considering the last option, it may be worthwhile to include a larger-than-normal battery for use with the gen-set.

If you're planning long-distance offshore voyaging, versus local coastal cruising, your electrical requirements (and especially the methods of satisfying those needs) will be different. When you're coastal cruising you'll often have access to shore power; this allows you to conserve your battery power and enables you to top off your batteries using your battery charger.

You'll most likely have more than one battery for domestic use. When this is the case, the installation is called a battery bank. It's preferable that all of the separate batteries in the bank are of the same amp-hour capacity, or at least similar capacities. If the sizes vary, then the smallest battery may control the system and can halt the charging process when it's fully charged; this can often occur well before its larger companions have reached full capacity.

Generally speaking, sailboats need fewer batteries than equivalent-sized powerboats do. Below are estimates for sailboats. For powerboats, add at least 50 percent to the suggested capacity. These estimates are not recommendations of actual amp-hour requirements but rather an indication of the numbers involved. If you're planning to carry the appliances that many consider as necessities, then you can use these figures as a starting point. Based on sailboat length and assuming there's a crew of two to four people, you're most likely to require the following domestic battery amp-hour storage capacity:

Boat Size	Amp-Hour Needs
28 ft. (8.53 m)	150 to 250
35 ft. (10.67 m)	400 to 600
45 ft. (13.72 m)	800 to 1,000
55 ft. (16.76 m)	1,200 to 1,500
65 ft. (19.81 m)	1,500 to 2,000

The connections between separate batteries are made in series or in parallel. Connecting batteries in series is done to increase the voltage, for instance if you connect two 12-volt batteries in series you will achieve 24 volts, not recommended on a 12-volt system! To connect two 12-volt batteries in series to achieve 24 volts, connect the positive pole number on one battery to the ship's systems, and connect the negative pole on the number 1 battery to the positive pole on number 2 battery the negative pole in the number 2 battery is connected to the ship's system, thus completing the 24-volt system. The same rules apply to connect two 6-volt batteries to achieve a 12-volt system.

Connecting batteries in parallel is done to expand the amp-hour capacity of a system; the voltage remains the same, but the system has access to additional amp-hours. To connect two or more batteries in parallel, connect the batteries positive to positive and negative to negative, then attach leads to negative pole on one battery and lead to system and one lead to positive pole on the same battery and to the system.

If you require large battery capacity, there's a sensible limit to the size of each individual battery. Unfortunately, in the case of large capacities it's seldom possible to keep each individual unit to a size easily handled by one person, so give this matter consideration when arranging your batteries. If you have more than one 12-volt battery, and you want to create a bank of batteries, then you would connect these batteries in parallel so they remain and act as one 12-volt battery of larger capacity. If you want to create a 24-volt battery (often used on larger pleasure boats and many commercial boats), then you can connect two 12-volt batteries in series, or four 6-volt batteries in series. Golf cart or similar deep-cycle, heavy-duty batteries are often available in 6-volt sizes and are becoming more widely used to make up large battery banks where large amp-hour capacities (for example, 2,000 amp-hours) are required. Most boats will have a number of 12-volt batteries connected in parallel to make up their 12-volt domestic battery bank.

Remember that you must balance your battery capacity against your power usage. It takes considerably longer to put back the amperage than to take it out. Batteries do not accept a charge at the same speed as they can discharge.

Deep-Cycle Versus Starting Batteries

The batteries you choose for domestic storage should be the deep-cycle variety. These batteries are constructed differently from those used for engine starting. Deep-cycle batteries are designed and built to accept a moderate load over an extended period. The plates are thicker, the cases are usually heavier, and they are better equipped to accept regular discharges of up to 50 percent and then be recharged on a regular cycling basis.

The construction of the starting battery is different from that of the deep-cycle type. The plates are thinner, and they're designed to release high power in short bursts. Once the engine is running, the charge from the alternator quickly replenishes the battery.

This is one reason why, when you check your engine-start battery, you'll often find that it's fully charged. In fact, you must be careful not to overcharge it even though your regulator is designed to prevent this happening. Because this battery seldom gives trouble, it's sometimes neglected. Make sure you regularly check the level of the water (electrolyte), the voltage level, and the general condition of the battery.

In the past, it's always been a rule that the engine-starting battery should be capable of being totally isolated. One reason is that you may want to leave the domestic battery system switched on to power an automatic bilge pump, alarm, or similar device. In some cases, you may wish to wire bilge pumps and alarms directly to the battery, so they are not accidentally turned off when you leave the boat.

Be aware that any 12-volt battery in operational condition will actually have a voltage higher than 12. If you're using a voltmeter, and you take a reading soon after you've stopped charging, your meter will most likely register more than 13 volts. After a few hours (without any discharge due to usage) your battery will read 12.8 volts if it's fully charged and somewhat less if it has not reached full capacity. A battery that reads 12.2 volts is 50 percent discharged. A battery that reads 11.6 volts is almost fully discharged and may be damaged beyond further use if you leave it in this condition for long.

Alternative Batteries

Ni-cad batteries are sometimes used as domestic batteries on boats, and they were installed on *K*I*S*S* when we purchased her. They worked well on this relatively low-tech sailboat. Ni-cads are expensive, but are reputed to have an extremely long life. It may be worth investigating this option if you're building a new boat, or refitting an existing one.

It's well to remember that ni-cad batteries do need recycling on a regular basis, and that they also present some health hazard in that they have to be disposed of as a hazardous waste.

Gel-cell batteries are lead-acid batteries, and are similar to the common wet-cell battery, but the differences in their chemistry and construction do give them some unique features. There is no need to add water, so the tops of these batteries stay clean. Unlike wet-cell batteries, the gel will hold its charge for months when left sitting with no load and no float charge. They can be stored in the off-season without the need for a constant float charge, and without fear of freezing. Gel-cell batteries will accept a higher rate of charge than the wet-cells do, and usually deliver better performance when connected to an inverter. The combination of acids in the gel-cell prevents sulfation and eliminates the need for battery equalization. Before you choose this type of battery, remember that 50 percent of the experts prefer wet-cell batteries!

Absorbed glass mat (AGM) batteries are becoming more popular. These batteries hold the electrolyte in a sponge-like material. You may want to investigate them if you're initially fitting a new set, or replacing an entire bank.

Finally, don't confuse gel-cell batteries with the so-called maintenance-free batteries. Water cannot be added and these batteries are totally unsuitable for marine use.

Battery Boxes

The first time you meet rough weather shouldn't be the time you decide that your batteries need to be installed more securely. Batteries, complete with fluid, weigh around 0.875 pounds (400 g) per amp-hour capacity. A 220-amp-hour, or 8D, battery weighs about 160 pounds (75 kg). It doesn't take much imagination to envisage what would happen if one of those monsters broke loose in a seaway. Batteries need to be installed in securely, and the best way is to house them in their own boxes. A battery box can be built out of ¾-inch (20 mm) waterproof plywood, and is best lined with fiberglass so that any spills are contained. The box should be bolted to, or otherwise securely fastened to, a suitable structural member.

When selecting the location for your batteries, remember that during the time you own the boat, they probably will need to be removed or exchanged for new ones. If the batteries are not already fitted with strong handles, make sure you install straps under them so you can remove the batteries from the box. Although many authorities insist on a vented lid for the battery box, we believe that provided the batteries are strapped in place, they are unlikely to jump out of the box, and the open top is better for ventilation. More importantly, it's one less obstacle to regularly checking the battery fluid levels.

Keep the terminals and the top of the case absolutely clean. One reason for the recommended battery box covers, is to prevent accidental shorting out of the battery and electrical system when some metal article like a spanner or wrench is dropped across the terminals. If you're considering a large battery bank, you should see if you can locate at least a large percentage of your batteries low in the hull, perhaps in the keel or bilge area. In this case, you'll need to make sure they don't contact the bilge water.

Battery Chargers

Most battery chargers are operated at alternating-current (AC) voltages of 120, 220, or 240.

A well-sdesigned and proven combination battery charger/inverter, such as this Heart unit, is an essential item in any well-found cruising boat; choose yours carefully.

They're usually left running when you are connected to shore power or an AC generator. There is a great variety of 12-volt DC battery chargers capable of delivering between 5 and 100 amps. When you run a 240-volt AC battery charger on 220 volts, you'll find that it will deliver only 80 percent, or less, of its rated output. The amount of amperage you need from a charger will be calculated at the same time as you are totaling amperage income from other sources such as the engine alternator, solar panels, a wind generator, and so on.

Single-stage battery chargers only deliver their full output when the battery is deeply discharged. For example, if you start charging a battery with a 30-amp charger (and assuming your batteries are 50 percent discharged at the start of the cycle) you'll note via your charging gauge that the needle immediately registers a 30-amp input.

But after a period (depending on the capacity of the battery bank), the input amperage needle will drop back to 20, 15, and eventually 1 or 2 amps. This is how most battery chargers are designed to work; they will give your battery as much power as they're designed to deliver only until the battery reaches around 80 percent of its capacity. Then the input becomes much less. You'll note that if you turn on a 12-volt DC appliance during this period when the charger is not delivering full capacity, the charge will increase to cover the amount of amperage you are using. We find this feature to be useful in giving a general estimate of the amperage used by a particular appliance.

The internal setting of your battery charger will determine how many volts your charger can deliver. It may be possible to alter a voltage that has been preset at the factory. Check with the manufacturer of the unit before you start making changes to these settings. If your charger delivers too high a voltage, it can cause your batteries to boil or gas, and you may permanently damage them. Grossly overcharged batteries have been known to explode, so take precautions when working on your batteries. As a minimum safety measure, always wear protective clothing and safety glasses.

Equalizing Batteries

This method of rejuvenating your batteries is one that should only be considered if you feel comfortable with your system and when you consider you have the experience to handle the process with complete safely. For a complete description of the process, see appendix 1, Equalizing Batteries, by Max Pillie, in my *Choosing for Cruising*. While a battery is being discharged, sulfuric acid in the electrolyte reacts with the lead plates in a chemical reaction that produces electricity and

lead sulfate. During recharging, electricity flows back into the battery and causes the reverse chemical reaction, which turns the lead sulfate back into lead and sulfuric acid.

With each discharge and recharge cycle, a small amount of lead sulfate will remain on the plates. If this sulfate is left in place for very long, it will harden or crystallize and eventually reduce the battery's capacity, increase internal resistance, and destroy the battery's ability to deliver an adequate amount of power. When this occurs, even an equalizing charge cannot remove the sulfate and the battery becomes useless except for recycling purposes.

GENERATING SETS

If you require a great deal of electricity, a diesel-powered generating set will be your next option. There are three types of power-generating sets

(continued on page 174)

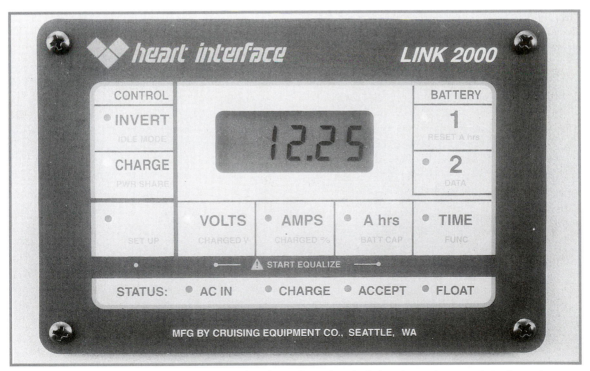

You will need an efficient control panel to monitor the various electrical charging and usage aboard your boat.

Electrical Systems in Metal Boats

The following is from notes written by Del F. Kahan, of Marinetics Corp., Newport Beach, California, and is included here with his permission.

The information contained here was prepared specifically in response to questions posed by many friends and associates in the marine industry: naval architects, marine engineers, production and plant managers, and individuals. All have been apprehensive about the special features that might be applied to aluminum- or steel-hulled vessels for which they are responsible. On several occasions, inquiries have been submitted after unfortunate and catastrophic experiences. It can be embarrassing indeed, to have a lovely vessel sink at the dock, suddenly lose bottom paint over a wide area, or suffer extensive underwater corrosion.

Generally, a metal-hulled vessel differs from one of fiberglass or wood (for the purposes of this text) only with respect to certain special precautions that relate to galvanic corrosion and electrical systems' insulation integrity. Basic electrical system concepts and design procedures should otherwise be identical.

Unless the vessel is to be moored and used in very pure freshwater (an unlikely circumstance in these times) either salt water or freshwater should be considered to be an electrolyte capable of accelerating galvanic corrosion—that which is attributed to dissimilar metals in contact, or electrically interconnected.

The designer's and builder's task, particularly with respect to aluminum hulls, includes selection of an appropriate corrosion-resistant alloy for the hull plating, proper welding alloy selection and procedure, and contact insulation with respect to dissimilar materials. Through-hulls should be nonmetallic, or suitably insulated. The propeller shaft should also be insulated from the hull through the use of appropriate nonmetallic bearings and coupling insulators. Cathodic protection of the hull through the use of sacrificial anodes such as zincs may be employed through the classical attachment methods or by means of "throw-over" zincs connected to the hull only when the vessel is dockside. Frequently, it is found that bottom-paint-lifting problems are simply the result of improper priming and painting procedures, and are not at all related to the "electrolysis bogeyman." Another phenomenon, deterioration of the trailing edges and other discontinuities, is frequently found to result from mechanical erosion due to cavitation or water turbulence. The above factors are mentioned here because it is common to blame the ship's electrical system for deficiencies that are totally unrelated.

Stray-current corrosion attributable to faulty DC electrical system installation or to subsequent deterioration can be prevented through proper system design and installation procedures. With respect to design, the author is of the firm conviction (reflecting both analysis and practical experience) that an isolated DC system *is neither essential nor desirable.* Typically, the smaller engines employed utilize single-terminal (engine grounded) electrical accessories and the cost to isolate these items and to maintain that isolation, is difficult to justify. The classical, negatively grounded DC system has been proven to be quite acceptable provided that certain simple precautions are adhered to as follows:

1. The negative ground shall be provided at a *single* point, the propulsion engine. Note: on a twin-screw vessel, a hull ground shall be provided at each engine—this will still be considered a single point.

    All circuit returns shall be by means of suitable insulated conductors, and shall terminate ultimately at the single point.

2. All circuit-protection devices (fuses or, preferably, automatic non-self-reset circuit breakers) and control switches shall be located in the positive conductors.

3. DC equipment should, for maximum insulation integrity, be mounted on insulating pads, off the ship's ground (hull). This need not apply to engine mounted (thus grounded) accessories such as the engine's starting motor, alternator, instruments, and warning senders, etc. All remote pumps, blowers, electronic equipment, etc., should have the cases and metallic mounting ears isolated from ground. The purpose of this procedure is to ensure that the deterioration of the internal insulation will not result in leakage of currents to and through the hull plating.

    Should it be deemed desirable to provide a radio-frequency (RF) ground *near* the radiotelephone transmitter, rather than to accept the DC single-point engine ground for the purpose, a blocking capacitor should be incorporated to confine the ground to RF currents only.

4. All wiring installation shall be made only with the best materials and procedures to insure high-quality integrity. Conductors must be carefully bundled and strapped in place and precautions taken to prevent chafe. The latter is particularly important where wire bundles are led around corners, past ribs or gussets, and through metallic bulkheads. Liberal utilization of protective neoprene hose, as a sheath, represents good procedure where hazards exist. Conductors that penetrate metallic bulkheads should be protected by means of plastic grommets or stuffing tubes.

It should be kept in mind that initial installation is not the only consideration. The effects of shock and vibration can cause shifting of improperly secured wiring. In addition, the activities of repair or servicing personnel with respect to other equipment (i.e., engine servicing) can dislodge or damage wiring unless suitable protection has been provided.

The disciplines essential to AC system installation are especially important. All of the principles described above must be conscientiously applied; in addition, special care must be directed toward the AC shore-power supply interface. There are those who promote the use of various forms of so-called "galvanic isolators" as a solution to the problems of the ship's ground connection to the AC grounding conductor (green wire) brought in with the utility shore-power connector. Some manufacturers of these devices are conscientious in their attempts to fashion well-designed products of this nature and to reinforce confidence in their product through sophisticated quality-control measures. Accordingly, a case can be made for the use of these devices with shore-power services brought aboard *fiberglass or wooden-hulled vessels* whose ship's ground system is intended to be connected to the AC grounding conductor (i.e., in accordance with ABYC or similar recommendations). With metal-hulled craft, the risk of any degree of failure or compromise of "isolation quality" is difficult to accept. By any measure, the most acceptable design principle mandates the employment of a high quality *isolation transformer* to ensure that no common electrical circuit will exist with respect to the shore-side utility power system. The best method for connection of the isolation transformer is in accordance with ABYC recommendations.

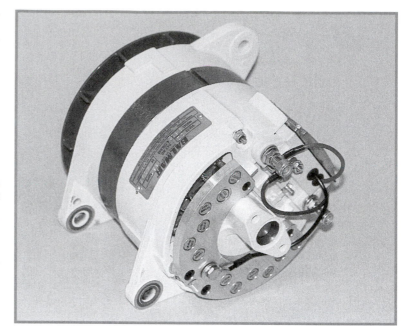

Large-capacity alternators like this Balmar Power-charger can add 75 to 100 amps to your charging system.

(*continued from page 171*)
capable of making the large quantities of AC electricity demanded by modern appliances. You may select a fully installed diesel-powered unit; a unit that is driven by a power take-off from the main engine; or a portable unit powered by gasoline (petrol). There's one additional type of high-capacity gen-set that is unique because it generates 12-volt DC power as opposed to most units, which deliver 120-volt or 220-volt AC current. Make sure you turn off all appliances, especially the 12-volt DC ones, before you fire up your generating set. When a generating set is first started there can be a surge of power that can harm your appliances.

Before considering installing these units, sailboat owners should estimate if their needs can be met by a combination of solar panels, wind-generated power, and the alternator on your main engine. Powerboaters will have greater requirements, and are not so inclined toward wind generators. Many powerboats have one or two solar panels of sufficient capacity to maintain the battery charge when the boat is not in use.

Although you may use some AC power, most of the electricity generated by a 120-volt or 220-volt AC unit is converted to 12-volt DC current via a battery charger before it is used on your boat. Perhaps it would be more efficient to start off with a 12-volt generating set and use the alternator's output to provide the minimal amounts of 120-volt or 220-volt AC you need, by way of an inverter (see Inverters, page 177). The 12-volt gen-set is covered later under its own heading.

Portable generators are inexpensive but they're not suitable for metal sailboats or power-boats. In most cases, they're very noisy. They introduce the need for you to carry gasoline (petrol) aboard and are not up to powering the range of appliances that made you consider a generating set in the first place.

For those on a budget, a power take-off (PTO) generator could be the answer. PTO units have a centrifugal clutch arrangement that enables them to keep generating at varying engine speeds. Suitable PTO generators, including the U.S.-made M90 Marine Cruising Generator, are capable of considerable output, and units of 3 kW to 6.5 kW are readily available. These units produce enough power to keep most appliance-happy cruising families satisfied.

If you've considered using your main engine and the regular alternator as a primary source of generating 12-volt DC power, it's as well to remember that you should have some load on the engine; in other words, we don't recommended that you run your diesel engine at low revolutions without some load being applied.

The load of a large alternator may be enough to offset the fact that the boat is stationary and out of gear. I have often wondered about the advice not to run a diesel engine without some load, when at the ski slopes one sees stationary diesel buses running sometimes for more than 24 hours. My advice is that if you plan to rely on the main engine to generate 12-volt power, then fit a decent-sized alternator to not only load the engine but also to get the job done as quickly as possible. The rule of thumb is that the horsepower required is twice the number of kW produced, hence a 100-watt alternator charging at 13.8 volts would account for nearly 3 hp. You might also consider having a special take-off pulley fitted to your main engine so that you could engage and disengage a sizable alternator at will.

For the larger boats, a conventional diesel-powered generating set offers power at a reasonable price. These units can supply AC power from around 3 kVA up to almost any size that you could require. The quietest units are powered by a water-cooled diesel engine with at least two cylinders. The entire unit must either be already installed in an well-insulated cabinet, or capable of being insulated and contained in a soundproof box.

Most gen-sets are reliable and deliver the amount of rated power promised by the manufacturer, so the difference between a good set and the best set comes down to noise. Try to hear more than one gen-set running before you make a final decision. Sound problems can come from the exhaust water rather than from the diesel or the generating unit; it's possible to reduce this noise greatly by using a water-lift exhaust muffler that can be arranged to exit the water below or above the waterline. In the case of the gen-set just arrange the muffler to exit below the water. Generally speaking most gen-sets are quiet and fuel-efficient. They can be tucked away in otherwise unused space in or near the engine compartment. But no matter how quiet and efficient your gen-set, you will not want to run it more than, say, two to four hours each day.

A generating system that produces large quantities of 12-volt DC power makes sense when you consider that most appliances likely to be found on even the most completely (electrically) equipped cruising sailboat can be run on 12-volt DC power. If you choose this option, you might want to install more batteries than you would normally. Powerboat owners, because of larger current demand, will probably prefer to install a 110-volt or 220-volt AC gen-set.

There are several 12-volt DC generating systems now available, including a combination unit manufactured by Balmar in the U.S. This unit is arranged to provide constant 12-volt DC power to operate a watermaker and a deep-freeze, as well as to keep the batteries in a constant state of charge.

All of the major components are readily available, and you may wish to build a unit to suit your requirements. If you're planning to use an all-12-volt-DC system, or mostly so, then you will need a battery capacity in the top end of the quoted estimates.

Most cruising boats with a regular AC-generating system fitted need to run it for two to three hours per day. With the all-12-volt DC system, it's estimated that you should only need to run your generating set for the same amount once every two to three days. This factor alone may be sufficient to encourage you to consider this setup. One disadvantage of the all-12-volt DC system is that it requires much heavier wiring and fuses. The main requirement is that you must be able to produce larger-than-usual amounts of 12-volt DC power, so your batteries can be replenished at a rapid rate. This is necessary to balance the two- or three-day charging cycle. Your 12-volt charging system will need to be able to produce between 150 and 300 amps to make the system work; it can be done.

The charging end of the unit will consist of one or more high-output alternators coupled with a dedicated, suitably sized, water-cooled diesel engine. The recommended procedure is to decide how much output you will require to charge your batteries in the desired time. Now match the output of the alternator(s) to this requirement and then select a suitably sized diesel engine. Between 10 and 20 hp should be sufficient to power the alternator(s). The engine will not require a transmission unit but you will need a shaft that can be bolted to the flywheel, and this in turn will accept the one or two pulleys used to drive the alternators via a suitable V-belt arrangement.

A reliable regulator will be part of this system. The last thing you want to do is to cook all those expensive batteries. You'll need to have the entire unit housed in a soundproof box similar to that used for an AC gen-set. The cost of this 12-volt DC generating set should not exceed the cost of a similarly sized AC unit. Your decision can be based purely on the convenience factor and on the requirements of your electrical system. For details of the availability of high-output alternators, see appendix 2.

SOLAR PANELS

When your boat is left unattended, you may find solar panels useful to keep the batteries charged. They have been successfully installed to run all types of appliances, including small refrigeration units. Solar panels (when they produce 1 amp or more) should be run through a regulator so that there's no chance of overcharging the battery. These devices are capable of taking power out of your battery at night; make sure you prevent a reverse flow of current by installing a blocking diode for each panel or bank of panels. Each diode uses 0.4 amp, so remember that when calculating input. If in doubt about your abilities in this area, have the units installed by a competent person.

Solar panels are becoming more efficient and can be mounted on many areas of your boat. You'll need to study the position of the sun in relation to the intended location of the panels. If you're able to rotate or angle the panels to take account of the boat's position in relation to the sun, they'll produce more electricity. You would probably soon tire of adjusting the angle of the panels several times each day, so you should calculate a reasonable average angle to suit the area where you're operating, and settle for around 75 percent efficiency. When you're mounting the panels, make sure you allow for air to circulate around the whole unit, otherwise the excessive

heat generated will seriously decrease the panel's output.

Once you've made the initial investment, the power you receive is free. Most solar panels have a long, maintenance-free life, usually 10 years or longer. As with most other capital expenses, you'll need to decide if you'll receive a reasonable return on your investment. In the case of solar panels, if you plan to be cruising at least 25 percent of the time, then they are a good investment. In any case, you should install a small unit that is capable of topping up the batteries when you're away from your boat.

The starting power of solar panels is 0.30 amps, which is ideal for battery replenishment. One panel per bank of batteries will avoid the need for a regulator in the system. Larger panels can produce up to 3.5 amps, ideal for the offshore sailor. If you consider solar power as a serious source of electricity, install several panels designed to produce a total of around 20 amps. Make sure to select solar panels whose rated voltage, at the temperature where you're operating, is at least 14.8. This allows for the blocking diode's 0.6-volt draw and gives net voltage of 14.2. This is the voltage required to fully charge lead-acid batteries.

WIND-POWERED GENERATORS

Cruising sailboats use wind generators more often than powerboats do. Many experienced cruising people argue that wind generators are more efficient and cost-effective than solar panels are. If your boat is intended for serious offshore cruising, then why not install both types of generating equipment and you can reap all of the benefits. The thought of those blades whizzing around will ensure that most people consider the safety aspects when deciding whether or not to install one.

To prevent damage to the charging unit and the blades, some types need to be shut down when winds reach 30 to 50 knots. Other manufactures include automatic speed control and shutdown. You should look for these features, as stopping the blades in high winds could be a risky operation. Most generators you will be considering will have blades of around 5 feet (1.52 m) in diameter. Don't let the above comments put you off considering a wind generator; they are a wonderful source of electricity and the warnings are intended to make sure you treat these wind machines with respect.

Wind generators do make noise; the amount depends on the model. We have noticed over the years that they are becoming quieter. The number of blades does not usually increase the output, but additional blades make for a quieter unit. Try to inspect the various models under operating conditions to see for yourself how much noise, and what type of noise, is involved.

Wind generators will require some maintenance. They are basically electric motors running in reverse, so they have all of the same components as an electric motor. Brushes, and even bearings, will need periodic replacement. Check with the manufacturer on what the maintenance procedures are, and how often replacement parts are required for their particular unit.

INVERTERS

It's well to note that inverters are users, rather than manufacturers, of electricity. They simply take one form of power and turn it into another, keeping a little for their trouble. The best models only consume around 5 percent during the conversion process.

There are many inverters capable of converting the 12-volt or 24-volt DC power stored in your batteries into 220/240-volt or 120-volts AC. They are generally available in sizes with outputs ranging from 50 watts to 2,500 watts. If you intend to run most of your electrical appliances from 120-volt or 220/240-volt AC power supplied by your inverter, then, before you purchase, you'll need to know the total power requirements of all the appliances you plan to run at any one time. If you have a relatively small sailboat, and are only intending to run one small AC appliance, then a simple strip-based 200-watt inverter may suit you best. One of these small units may cost

you as little as $150 (£100) or less. Owners of larger liveaboard cruising boats often underestimate their requirements, so it's most important that you calculate your expected needs carefully. Allow some room for expanded usage. You will need the 12-volt DC battery storage capacity to back up this usage, and this will temper your appetite for AC appliances. Remember to convert your requirements to the same units, either amps or watts, before you start to estimate your total requirements; see the conversion formula at the start of this chapter. There are several manufacturers of these appliances—see appendix 2.

In early models, the current produced by inverters was not the same as that supplied to your home by the local power company. The inverter produces a "square," "stepped," or what is generally referred to as a "modified" sine wave. An onboard generating set delivers the same pure sine-wave power that your local power company generates. Why do you need to know this? Because the power from an inverter may not properly run certain AC appliances; problems may occur when inverters are coupled with television or computer screens, radar, and similar units. These problems are being addressed and largely overcome, but it's wise to check with manufacturers regarding the compatibility of their units with the appliances you wish to operate. Since 1998, there has been a vast improvement in the way inverters operate. You should be able to find one that will suit your requirements and will also give you trouble free service.

When you're considering what appliances you can run on your inverter, you'll need to consider the starting amperage required by many pieces of electrical equipment. For example, an electric drill that operates on 1,000 watts will normally take a considerably larger amount of power during the first few seconds of operation to get going. This is sufficient to create an overload and trip out the whole circuit. Because inverter technology is constantly changing, you should investigate the various makes and models to ensure that the unit you select will properly run your AC appliances.

MULTIMETERS AND HYDROMETERS

To assist in managing your electrical supply and demand, you need one or more test instruments. They will enable you to check the state of charge of your batteries and keep track of the general health of your electrical system.

One of the first items you should acquire is a handheld multimeter. Most of these instruments not only read volts on the DC and AC scale, but also read ohms and amps. Most units are capable of reading a wide range of voltages from a small percentage of 1 volt through to 500 volts AC or more. On a cruising boat, the main interest will lie in the 12-volt DC, and the 120- or 220-volt AC ranges. Multimeters are available in two basic configurations, analog or digital. Like many people, we started off with an analog instrument. However, we soon found that the digital version was capable of being read more accurately. These instruments are relatively inexpensive and good-quality ones are available for a little as $22 (£15). This instrument can be used to test circuits and is the first thing you reach for (after you've checked the fuses) when any electrical appliance or instrument fails to operate.

For those of us who need to know the exact state of our batteries and associated equipment at all times, there are a number of monitoring instruments that can be permanently installed in the electrical system. These instruments provide information on demand.

The E-Meter is manufactured in the U.S. by Cruising Equipment (see appendix 2) and is marketed in the U.S., Canada, and the U.K. under the name Heart Interface Link 10. The E-Meter measures most of the battery functions of interest to you. It measures the amp-hours remaining in your batteries. It measures voltage, amperage, and the time remaining until the battery would be discharged. The remaining amp-hours can be displayed on the light-emitting diode (LED) display, or as a percentage of the battery capacity. The meter is powered by the battery system to which it is attached, but the drain is so low as to be negligible in most systems.

There are many other battery-monitoring devices that keep an eye on every battery function. I have featured the E-Meter/Heart Link 10 because it represents such outstanding value for the money. There are battery monitors that have even more functions than the E-Meter, and you may find these useful.

The hydrometer is another measuring instrument that you should have on board. This device consists of a glass tube with a rubber bulb on one end and a thin tube on the other. Inside is a float, marked off in one or more scales designed to give various readings. When used to draw off a small amount of electrolyte from each cell, it depicts the state of charge. If one cell registers a reading considerably lower than another, then you may well have a problem, not only with that cell but also with the battery. One dead cell will render the whole battery useless, and it will have to be replaced.

Many hydrometers also have a scale to measure specific gravity. This scale can be used to test, among other things, the state of the coolant in your engine's heat-exchanger system. As temperature can play a part in the operation of your batteries, some hydrometers are fitted with a thermometer. In our opinion, this is overkill and there are less expensive ways of determining and factoring in the temperature.

The fluid you draw off the battery when testing with a hydrometer has a high sulfuric acid content, so be aware that it's capable of burning your skin and eyes. Make sure you are adequately protected. Your clothing and fabrics used in the interior of your boat are especially vulnerable to even the smallest amount of battery acid. Always rinse out the instrument in fresh, clean water after use; don't put contaminated water down the sink. Always use a separate glass jar for rinsing, and dispose of the water in an appropriate manner.

Now that you have some understanding of the complexities of the subject of marine electrics you may wish to study further; the subject is fully covered in several specialized books—see appendix 1.

15
APPENDAGES, FITTINGS, AND ALTERATIONS

Skegs are usually fitted to sailboats with fin keels, and sometimes to powerboats. On fin-keel sailboats, we consider skegs to be preferable to unsupported spade rudders. On powerboats, skegs can often improve the directional stability. You may want to add a skeg, even if your metal boat was not designed with one.

If your sailboat plans call for a skeg and rudder combination, you'll need to assure yourself that the arrangement will stay with the boat at all times. Skegs are vulnerable and are more easily damaged than a boat that has a longer keel combined with a heel-supported rudder.

On sailboats where a skeg is fitted, it usually occupies about one-third of the total area of the rudder-skeg combination. Even though we have been guilty of designing single-plate skegs and rudders on sailboats, we've learned that this arrangement is far inferior to an airfoil-shaped appendage. Fortunately, if you have a single-plate skeg and/or rudder, it's a simple matter to add some support fins and outer plating.

Assuming your boat is designed to be fitted with a skeg, it's important that it be built strongly enough to withstand a reasonable amount of rough treatment. It would be possible to design and build a skeg so strong that it would tear the bottom out of the hull before the skeg was severely damaged. This type of overkill may cause you to lose the boat. How strong is strong enough, but not too strong?

First, we consider it important that the skeg be built onto the hull after the plating is completed. The skeg should not be a hollow appendage that is open at the top, similar to the keel. A keel structure has to be strong enough to withstand anything that the elements can offer. Most keels on metal boats will survive grounding but, unfortunately, a skeg is not large enough to have the same strength.

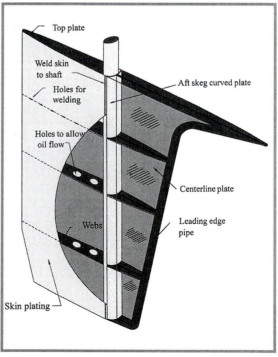

One of several ways to build a metal skeg and rudder.

This is how the rudder webs are welded to the shaft.

Most metal hulls have a substantial center-line bar on which to weld the centerplate for the skeg. The centerplate can be the same shape as the skeg and can be welded directly to the bar. You could have the plate continue up through the hull and then have a number of web floors to reinforce the plate. This latter arrangement is getting over-strong and likely to take some of the hull plating with it if ever you have the ultimate skeg-damaging collision.

You can see by the foregoing that designing and building a skeg is no simple matter. If you make it too weak, you may lose the skeg; if you make it too strong, you may sustain hull and rudder damage in the event of a serious collision. This is one reason why, in some of our latest cruising sailboat designs, we're now leaning toward a modern version of the long keel, with a heel supporting the bottom of the rudder. Generally speaking, powerboats do not have any of these problems.

The drawing on page 179 represents our idea of sensible skeg construction. Installing the fore-and-aft profile centerplate may make it just too strong. We would follow the elements shown

The skeg and rudder shown here were built using the methods shown in the illustration on page 179.

Note the stiffeners on the transom and webs that support rudder tubes on this steel Waverunner 44.

in this sketch. In some of our earlier designs, we allowed the skegs to have propeller apertures. Our current thinking is that the security for the propeller comes at too high a price. It's almost impossible to include the cut-out without seriously weakening the skeg.

The leading edge of the skeg can be whole pipe, split pipe, or rolled plate. Your plans may incorporate a "fence," which is like a fin that runs parallel to the DWL and usually extends from the front of the skeg to the aft end of the keel. The skeg can have the leading-edge pipe continued around and forward to form the bottom of the fence. The aft edge of the skeg is best constructed using an open-faced, large-diameter split pipe or rolled plate. The after end needs to be open enough to allow the rudder to swing at least 40 degrees in each direction. The centerline plate will support the airfoil-shaped half webs that are arranged on each side of the plate. If the centerline plate is omitted, you can have full-width webs attached to the leading and trailing edges of the skeg. The bottom airfoil web is usually ½-inch (12 mm) plate and can support the rudder-bearing cup.

To install the plating on the skeg, you'll need to make slots in the plate so you can weld through them and attach the plate to the webs. After fully plating the skeg, you may wish to install a fillet at the top on both sides where the skeg joins the hull. The fillet should measure, say, 4 inches to 6 inches (100 mm to 150 mm) and be installed at 45 degrees between the hull and the root of the skeg. Fair off the forward end of the fillet that will be welded to both the skeg and the hull plating.

SAILBOAT RUDDERS

Build the rudder in a manner similar to that used to make the skeg. The leading edge of the rudder will be either solid round material or a hollow tube of suitable strength. Your plans will indicate the size and type of material recommended for the rudderstock. Take care not to introduce stress into the stock when welding the webs and the plate to it. Some builders fit drain plugs to their rudders and skegs and fill them with oil. The idea is to prevent corrosion inside. In some publications, we've seen concrete recommended as a fill for rudders and skegs. Don't follow this recommendation. Our experience with concrete in boats, including metal hulls, is that it can cause corrosion from inside the hull, so don't include this material anywhere in your metal boat. A fill with foam, similar to that used as insulation inside the hull, may be of some benefit.

You may wish to have an arrangement that allows you to remove the rudder without removing the skeg bearing or lifting the entire boat. You can arrange flanges bolted together to make the removal of the rudder a simple matter. If you use flanges in the system, make sure they are of sufficient strength and have at least five bolts equaling the cross-sectional area of the rudder shaft. If you have flanges and bolts, then you must wire the nuts together so there is no risk of the bolts coming loose and allowing the rudder to part company with the boat.

In the bottom cup bearing you may insert one or more metal balls as a bearing surface for the bottom of the rudderstock. If you use this system, make sure that the hanging arrangement for the rudder is such that it cannot part company with the boat if the balls fail.

POWERBOAT RUDDERS AND STEERING SYSTEMS

Hydraulic steering systems can more easily be interfaced with autopilot systems, and for this and other reasons they're generally preferred for most powerboats. This whole question of steering systems and choosing the right system for your boat is covered in our books *Choosing for Cruising* (sailboats) and *Choosing a Cruising Powerboat* where more space is available to cover the subject in considerable detail.

Powerboat rudders are usually cast from alloy, and the size of the blade and shaft has to be carefully calculated to allow your boat to be steered within a range of speeds. The problem is that the larger rudders that would be ideal for handling the boat at slow speeds are not suitable for a boat operating on a plane. It's essential that you have the correct rudder size to suit the type of hull and expected performance characteristics of your particular boat. Consultation with the designer of your boat, or better still with a rudder specialist, is essential if you're to have a successful match.

SAILBOAT TRANSOM STEPS AND SWIM PLATFORMS

Most sailboats can be improved with one of these features. The platform will need to be designed so it's still clear of the water when the boat heels to its maximum sailing angle. On sailboats, the swim platform and boarding steps are usually incorporated into the construction of a "reverse" or "sugar-scoop" transom. If you're building from

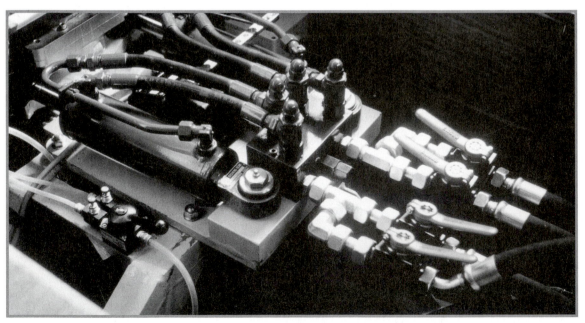

Hydraulic steering coupled to a self-steering arrangement will require some substantial pipe work, as seen here in a steel Roberts 53 sailboat.

This Roberts 64 sailboat incorporates a set of transom steps.

new, then the whole arrangement can be designed into the stern. If you are planning to add these features to an existing metal boat, then careful thought will be required before you start to alter the transom.

If the after end of the transom is too high from the water, say more than 1 foot, 6 inches (457 mm), then you'll need to include a boarding ladder in the arrangement. If you're having a boat designed, or altering an existing design to suit your particular requirements, it's worthwhile noting the height of the bottom of the transom above the water. It may be possible to modify the design so a separate boarding ladder isn't required.

The sugar-scoop stern is fashionable at present. Be careful if you're planning to have one of these added to the stern of your sailboat; we've seen some poorly designed additions that have spoilt an otherwise attractive design.

POWERBOAT SWIM PLATFORMS AND BOARDING LADDERS

In some places the swim platform is referred to as a "duck board." We confess to not having given this matter much thought until we finally owned a powerboat fitted with one of these appendages and then noticed how the ducks find them ideal for roosting. This isn't a

The transom arrangement on this Roberts 53 makes boarding and unloading a dinghy just that much easier.

problem, as the birds seem to know which boats are unused, and concentrate their unwelcome attentions on those vessels.

A large percentage of powerboats feature some form of swim platform and most are fitted with a boarding ladder at the stern. Anyone familiar with boating will be aware of the usefulness of these features, and if you're building a new boat or refitting an existing metal craft, the design and construction of this part of the hull should receive your serious consideration. We've also seen a set of steps incorporated into the bow of a powerboat. These simple, U-shaped stainless-steel steps enabled a crewmember to step from the boat to the shore more easily. This arrangement is worthwhile considering if you're planning extensive cruising in canals.

Recently, there has been a trend to carry the hull underwater sections past the regular transom and thus provide a base for the swim platform. This additional underwater volume will need to be considered with the rest of the hull if the boat is to retain its designed fore-and-aft trim. One way to ensure that there are minimum trim problems is to use this extended hull volume as liquid storage, either as a holding tank or as a way to increase water or fuel capacity. The holding tank option is the most popular solution—and dare we say you'll have more control as to when and how this form of ballast is discharged?

Another option when considering a swim platform is to have the structure built with a pipe frame that may be permanently left in position, or designed to fold upward when not in use. The fixed version is easier to build and maintain, and unless you have some reason that forbids its use (such as marina costs or space restrictions) then this is the type I

recommend. A pipe swim platform can be built out of 2-inch-diameter (50 mm) heavy-wall pipe, and can be an attractive addition to your boat. Suitably spaced 2- by 2- by ¼-inch (50 by 50 by 6 mm) angle can be used to support a system of teak planking.

The top of the swim platform will need to afford easy access from the water. In some cases, this may involve a calculated guess as to where the final waterline will be located. In any case, transom steps or, more likely, a boarding ladder will be needed from the swim platform to the main deck.

BOWSPRITS

Although they're usually confined to sailboats, short bowsprits can often be usefully incorporated into a powerboat hull. Construction would be similar in either case but the sailboat version will need extra strengthening to take the loads imposed by the sailing rig.

The simplest and most effective form of bowsprit on a metal boat is one built of heavy-walled pipe to form a U-shaped or similar structure. The ends of the U are anchored to a suitably reinforced section of the plating near the bow. The illustration shown here will give you a reasonable idea of what we consider to be the basis for a sturdy bowsprit. The structure may incorporate rollers to accept the anchor chain. Your bowsprit should provide an ideal place on which to stow the anchor. The anchor should be stowed

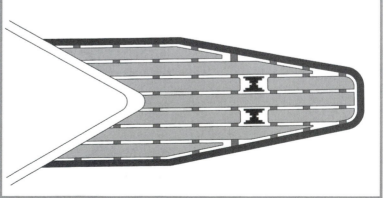

A pipe bowsprit is easily fabricated from the same metal as your hull; this is one place where you can avoid the use of dissimilar metals.

This bowsprit was installed on a beautiful Centennial Spray 34 launched in the U.K.

This arrangement combines a bowsprit, a sturdy pulpit, a jib boom, and an anchor-line reel for the second anchor.

far enough ahead of the bow so as to be out of the way, while remaining ready for immediate use.

In the sailboat version, tangs will be needed to accept the lower end of the forestay. The ideal material from which to build the main pipe structure is 316 stainless steel. The high cost of this material in the sizes and weight required means that you'll probably be using mild steel, aluminum, or copper-nickel, depending on the metal used to build you boat. It's preferable to use stainless steel for the tangs and other areas of the bowsprit where normal usage would soon wear away the paint and cause future maintenance problems.

The working platform of the pipe bowsprit can have L-angle installed as supports for the teak decking. Some form of bobstay may be required, depending on the strains imposed by your particular sail plan. In some cases where the bowsprit is no more than an extension of the bow/foredeck area, and intended to make the handling of anchors and ground tackle as simple as possible, then a bobstay may not be required. If the "U" is wide enough where it's attached to the hull, then side stays may not be required.

DAVITS

These dinghy-stowage devices are sometimes seen on sailboats. Davits on sailboats can be a mixed blessing because all too often they're of crude design and construction. Davits can increase the available deck area by moving the dinghy out of the way, but they may impede the operation of a self-steering windvane and can cause problems when you're sailing in a following sea. As davits may sooner or later require some repairs, you may consider it preferable to bolt them in place rather then weld them directly to the deck. There is one type of davit that may be suitable for all types of boats and that is one where the dinghy is lifted from the water in the normal manner and then flipped over to lie upside down on top of the davits.

We'd like to mention the fittings known as "snap davits." They're generally bolted to a swim platform, and matching fittings are glued or otherwise attached to the dinghy. The dinghy is positioned so the attachment points match up. The dinghy is now in a position to be pulled upward and sits parallel to the vertical transom. The dinghy actually hangs on these snap hinges outside or aft of the swim platform, thus allowing reasonable access to the platform. This arrangement is an alternative to fitting regular davits. You should decide if the disadvantages of restricted access to the swim platform and some restriction of aft vision by the dinghy outweigh its advantages.

Regular davits can be built of mild steel, stainless steel, or aluminum and can be constructed of pipe, rectangular tube, or sheet metal. If you have a generous budget, then it may be simpler to purchase ready-made davits. The rest of us will need to decide which design and construction method would best suit our needs. For other reasons, your dinghy should be as light as practical, so it shouldn't be necessary to build the davits of such heavy construction as to add unnecessary top hamper to your vessel. Try to match the style of the davits to the style of your boat. This is one of the many areas where it is possible to spoil the overall appearance of a boat by adding an ugly item that is there for all to see.

Because of the variety of dinghies likely to be carried, it is impossible to give detailed advice on constructing davits. If you study other boats with off-the-shelf or custom-built davits, you should be able to gain sufficient information to enable you to build a set for your boat.

MAST STEPS

No matter whether your mast is deck-stepped or keel-stepped, it will need some kind of device to secure its lower end. Many commercially manufactured masts come complete with a cast-aluminum step. It's fastened to the deck and the mast simply sits in this cup-like arrangement. Make sure that your deck-mounted step has the ability to drain the water that lodges around the bottom of the mast.

Examine the mast-support post—it may be 2-inch to 3-inch-diameter (50 mm to 75 mm) metal pipe—to ensure that it is up to the job. Your mast's under-deck support may be in the form of a beefed-up bulkhead. Check your plans for details. If your mast is stepped on the keel, check if you have an arrangement that will allow you to alter the rake of the mast (this will change the fore and aft location of the foot).

You may also consider a tabernacle mast step, a vertical trunk that accepts a deck-stepped

The sturdy tabernacle on this Roberts 53 is in keeping with the rest of this beautifully built boat. It's built to go anywhere.

CHAINPLATE DETAIL:

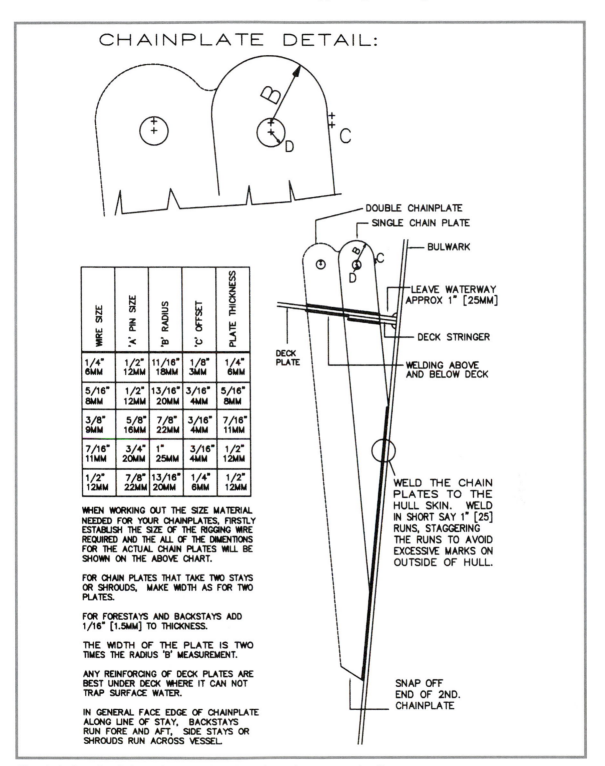

DOUBLE CHAINPLATE

SINGLE CHAIN PLATE

BULWARK

LEAVE WATERWAY
APPROX 1" [25MM]

DECK STRINGER

DECK PLATE

WELDING ABOVE
AND BELOW DECK

WELD THE CHAIN
PLATES TO THE
HULL SKIN. WELD
IN SHORT SAY 1" [25]
RUNS, STAGGERING
THE RUNS TO AVOID
EXCESSIVE MARKS ON
OUTSIDE OF HULL.

SNAP OFF
END OF 2ND.
CHAINPLATE

WIRE SIZE	'A' PIN SIZE	'B' RADIUS	'C' OFFSET	PLATE THICKNESS
1/4" 6MM	1/2" 12MM	11/16" 18MM	1/8" 3MM	1/4" 6MM
5/16" 8MM	1/2" 12MM	13/16" 20MM	3/16" 4MM	5/16" 8MM
3/8" 9MM	5/8" 16MM	7/8" 22MM	3/16" 4MM	7/16" 11MM
7/16" 11MM	3/4" 20MM	1" 25MM	3/16" 4MM	1/2" 12MM
1/2" 12MM	7/8" 22MM	13/16" 20MM	1/4" 6MM	1/2" 12MM

WHEN WORKING OUT THE SIZE MATERIAL
NEEDED FOR YOUR CHAINPLATES, FIRSTLY
ESTABLISH THE SIZE OF THE RIGGING WIRE
REQUIRED AND THE ALL OF THE DIMENTIONS
FOR THE ACTUAL CHAIN PLATES WILL BE
SHOWN ON THE ABOVE CHART.

FOR CHAIN PLATES THAT TAKE TWO STAYS
OR SHROUDS, MAKE WIDTH AS FOR TWO
PLATES.

FOR FORESTAYS AND BACKSTAYS ADD
1/16" [1.5MM] TO THICKNESS.

THE WIDTH OF THE PLATE IS TWO
TIMES THE RADIUS 'B' MEASUREMENT.

ANY REINFORCING OF DECK PLATES ARE
BEST UNDER DECK WHERE IT CAN NOT
TRAP SURFACE WATER.

IN GENERAL FACE EDGE OF CHAINPLATE
ALONG LINE OF STAY, BACKSTAYS
RUN FORE AND AFT, SIDE STAYS OR
SHROUDS RUN ACROSS VESSEL.

The chainplate detail shown here can be adapted to suit most metal sailboats.

mast and often allows it to pivot fore and aft. It can be manufactured of cast aluminum or fabricated from stainless or mild steel. Naturally the design of the tabernacle will need to match that of the mast and gear it's expected to support. When we say that it can be built from ¼-inch (6 mm) plate, you'll have to determine if that's suitable for your particular situation.

CHAINPLATES AND TANGS

Because of the wear and tear imposed on chainplates and tangs, they should be fabricated from 316 stainless steel. If you build chainplates or tangs out of mild steel that is subsequently painted, you'll find that the paint will wear away and corrosion will soon appear. Most metals, other than stainless steel, are also unsuitable for making these parts. When you paint the boat, make sure you extend the paint up 2 inches (50 mm) on to the stainless fittings; this will prevent any corrosion caused by the proximity of two dissimilar metals. Most chainplates and tangs will be made from plate of a minimum thickness of ¼ inch (6 mm), but consult your plans for exact sizes. Some designs call for the chainplates to be made from solid round stainless-steel bar. Watch for crevice corrosion. Reread the section on stainless steel in chapter 3. Its strengths and weaknesses should be kept in mind when using this material.

Avoid chainplates that are simply welded to the outside of the hull; they look crude. They're also corrosion traps because they're welded on top of another metal. In our opinion, welding even similar metals one on top of the other is bad practice. For instance, if you're welding a cleat to the deck, either reinforce the plate with a section of heavier metal let into the deck or use a cleat where you weld the legs of the cleat to the deck. The same advice applies for parts, such as stand-pipes, that you weld to the hull deck and superstructure. If the area needs reinforcing, then let a section of heavier plate into the area rather than weld another piece over the first. Failing to follow this advice will allow corrosion to form between the two layers of plate. Make sure the chainplate angle is in line with the load of the shroud or stay. Check fore-and-aft angles and loads, as well as the obvious athwartship ones. All loads of this type should be in sheer, avoiding all twisting or bending loads.

CLEATS

Make sure your cleats are adequately sized to handle your lines. Cleats may be made of aluminum or stainless steel. Painted mild-steel cleats would corrode due to the paint being worn off when the cleats are in use. Try to position them in such a way as to minimize the chances of stubbing your toes. In many cases, cleats have to be in a certain location, but you can usually manage to avoid placing them in the most dangerous places. Fastening the cleats to decks, coamings, and cabintops should be a simple matter of welding them in place.

Always use 316 stainless steel when making these items. It's worth taking the fabricated cleats to a metal shop and having them polished, as the finish will be long-lasting. One of the many advantages of building a metal boat is the fact that you can weld most cleats and fittings directly to the deck or other surface. Your plans may include the exact locations of the sail-handling cleats or you may confer with your rigger and/or sailmaker for suggestions in this area. In a sailboat, you'll have a variety of cleats including ones to accept the various sheets and halyards.

Both sailboats and powerboats require mooring cleats and they should include one each side in the following locations: one near the bow, one amidships, and one near the stern. The midship pair are sometimes omitted, which is a pity because they're often the most useful. If your boat is over 40 feet (12.19 m) long, you may require additional mooring cleats. It's always advisable to install a substantial cleat on the foredeck; it can be used for towing and other purposes. Even if you have a substantial anchor winch, the centerline cleat can be used when setting additional anchors. Always make sure that

This bollard doubles as a ventilator.

any cleats, bitts, or other fittings welded directly to the deck or superstructure are fully welded to the surface. Don't leave gaps where moisture can creep underneath and start corrosion. That advice applies to all fittings welded to a deck, coaming, or cabintop. A thickened section of plate under the cleat or other fitting may be required; in any case, this is just good practice.

BITTS AND BOLLARDS

On our boat, we prefer mooring bitts to cleats. Cleats are fine for handling sails, but when you have the weight of the entire boat plus a surging action wanting to separate a mooring line from your boat, a set of bitts is preferred. Six of these fittings should suffice on boats up to 55 feet (16.76 m) in length: one pair up near the bow, one pair amidships, and another near the stern. These bitts make the best termination for your mooring lines and will provide a perfect arrangement should you decide to take your sailboat through some of the canals and waterways of Europe, the U.S., and elsewhere. As with all stainless fittings that you can weld directly to the boat, don't forget to paint an inch or two (25 mm to 50 mm) up the sides of the stainless fitting to ensure no corrosive action will take place between dissimilar metals.

Bollards are deck fittings featuring a tubular base with a solid pin set at right angles—a sort of cross between a cleat and a set of bitts. One advantage of bollards is that they're popular on powerboats, so they're easy to obtain ready-made in stainless steel. Of course you can make your

Stainless-steel bollards are sensible and attractive on any metal boat.

This bollard and fairlead combination works well; it would be improved if built from stainless steel.

own from tube and solid rod. As with many fittings, you may decide to purchase one as a pattern and then make as many as you require, thus saving yourself a great deal of cash.

STANCHIONS AND GUARDRAILS

Stanchions and guardrails as well as pulpits and pushpits, are best fabricated from stainless steel. However, if the cost is too daunting, then galvanized and painted ones will be the next best thing. Some builders construct stanchions and chainplates as a combination fitting. In our opinion, it's better to separate them as they need strength in different areas. There's much discussion as to whether you should weld the stanchion directly to the deck or mount it on a plate that is, in turn, bolted in place. Some experts suggest that an oversized pipe socket to accept the stanchion be welded to the deck. Our opinion is that provided the stainless variety, as mentioned earlier, are painted at the attachment point, then these and mild-steel stanchions are best welded directly to the deck.

If you want the ultimate connection, you could have 2½-inch (35 mm) square plate, or a disk of ¼-inch (6 mm) plate, beveled on the edges so the thicker portion stands proud of the deck and then welded in place. The stanchion is simply welded to this thicker, reinforced, and raised plate. The water will naturally run off the area of the stanchion-deck join and minimize the chance of corrosion.

If your boat is large enough, you may wish to consider installing guardrails as opposed to stanchions and wire lifelines. Any sailboat over 40 feet (12.19 m) should be able to "carry" them. Any powerboat, even of smaller size, seems to look right when fitted with guardrails. To look right, the rails should be of smaller diameter than the stanchions. Rails of about 75 percent of the stanchion size seem about right. The diameter of the stanchions will depend on the size of boat. Any "security fence" around the perimeter of your decks that is less than 28 inches (711 mm) high is dangerous. You need stanchions that are 36 inches (914) mm high. This is perfect for security, but would look too high on some boats.

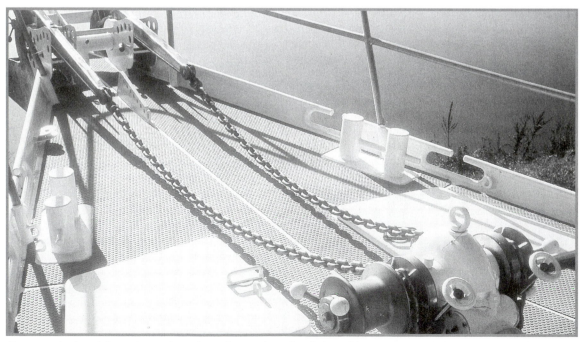

If you need a break from the main project, then make a few fittings. These were made by Herbert Fritz for his steel Roberts 53. Fritz must have done a good job; this boat has now successfully completed a circumnavigation.

If possible, combine your stanchions with at least a low bulwark, and this will keep the apparent overall height of the stanchion/bulwark within reasonable limits. Don't forget access in your stanchion arrangements. You should have a "gate" each side, near the most obvious exits from your sidedecks. If you opt for stanchions and wire lifelines, make sure you have either small-diameter pipe fitted through the stanchions to carry the wire, or use some method to avoid water getting into the stanchion and causing corrosion at the base. Use flexible stainless-steel wire for lifelines; galvanized wire will not last long. The off-the-shelf, plastic-coated variety is dangerous.

PULPIT AND PUSHPIT

The pulpit and pushpit can be built of the same metal as the stanchions but use pipe of a slightly larger diameter. You can study other boats as to the latest trends and designs of these items. The pulpit is best arranged with an opening in the most forward area so you can exit and enter the bow when moored bow-to, as is necessary in some areas. This arrangement will combine well with a short bowsprit or platform. The pulpit can

This is one way to make a strong and inexpensive forestay fitting; again, stainless steel would improve its durability.

be a little higher than the guardrails without spoiling the overall line of the hull.

The pushpit, or stern pulpit, needs a gate for aft access to the boarding ladder or swim platform. Before designing and fabricating this safety feature, study other boats similar in size and style to your own.

BOW FITTING

Your bow fitting is best constructed from 316-grade stainless steel. Your plans may include specific details on how to construct this item. On a sailboat, the bow fitting will most likely include tangs for the forestay and an attachment for the furler or tack of the jib.

Depending on the arrangement for your boat, you may

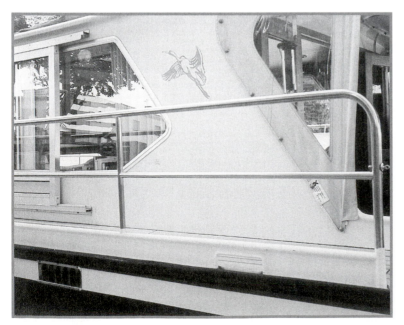

Stainless-steel pipe rails, pulpits, and pushpits are recommended on all metal powerboats and can be a great asset on larger sailboats.

This sturdy stainless-steel bow fitting is up to the job.

not become mixed. Generally the main anchor, a plow or Bruce style (no relation!), is kept stowed on bow rollers or a small bowsprit, ready for use. The secondary anchor, usually a Danforth type, is stowed in the locker along with its rode. Some anchor lockers are arranged so that the chain runs through a tube down toward the center of the boat. This puts the weight where it can contribute to the stability of the vessel. If you decide to arrange your anchor chain in this manner, make sure that you can reach into the locker to assist the chain to stow neatly. Also ensure that it can't get loose in the event of a knockdown. You may want to consider carrying a third anchor at or near the stern, where it can be useful when you wish to anchor fore and aft.

HAWSE PIPES

Formerly the preserve of larger vessels, hawse pipes are now often seen on powerboats as small as 30 feet (9.14 m). If you carry only one bow anchor, and your hawse pipe is only on one side, it can be a problem when you're anchoring in certain wind and sea conditions, as the chain can chafe the bow. In a smaller boat, the hawse pipe should be located in the bow itself and placed on the centerline. Where you are able, have an anchor locker with a bulkhead down the centerline, and then carry two bow anchors, each in their own hawse pipe. This arrangement is worth considering, especially on a larger powerboat. Make sure the actual hawse pipe is large enough for the chain, about three to four times the diameter of the chain should be about right. Don't install a hawse pipe so that the chain has to make difficult bends before it stows itself in the chain locker.

When your boat is fitted with one or more hawse pipes, you'll need to prevent the anchor from damaging the hull paintwork or even scoring the hull. A light stainless-steel plate is usually placed around the area where the anchor will reside. In addition, you should fit a floating ring that stows permanently over the chain and lies between the anchor and the hull.

also incorporate rollers, one for the anchor chain and another for the anchor line. If you wish to stow the anchor on the bow roller, then a Bruce or CQR anchor may be arranged in that manner.

ANCHOR LOCKER

You will want to decide if you want a self-draining anchor locker, which has drains at the bottom of the locker and which is sealed off from the rest of the boat. Water can drain out; it can also flush in through the drain holes. I prefer a locker that drains through a pipe to the bilge where the bilge pump is located.

Many cruising boats carry two anchors in the forward anchor locker; however, very few are divided so that the anchor lines and/or chains do

Especially in a sailboat, we'd favor a small bow platform or bowsprit, and then the anchor and chain would be more accessible at all times.

LENGTHENING A METAL BOAT

We should at least mention the possibility of your altering a boat you already own, or one you can acquire at the right price. By "altering" we mean shortening or lengthening an existing boat. (In our opinion, widening a boat is almost impossible, so unless you have some information that has eluded us all these years, then you had best put that idea aside.) It's simpler to make these alterations to a boat built of metal than it is to make similar modifications to one built of fiberglass or timber.

It's uncommon to consider shortening an existing powerboat, so we will confine our remarks to the possibility of lengthening a sailboat or powerboat. Steel, aluminum, and copper-nickel all present about the same amount of difficulty, so they can be considered at the same time. There is one exception to the above statement. This concerns the shortening of barges and similar vessels. Many Dutch and other European working barges are shortened when they are converted from commercial to pleasure usage.

Thousands of large metal powerboats have been lengthened. This usually occurred when the owners decided that it was less expensive, or in some way more desirable, to increase the size of the boat than to buy or build a new vessel. There are many factors to be considered before you commit to changing the dimensions of your metal powerboat. First, where to make the addition. Many owners often mistakenly believe that to increase the length is just a matter of adding a few feet to the stern. Although many boats are lengthened in this manner, it's worth exploring all the options before making the final decision on how you'll tackle the project.

It is possible but expensive to add sections into the center or other than the aft end of a metal vessel. People who have the means to buy large boats and then totally gut the interior some-times take the opportunity to lengthen the boat at the same time. Remember, any vessel that's lengthened should have a new, complete set of stability and other relevant calculations prepared for the altered vessel.

If you opt for extending the stern, here are a few items you will need to consider. Will the engine room need to be moved? How about the rudder(s)? How will they be affected? And the steering location: will the new longer hull be harder to steer from the current steering station? How will the hull lines be continued and how will this affect the handling? Will the fore-and-aft trim of the vessel be affected, and how can we overcome any problems in any of these areas? Many of these factors will need to be discussed, preferably with the original designer, or, if that's not possible, then you should seek the help of a suitably qualified naval architect.

The reason that extending a powerboat by lengthening the stern is such a popular option is that usually it means that the interior accommodation, electrics, and plumbing can be similarly extended without disturbing the existing arrangements.

It's harder to lengthen a sailboat. Here we have a whole new set of factors to consider. The position and length of the keel, the amount and location of the ballast, the location of the auxiliary engine and the possible increase in the size of the rig are all factors that need consideration when increasing the size of a metal sailboat. If you plan changes in these areas, you'll need the services of the original designer. It's our opinion that lengthening a sailboat is probably not worth the trouble.

ALTERING CABIN STRUCTURES

The cabin is one area where you may be able to improve your existing boat. First, on no account raise the overall height of the cabin structure without seeking professional advice. You may totally destroy the handling and performance of your vessel if you raise the cabintop beyond

Most powerboat hulls need some form of spray rails to prevent water climbing up the bow or throwing excessive spray back over the crew. You will be surprised just how effective a rail such as the one pictured here can be in keeping spray off the decks.

sensible limits. The most common change made to cabins is the addition of a pilothouse. While this can be a worthwhile addition for many boats, it's one that needs to be carefully designed before changes are made. Keep it light and keep it low. See Building or Adding a Pilothouse, chapter 9.

BALLAST AND TRIMMING

It's impossible for the designer to know how the builder keeps track of the materials used to build the boat. Only the builder knows what has been added to the basic construction materials and gear specified in the plans.

If you want your ballasting to be correct, and as efficient as possible, keep accurate records and generally follow the designer's recommendations as closely as possible. It may be worth having the hull weighed before installing the ballast. The crane that is used during the moving of the boat from the building location to the launching site can often undertake this weighing operation. Perhaps a small side trip to a weighbridge could achieve the desired result. With the minimum of planning, it should be possible to add the ballast just prior to launching the boat.

When you do install the ballast, make sure that you install it by weight not by volume. Weigh each portion as it's installed in the keel. This is a time-consuming and thankless task, but you may be rewarded if you need to trim the boat, add tankage, or otherwise change the ballast arrangements.

In a metal sailboat or trawler yacht, the keel sides, the bottom of keel, and the web floors all form part of the ballast. In some cases, such as in ultra-shallow-draft boats, the bottom plating is considered to be part of the ballast. Back in the early 1970s, we didn't make this sufficiently clear, and this caused some builders of our designs to install more ballast than was intended. Fortunately, this didn't materially harm the handling of the boat. But there's no doubt that in many cases carrying too much ballast can detract from performance.

No matter who designed your metal boat, make sure you know how much ballast has to be added in addition to that already created by the keel and supporting structure. Of course, this advice mainly applies to steel and copper-nickel hulls; aluminum hulls require the full amount of ballast quoted by the designer. In any case, during the construction stage, it's wise to only install between 70 and 80 percent of the total ballast required. The remainder can be added for trim ballast, as and when required.

Another point to remember is that there may be some confusion over the quoted displacement/ballast ratio. Total the amount of the "naturally acquired" ballast and the added ballast before making any judgmental comparisons in this area.

Over the years, many different materials have been used as ballast. Today the choice lies between lead, cast iron, and scrap steel. Cast iron is now about the same price as lead. It's mostly used as bolt-on ballast, and consequently it's less suitable for metal boats. The designer may have already chosen your ballast material after taking its relative center of gravity into account when figuring the stability of the vessel. Always consult the designer before making any changes to the amount, type, and location of ballast.

Some builders have found it convenient to install the ballast at an early stage. If you're building upright, it may be a good idea to install the bulk of the ballast before the final bottom plate is installed. This means you don't have to carry the ballast material up and over the sides of the hull. Some builders have constructed the keel separately and, after setting it in position, have installed most of the ballast before even setting up the frames. All these factors should be taken into consideration before you decide to build your hull upright or upside down.

Lead Ballast

Lead weighs 710 pounds per cubic foot (3,466 kg per cubic meter), and this, combined with its low melting point of 621°F (327°C), makes it the superior ballast material. If you're building on a tight budget, then all of the advantages may be purely academic. The price for lead will vary from one dealer to another, so it's worth shopping around. You may collect scrap lead from a variety of places, including garages and tire outlets where those small lead weights are used to balance the wheels on your car.

When considering the ballast material, the boat design will be a factor: shoal draft favors lead ballast, while a deeper draft accommodates the scrap-steel option. No matter which draft option you choose, lead is best. Lead ballast is more expensive than steel, but it can be installed in a smaller space, which, in turn, will leave more room for the stowage of stores and perhaps the installation of additional fuel and water tanks. As mentioned elsewhere, the storage of canned goods and other relatively heavy stores under the sole is a very practical idea. The weight is located

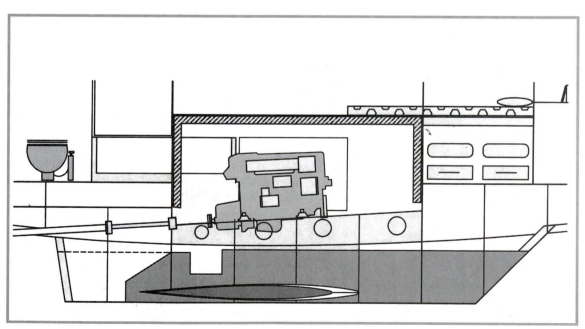

Wing keels are relatively easy to fabricate on a steel boat.

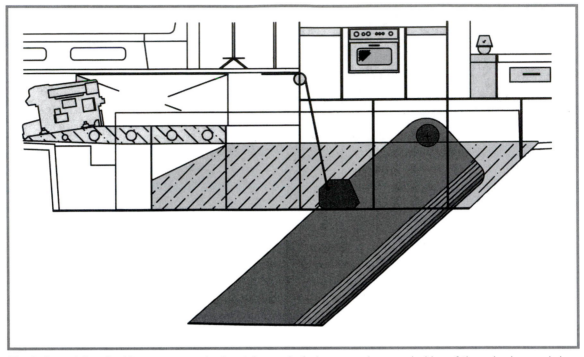

The ballasted drop keel is one way to obtain minimum draft; however, the complexities of these keels are obvious even in the simplest form, as shown here.

where it will provide some benefit as ballast. The stores are much less likely to be thrown about in rough weather than are similar stores located above the waterline.

Another reason to choose lead ballast is that it will definitely add to the resale value of your boat. It should be remembered that almost every boat is sold sooner or later. By installing lead ballast, you're helping to protect your investment.

The lead may be installed in standard pigs, or melted and recast into shapes of a suitable size and weight and then installed into the keel. Melting lead can be a hazardous operation, and you should take the utmost care when you're handling it. Wear gloves and other protective clothing including a breathing mask. Masks used for avoiding paint fumes are not suitable, and special respirators are available that will filter out the lead particles and gases given off during the melting process. Totally avoid the fumes that lead gives off.

To melt lead, you'll need some form of ves-

sel to hold the chunks while heat is applied. The type, size, and complexity of the melting pot will depend on the amount of lead you plan to melt. Less is better, so try to choose one of the installation methods that requires the least melting before the lead is installed in the keel. For example, lay large chunks or pigs in the keel and then use small amounts of molten lead, poured over and around these larger pieces, to solidify the whole mass. For large melting jobs, an old cast-iron bath is ideal. They used to be available from the wreckers. These days, however, many of these older items are prized as artifacts and are no longer available for other uses.

If you have to construct a melting pot, it should be about 2 feet, 6 inches (762 mm) in diameter, or 2 feet (610 mm) square. Make it about 3 feet (914 mm) high and raise it about 2 feet, 6 inches (762 mm) from the ground. Either use strong pipe legs or a similar very strong structure to support your melting pot. The melting pot will need to have plate walls at least ¼ inch (6 mm)

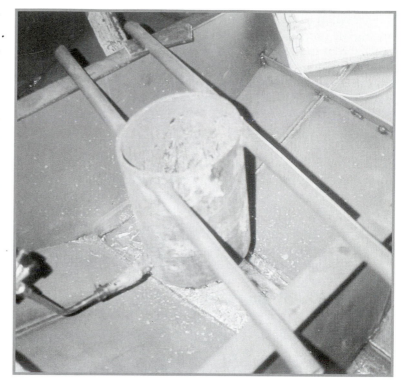

This homemade lead-melting device is fine for installing the final, relatively small amounts of molten lead used to bind the lead pigs into one mass.

thick. Don't use oil drums or similar containers; they'll be far too light for this purpose. At the bottom of your melting pot, you'll need to install a tap or valve to allow the molten lead to be drawn off as required. A pouring bucket or ladle will be needed to transfer the lead to your mold or directly to the keel for pouring over the large solid pieces that you have already installed.

If you require only a relatively small amount of molten lead, then the melt-and-pour-in-place arrangement may suit you better than a melting pot situated some way from the keel. As lead solidifies rather quickly, and as you need to eliminate voids between your large pieces and the molten filler lead, make sure you install the lead in small amounts and in a sequence that will achieve the desired result. There should be no voids, and using this method the lead can be "welded" together.

Many builders have made patterns of the keel areas between the webs where ballast is to be installed. Heavy pine planking, say 1¼ inches (35 mm) thick, can be used to build a mold for these blocks of ballast. Using a well-constructed melting pot and an adequate ladling or pouring bucket, pour and mold each section. A lifting eye or wire loop can be installed in the top of each lead block and the completed ballast section is then installed in the keel. The keel will still need to be lined to avoid the lead's interacting with the steel, aluminum, or copper-nickel. (See below.)

Never melt the bulk of the lead directly into any keel, not even a steel one. The heat of the molten lead will surely buckle the sides of the keel. The heat could ruin the shape and structure of the keel. Lead can be cut, but with some difficulty; it tends to clog up the teeth of a saw. Some boatyards have used chainsaws to cut lead; this seems to add one hazardous operation to another. An oxyacetylene torch can be used to burn off chunks of the material. You can weld angle or plate over the ballast so that in the event of a 'knock-down' you can be sure that it stays in place. Another method of securing the ballast is to cut holes in the web floors and allow the ballast to extend from one keel compartment to the next. There are many simple and ingenious ways to ensure that the ballast is effectively one unit and will stay in place under all conditions.

It's desirable to make some provision to separate the lead ballast from the interior of the keel plating. This applies to all metals. One method is to coat the inside of the keel with tar epoxy, but watch out for the fumes as you install the molten lead ballast. Another method is to line the inside of the keel with sheet zinc before installing the ballast. The zinc will melt when the molten lead touches it, and will float up the insides of the keel, giving the inner surfaces a coating and protecting them from any interaction with the lead. Bitumastic is another material that has been successfully used to line the steel keel before the lead ballast is installed.

Ballast Mixes

It's possible to purchase ready-mixed ballast, usually in granule form. This ballast is very easy to install but, because it has been "processed" for your convenience, it's relatively expensive. A check of the classified advertisements in your local boating magazines should reveal the suppliers of this type of ballast.

Scrap-Steel Ballast

If you're installing scrap-steel ballast, you should obtain the largest possible pieces of material that you can conveniently place between the webs in the keel of your boat. One material that's particularly suitable for installing in keels consists of the pins used in the tracks of crawler tractors and other earth-moving equipment. These track pins are usually about 12 inches (305 mm) long by 2 inches to 3 inches (50 mm to 75 mm) in diameter, and have proven in the past to be ideal as ballast material. The pins may be set either on end or on their sides. You'll need to insert small steel rods in between the round pins to achieve as solid a mass as is possible.

When using scrap-steel ballast, it's most desirable that you obtain a ballast density of 350 pounds per cubic foot (1,708 kg per cubic meter). This is a minimum figure, and it may be useful to make a test "brick" of the materials you have available. Weigh the brick to make certain it reaches the proper density. If you use scrap-steel punchings, you may have a problem in reaching the desired density, so larger pieces of metal are preferred. Railroad track, combined with other steel materials, may be suitable.

After the scrap-steel ballast has been installed, and small pieces of steel have been added to ensure a minimum of voids, it will be necessary to bond the whole mass together. You must be sure not to trap air in the ballast mix, otherwise you'll have corrosion problems with the ballast. If you have voids in the ballast, bilge water will find its way to the lowest point and it can set up a corrosion process that may remain undetected until serious damage is done, either to the ballast itself or, more importantly, to the keel. Hot pitch or similar material can be poured over and into the ballast and it will effectively find its way into the same voids that would harbor bilge water. The pitch will fill and seal off the voids and prevent corrosion problems. Tar epoxies, or other suitable epoxy materials that have been thickened with suitable fillers, can be used in place of the hot pitch. This would give a superior, but more costly result.

The pins from crawler tractors make excellent ballast in boats able to accept the lesser density of steel ballast.

Most Spray designs will accept scrap-steel ballast, thus considerably reducing the cost of the hull. This round-bilge steel Centennial Spray 38 was built in Sweden.

Securing the Ballast

In the past, some builders have used cement (or concrete) for bonding the lead or steel ballast and locking it in position. We have often warned against this practice, and recently have been made aware of two examples where the cement caused the steel to rust out from the inside. In one case, this caused the loss of the boat and, in the other, all the bottom plating had to be replaced. *Never use cement or concrete in your ballast mix.*

After the ballast is installed (except the trim ballast) you may consider welding L-angle or other reinforcing across the top of it. Some builders have plated over the ballast. The timing of this operation is difficult as you need to have

the trim ballast installed, and by this stage you have all of the exterior paintwork completed. The welding of the plate over the ballast will disturb your paint job. Careful planning is necessary to overcome this and other scheduling problems.

When you've completed the installation of the primary and trim ballast, you can seal off the top of the ballast with epoxy filler troweled to a smooth finish. A thin plywood liner could be used to complete the finish of this area above the ballast, making an ideal storage compartment. You'll need to make provision for the flow of bilge water. In modern, well-maintained metal boats, the amount of bilge water will be small and mostly caused by preventable condensation.

16
CHOOSING THE DESIGN—SAILBOATS

Before buying or building your metal boat you should pause and ask yourself why you want a boat and what you will do with it. For what it's worth, during 35 years in the marine industry we've found that most women would prefer a power-boat, while most men prefer sail. Be sure to discuss the decision thoroughly with your partner or family before writing any big checks. (The sizes of the boats I refer to here are between 35 and 65 feet [10.66 and 16.76 m]. My opionion as stated above is the result of discussing the preferences of power versus sail with literally hundreds of couples. The fact is that many women only *go along* with their partners when they want to have a sailboat. In many cases, eventually the lady gets her way or the male partner cruises alone.)

SIZE

When it comes to choices, size is an obvious place to begin. If you're building in aluminum, then you can build as small as you wish. If you choose steel or copper-nickel as your basic building material, then we feel that 24 feet (7.31 m) length on deck (LOD) is the practical minimum for both power and sail designs. On the other hand, you should only build as large a boat as you need. A well-equipped sailboat of 55 feet (16.76 m) LOD, can be handled by a fit male-female couple without outside assistance. There are many examples of sailboats of this size sailing the world with two persons thoroughly enjoying the cruising experi-

ence. In our opinion, this is the upper size limit that any couple or small family should consider. Our advice is that a boat between 40 feet (12.19 m) and 46 feet (14.02 m) is the perfect size, if you can afford it.

STABILITY

There are three primary kinds of stability: initial or form, positive, and ultimate.

Initial or *form stability* refers to the shape of the hull and the amount of effort it takes to heel the boat to the point of capsize. This factor ignores the ballast and other factors, which contribute to other forms of stability. A wide-beam boat with a boxlike hull would be expected to have the most form statility. *Positive stability* or *range of positive stability* is calculated by the designer and reveals at what point the hull would lose its natural tendency to remain or return to the upright position. This type of stability is measured in degrees, and an acceptable range for most vessels is between 110 and 150 degrees. *Ultimate stability* is the factor that measures whether the hull will return to its upright position from a complete capsize. This factor is more related to positive stability than to form stability.

First, let's make it clear that a high range of stability doesn't necessarily make a great cruising boat. Conversely, neither does a lower range of stability make a bad cruising vessel. Positive stability does play an important part in the success or otherwise of any cruising sailboat, but a high number is not the be-all and end-all that some would have us believe. It's important, yes. But the most important design feature? Not necessarily. There are many other equally important factors that go into making a good cruising boat. These include general hull shape, sea-keeping ability, initial stability, the number of openings in the hull and their placement, the integrity of the deck and superstructure, and many other design features.

The most important thing about stability calculations is that they must be accurate. Often, the numbers quoted in magazines and sales brochures are not correct. Many, if not most, are based on "light ship" conditions and most fail to take into account all the weight that accumulates in the real world of offshore cruising. If you feel that these calculations are important to you, be prepared to pay around $2,500 to $4,000 (£1,600 to £2,700) for a complete "Stability Book." When properly calculated by a qualified person, this extensive document can tell you a lot about your boat. If the boat already exists, you'll need to take certain measurements and supply a considerable amount of information to the person making the stability calculations.

How much stability should a cruising boat have? What is the right number? First, smaller boats need a higher number. For those who rely on this calculation, the farther you sail south or north, the higher the number should be. Taking a cross-section of

available sailboats, you'll fine that the range of positive stability is between 110 and 150 degrees from the vertical. In our own case, the Voyager 495 has a positive stability range of between 130 and 140 degrees depending on the keel configuration, rig, tank sizes and several other options. We feel that this is very satisfactory considering the size the boat and other factors.

PRISMATIC COEFFICIENT

This important hull calculation is often quoted, so we'll include some explanation here. If you wish to expand your knowledge of hull characteristics, performance prediction, fuel economy, etc., then refer to appendix 1, Recommended Reading, which lists books on both powerboats and sailboats. These books contain formulas, detailed hull analyses of various hull types, and other information.

The prismatic coefficient is usually indicated as PC or CP. It's a figure that represents the underwater portion of the hull. If you take a block

This round-bilge steel hull was built from the fiberglass lines, which feature a hollow "heel." This is difficult to build in metal and this type of hull/keel intersection should be avoided by all but the most experienced builders.

of wood that has the maximum length, width, and depth of the hull, with the shape of the midsection carved throughout its length, and then carve the underwater shape of the hull from this block, the PC is the relationship of the volume of the finished block as opposed to the block originally carved to the midsection shape throughout. Thus, the number represents the fullness or fineness of the ends of the hull. The more you carve away the ends, the smaller the PC number becomes. In sailboats, PCs can range from just below 0.50 for a fine racing hull to 0.60 for a motorsailer. Most cruising sailboats will have PCs that fall between 0.53 and 0.59. In powerboats, the figure will range from 0.60 to 0.75.

HULL TYPE

Developed Hull Surface

In chine hulls, some "round" will naturally be incorporated when the hull is built. In the days before computer-aided design it was necessary to develop the hull by triangulation or conic development. These processes were needed to ensure that the flat plating would indeed conform to any compound curves in the hull. This involved considerable calculation on the part of the designer or loftsman. The alternative was a very boxy hull without any compound curves. Computer design and lofting has changed all that. Now it takes just a few minutes to transform a set of straight sections into a beautifully faired, "developed" hull that will accept the plating with ease. My favorite expression is: the plating simply drapes over the structure that is formed by the frames and stringers. This assumes that you are building the hull upside down.

Single Chine

This hull form is best for planing or semidisplacement powerboats. It's also recommended for some displacement-hulled trawler types, where it can be used to advantage. Trawler-type motor sailers can sometimes benefit from using this hull form.

Double Chine

This configuration is often used as the basic shape for sailboats. One of the main attractions of this hull form is that, compared to single chine, it allows superior hull shapes to be built in metal without resorting to rolling the plate. Generally, these double-chine hulls take on a "developed" hull form and have considerable round in the sections up towards the bow. Double-chine hulls have their own beauty; but you either love or hate this hull form.

Radius Chine

Metal boatbuilding, especially of sailboats, changed forever when designers switched to computer-aided yacht design. One of the first benefits was the development of the radius-chine technique. This construction method could not be practically achieved without the aid of computer software and special training. We are forever in the debt of Grahame Shannon, who developed the Auto Yacht computer yacht-design programs that made this technique possible. While radius-chine methods can be used to build fiberglass or wood epoxy hulls, their biggest impact is in the ease with which they allow beautiful, rounded, metal sailboat hulls to be constructed. These hulls are usually impossible to distinguish from their fiberglass counterparts.

The secret lies in the computer fairing that provides a constant radius from the stern through to the bow. This allows plate that has been pre-rolled to a predetermined radius to be installed without fuss or the degree of difficulty associated with round-bilge hulls. The secret of radius chine is that it fairs the radius through the bow. Previous attempts at this type of hull form have tried to fade out the chine before it reaches the bow. This can result in an unfair or flat spot in the forward area of the hull.

The radius chine, as developed by Grahame Shannon, is the perfect metal boat hull-building technique, particularly suited to (but not restricted to) sailboats. As we have seen, excellent results can be achieved by any person with minimal metal-working experience. Full details on building hulls using this and other hull building methods appear in chapters 6, 7, and 8.

Other Chine Configurations

Before the advent of the radius chine, builders had sought to "soften" the double-chine hull by the addition of mini-chine panels, or by introducing rounded sections of split pipe at the chine. These softening techniques required a considerable increase in the amount of welding. Not to be confused with the foregoing is the alternative to use solid round bar of 1 inch (25 mm diameter) in place of the flat-bar chine stringer. The solid round can soften the chine, but it makes it more difficult to obtain a perfectly fair chine line. The round bar also needs special attention to prevent water lying on top of the chine bar inside the hull.

Some designers have designed multi-chine hulls that try to approximate a round-bilge form. We don't favor these many-chined hulls. They are expensive to build and usually, at least to our eye, give a fussy appearance. The popularity of double-chine hulls has been somewhat eroded by the development and ease of construction of the radius-chine hull form.

Round-Bilge Hulls

This method is best suited to sailboats and full-displacement, long-range powerboat hulls. This hull building method requires previous metal-working experience. It's possible for a

competent metal worker with little or no boat-building experience to produce a fair and attractive round-bilge metal hull.

There are relatively easy round-bilge hull shapes, there are virtually impossible shapes, and there's everything in between. Unless you're an experienced metal boat builder, avoid the difficult shapes, such as rounded "golf-ball" sterns, hollow-heel garboards, and the like. There are simpler shapes that will provide you with an easy-to-build, seaworthy, and attractive round-bilge metal hull.

Selecting the Hull Form

So, among these alternatives, which is the best hull form? There are several factors to consider, including the use you have in mind, ease and cost of construction, and estimated resale value. We

Note the rigging arrangement used on the cutter Spray of Del Quay, *a steel Spray 40.*

This photograph of a large round bilge steel sailboat clearly illustrates how a conical bow can be formed.

43, the Mauritius 43, and others of the same family. The above-mentioned designs were replaced by the popular Roberts 432. Other designs have been left out of some catalogs and lists simply because they just were not popular enough to warrant their inclusion. We give you these examples because you must be careful not to build or buy a metal boat (or any boat for that matter) until you're sure of its design history and the designer's current opinions. Most naval architects and yacht designers are very frank about the merits and shortcomings of their boats. The well-established designers can afford to be frank; they have many great boats to balance any less-than-successful designs.

would choose radius-chine because it has many advantages and no major points against it—in other words, a near-perfect sailboat hull configuration. However, we would add this exception: the Spray designs are not suitable for building in this technique, and we greatly admire the Spray and its derivatives. These boats can only be built with multichine or round-bilge hulls. (See the Spray Series sidebar, pages 206–14.)

Many hull types, especially the modern computer-designed variety, can be matched with either long or short keels. To be effective, a sailboat with a short or medium-length keel needs a skeg/rudder combination.

Make sure you are selecting a design that is not only proven, but also proven to be a satisfactory all-round performer. The smaller the crew in relation to the size of the boat, the more important it is to have a well-balanced hull, keel, and rig combination.

With our own cruising-sailboat designs, we have updated some; for example, the Roberts 53 was first designed in 1969, and now is more popular than ever. We doubt the owners of the original boats would recognize the design as it is today. Other updated designs include the Roberts

This German-built Spray 40 has been cruising for many years and is a fine example of the durability of steel as a boat-building material.

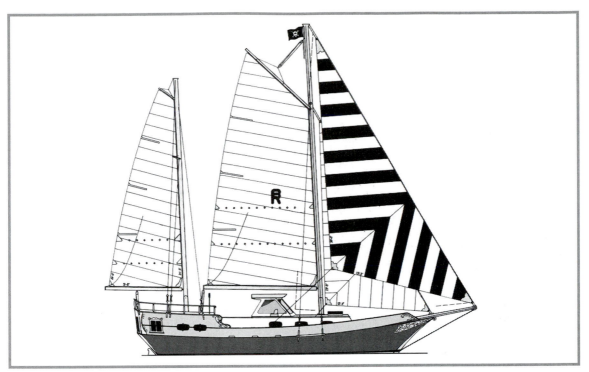

The Spray 40C is one of the most popular of the Spray range. Hundreds are cruising in all parts of the world. This boat can be built in steel, aluminum, or copper-nickel.

Ulrich Kronberg, editor and publisher of the German yachting magazine Der Palstek, at the helm of his owner-built Spray 40, Mirounga.

The Spray Series

Sailing Alone Around the World, Joshua Slocum's account of circumnavigating in his sloop *Spray,* is standard reading for any cruising sailor. Over the last 100 years, it has been the inspiration for many of those who go to sea in small boats. Some years ago, our design office was approached by a *Spray* enthusiast who wanted to know if we could prepare plans for the *Spray.*

For those of you not already familiar with the story, in 1892, Joshua Slocum, at age 51, was given an aging and decrepit sloop called the *Spray.* The captain spent the next few years rebuilding the vessel. He removed the centerboard and replaced almost every piece of timber in the hull and deck. All of the materials used were collected around Fairhaven, Massachusetts, where the vessel had lain in a field for several years. The *Spray's* lineage is clear when one examines photographs of old and still-sailing examples of the North Sea fishing boats that have worked off the coast of England and France for at least 150 years.

Slocum's *Spray* was reputed to have served as an oyster dragger off the New England coast. Slocum sought to improve the seaworthiness of his acquisition by adding freeboard so the vessel would be better suited to the deepwater sailing that he obviously had in mind.

After a year of commercial fishing on the Atlantic coast, and generally proving the worth of his new boat, Slocum decided to undertake a voyage that even today is not undertaken lightly. Slocum's trip proved a resounding success. Not only did he achieve what he set out to do—the first single-handed circumnavigation of the world—but he proved the many fine features of *Spray.*

We were not the first to consider a replica of *Spray*—copies of the boat had already been built in other materials. Replicas included the *Pandora,* which was built in Perth, Australia, in about 1908. This vessel sailed from Australia to New Zealand and then on to Pitcairn and Easter Island. From Easter Island, *Pandora* sailed for Cape Horn, arriving off the Horn in January, 1911. A week later, it was struck by a huge wave that rolled it over completely. (It's worth noting that it did right itself after being capsized.)

Replicas have also been built in the U.S. The late John G. Hanna, well-known naval architect of Dunedin, Florida, designed modified versions of *Spray* that were built in sizes ranging up to 100 feet. Another well-known U.S. boat designer and builder, Captain R. D. (Pete) Culler, built two (continued on page 208)

This steel Spray 27, MS Voncille, *was built by A. J. Culp, of Santa Maria, California, in 1989. This boat is now schooner-rigged and has cruised extensively along the California coastline.*

The steel multi-chine Spray 33 Bellavia was built in the U.K. and sailed to the U.S. She is now a regular sight cruising the waters of the Caribbean.

There are over 400 examples cruising throughout the world. This design is a smaller version of the original Spray and shares many of the same features. Either can be built in steel, aluminum, or copper-nickel. These designs are available in double-chine or round-bilge hull form. A large variety of deck layouts are available, including center cockpit, aft cockpit, and pilothouse versions.

Available sail plans for the Spray 33 include Bermudan cutter and ketch, gaff cutter, schooner or ketch, or junk schooner.

LOA	37'8" / 11.48 m
LOD	32' 11" / 10.03 m
LWL	26'7" / 8.13 m
Beam	12'0" / 3.66 m
Draft	4'0" / 1.22 m

One of the many advantages of the Spray design is that most models can be beached for bottom painting and maintenance.

(*continued from page 206*)
Sprays, one for his own use, and another for Gilbert Klingel. Captain Culler owned his Spray for 23 years and in various writings both he and Mrs. Culler spoke very highly of the Spray's seaworthiness and comfort.

We eventually uncovered enough information to convince us that the proposition was practical. About this time, we were fortunate in securing a copy of Ken Slack's book, *In the Wake of the Spray,* which provided a wealth of information. (Much of the information in Ken's out-of-print book is now included in our book, *Spray: The Ultimate Cruising Boat.*)

It's worth reflecting on the fact that *Spray,* as Slocum sailed her, would be unacceptable to most cruising sailors of today. First, Slocum's accommodations were basic. He had the after-cabin fitted out with two berths, a sea-chest, and book racks. The forward section of the vessel was used as a cargo hold, and nowhere were there provisions for the modern cooking and toilet facilities that are considered essential by today's sailors.

Because of the volume provided by Spray's hull, it was a simple matter to arrange alternate accommodation plans to allow for the varied tastes of today's cruising fraternity. During the design stage, we decided that instead of having the oversized cutwater at the bow, it would be preferable to fair in the forward sections above the waterline, and, hopefully, to improve the appearance. These minor changes would in no way adversely affect the sailing performance of the design.

Since those early days, we've gone on to design many new versions of *Spray.*

Spray 36A. This is one of several versions of this popular design. Over 400 Spray 36s have been built in steel and aluminum. Examples of this design are found in most popular cruising locations around the world.

LOA	41'0" / 12.50 m
LOD	36'10" / 11.22 m
Beam	12'0" / 3.66 m
Draft	4'0" / 1.22 m
Displ.	24,400 lb. / 11,068 kg
Hull form	chine or round-bilge

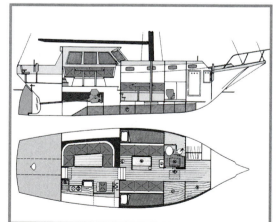

Spray 36B. This aft cockpit combined with a pilothouse arrangement has proved popular with those who prefer single-berth arrangements. A double could be worked into the forward area if preferred.

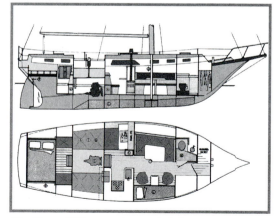

The Spray 36A, a center-cockpit layout.

**ROBERTS
CENTENNIAL SPRAY 34**

*A well-set-up gaff cutter can be a handy rig on smaller cruisers. This is a Centennial Spray 34.
These new Sprays have been designed to be built using round-bilge steel or aluminum.*

LOA	*34'9" / 10.59 m*
LWL	*30'11" / 9.45 m*
Beam	*13'0" / 3.96 m*
Draft	*4'9" / 1.45 m*
Displ.	*27,000 lb. / 12,247 kg*

Launched at Great Yarmouth, U.K., this round-bilge Centennial Spray 34, Joshua, *sailed to Scotland; it was ultimately bound for Portugal, where it was to be used for part-time charter.*

An experienced metalworker can build a round-bilge hull like this Centennial Spray 34.

The Centennial Spray 34 is rigged as a gaff schooner, but any rig can be used to power this boat. Custom accommodation arrangements may be drawn to your requirements. Center cockpit, pilothouse, and other similar arrangements are available for these new designs.

To celebrate the 100th anniversary of Slocum's record-setting voyage, we designed a new Centennial Spray series. These boats embody all of the desirable features of the Spray plus incorporate the improvements we have gleaned over 30 years of designing, building, and sailing these boats. Sprays are available from 34 to 75 ft. (10.36 to 22.86 m) and these designs are in correct proportions to the original Spray.

If you have the experience to build a round-bilge hull, you may opt for the Centennial Spray 38. This boat will accept a variety of rigs, including the all-out traditional gaff ketch shown here.

The Centennial Spray 38 was designed for round-bilge steel, aluminum, or copper-nickel construction. You could fit this hull with a pilothouse and choose between a center and aft cockpit configuration. The possibilities are endless.

LOA (hull)	38'6" / 11.73 m
LWL	33'1" / 10.08 m
Beam	14'1" / 4.29 m
Draft	4'10" / 1.47 m
Displ.	35,638 lb. / 16,174 kg

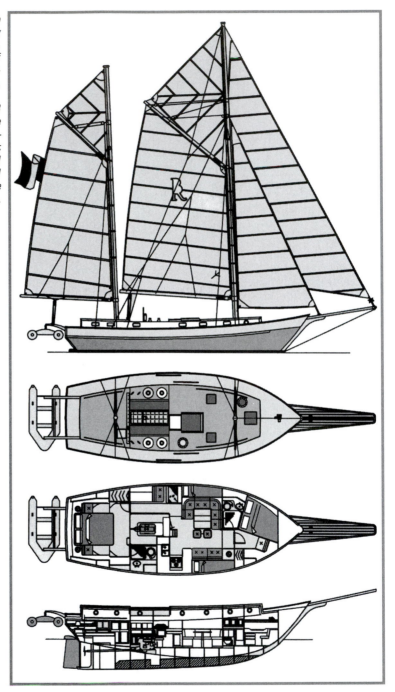

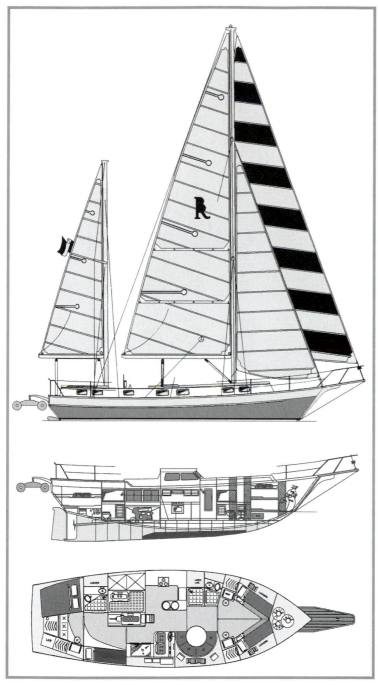

For those with a large family or thinking of charter work, the Centennial Spray 45 design comes with a variety of accommodation plans, including a center-cockpit version (shown), a pilothouse version, and even a trawler yacht capable of world cruising.

The Centennial Spray 45 was designed for round-bilge steel, aluminum, or copper-nickel construction. You could fit this hull with a pilothouse and choose between a center or aft cockpit configuration.

LOA (hull)	45'6" / 13.87 m
LWL	40'9" / 12.42 m
Beam	15'6" / 4.72 m
Draft	5'0" / 1.53 m
Displ.	49,000 lb. / 22,226 kg

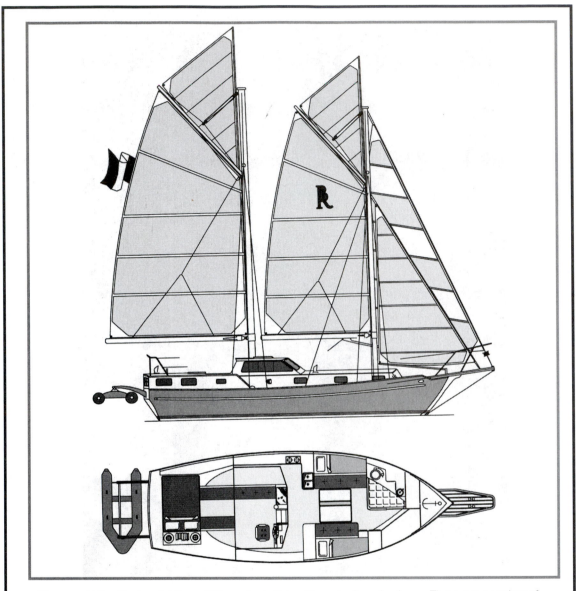

The round-bilge Centennial Spray 36 can be built in either steel or aluminum. There are a variety of rigs and accommodation plans available. The hull is designed to be built in all strip planking or using a combination of strip plank covered with one or more layers of veneer. The large-scale building plans and full-size patterns include all information necessary to build this boat, including patterns for casting the ballast.

LOA	36'4" / 11.05 m
LWL	32'4" / 9.85 m
Beam	13'0" / 3.96 m
Draft	4'3" / 1.30 m
Displ.	28,000 lb. / 12,700 kg

STERNS AND TRANSOMS

Each of the many types of sterns has its benefits and drawbacks. Although not strictly accurate in nautical terminology, the names stern and transom are often used to describe the after end of the hull. Not all sterns have transoms. In fact, not all transoms are at the stern. You will hear terms such as canoe stern, transom stern, rounded stern, poop stern, cruiser stern, chevron stern and, more recently, sugar-scoop stern. The shapes and names of the after end of the hull have changed over the past years. Some changes are caused by racing rules, others through fashion. Many sterns have been developed through experience, and these are the ones that concern us here.

Most sailboats today have either a traditional transom or reverse-transom stern. One relatively recent development is the advent of the sugar-scoop stern, which incorporates a vertical transom within a reverse-angled ending to the hull. This arrangement usually features steps for boarding from the water, or when the boat is moored stern-to. The reverse transom is also often fitted with steps built into the transom itself. In fact, steps are one of the most important benefits of the reverse transom.

On powerboats, the underwater section of the hull may be carried aft to form a boarding or swim platform. The underwater area is sometimes used for holding tanks, or for storing other liquids. If you wish to extend the underwater section of a powerboat hull in this way, consult the designer first. You may upset the fore-and-aft trim of the hull. The tankage may only partially offset the extra buoyancy provided by the extended underwater section.

Rounded or ball-shaped sterns are difficult to build in metal, so this feature is best left to the professional builder. If you're planning to build your own metal boat, make sure you select a design that has a "buildable" stern or transom.

BOW SHAPES

Before the advent of hulls faired and developed by computers, we often designed bows on metal powerboat hulls that were very difficult to build. During the 1960s and 1970s, flared bows were the norm on fiberglass hulls, so that is what our clients wanted. Today, most builders are more enlightened, and appreciate the beauty of a hull with properly developed forward sections. These bows, when combined with spray chines, have the same effect of keeping the boat dry. They are also much easier to build.

Junk or lug rigs are popular in some areas, and can provide an inexpensive and handy rig when installed on a Spray or similar design.

The PCF 40 is based on a trawler hull and is a true motor sailer. Many of these boats have been built and one sailed from Australia to Ireland—not a recommended use for this type of vessel.

The pilothouse can be reduced in height by lowering it into the main deck, if you're looking for a lower profile—there's adequate height in the engine compartment to accept any power plant you're likely to install (50–100 hp).

LOD	*40'0" / 12.19 m*
LWL	*35'0" / 10.67 m*
Beam	*13'0" / 3.97 m*
Draft	*4'3" / 1.3 m*
Displ.	*31,000 lb. / 13,950 kg*

Conical bows are less suitable for sailboat hulls than for powerboat hulls. In the powerboat, the cone starts with little or nothing at the forward end of the chine and ends at the deck. This gives an attractive, rounded shape to the bow, especially when seen in plan view. The resulting shape plays a part in keeping the foredeck dry, adds some buoyancy, and increases the deck space up forward. This extra space is often most appreciated when handling anchors and ground tackle in adverse conditions. Not strictly part of the bow, a short, "anchor-handling," U-shaped, pipe bowsprit is an asset on any sailboat or powerboat.

Sailboat bows come in all varieties; fortunately the few designs (not ours) that featured flared bows have long-since disappeared. Overhangs come and go out of fashion, and bow profiles vary from clipper, through straight, to convex. The bow on the design you decide to buy or build will already have been carefully styled by the designers, and our advice is not to try to improve on their efforts.

From station 2 forward, be very wary of sailboats that are too full, or have large flats; they may pound excessively. Some fullness is required in the bow sections, but it must be moderate. This is a good time to say that if you're considering a wholesome, and perhaps fast, cruising boat, then you should avoid the excesses, fashions, and rule bending of the racing fraternity. Nothing looks more dated, or is harder to sell, than a boat that was built to a racing rule that has long since passed into obscurity.

MOTOR SAILERS

What is a motor sailer? This term has been used to describe a variety of vessels, from a regular sailboat that happens to be fitted with an oversized engine to a powerboat that has a small steadying sail. The term motor sailer used to mean a boat best described as a 50/50, that is 50 percent motor and 50 percent sail. Occasionally, one would hear boats referred to as 60/40, or by some similar definition.

The Pacific Coast Fisherman 40 best expresses my interpretation of the term motor sailer. The PCF 40 is a single-chine, displacement trawler, a fishing-boat hull that has been fitted with a modest but effective sailplan—one recently sailed from Australia to Ireland. The *Spray*-type hulls, while being good performers under sail, also make excellent motor sailers and are noted for their precise handling under power.

More recently, you're likely to hear the term motor sailer applied to a variety of sailboats equipped with varying sizes of auxiliary power. Considering the term motor sailer in its more recent usage, we'd say that a boat fitted with an engine with more than 2½ hp per 1,000 pounds displacement, (1.86 kW per 454 kg) might be termed a motor sailer.

You should consider the hull form, rather than the general terminology, when you're making your decision as to which hull is most suitable for your type of cruising. If you're considering cruising in the canals of Europe, with the odd foray into the Mediterranean, then a motor sailer in its true context could be the right choice.

The Roberts 58 can be powered to qualify for the term motor sailer. *This radius-chine aluminum version was built in Belgium.*

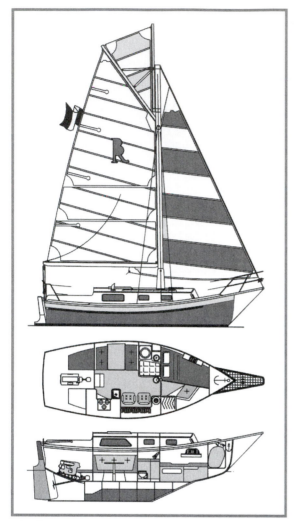

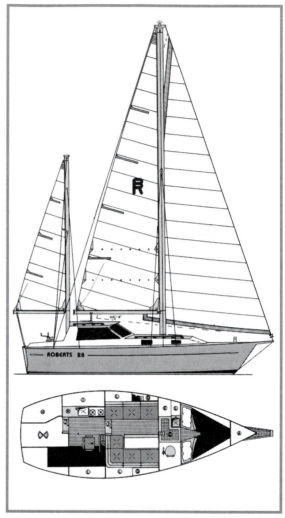

The Tom Thumb 26 uses "frameless" construction techniques in either steel, aluminum, or copper-nickel or a combination of any of these metals and is an ideal first project for a "go-anywhere" boat. This design has been built in several different configurations, and the plans include alternate accommodation plans and a choice of rigs, including Bermuda sloop, gaff cutter; and a cat rig.

LOA	25'11" / 7.92 m
LWL	23'9" / 7.24 m
Beam	10'4" / 3.15 m
Draft	4'0" / 1.22 m

This Roberts 28 can be built in steel or aluminum and makes a comfortable small pilothouse cruiser.

LOD	27'8" / 8.43 m
LWL	24'2" / 7.37 m
Beam	10'2" / 3.10 m
Draft	4'9" / 1.45 m

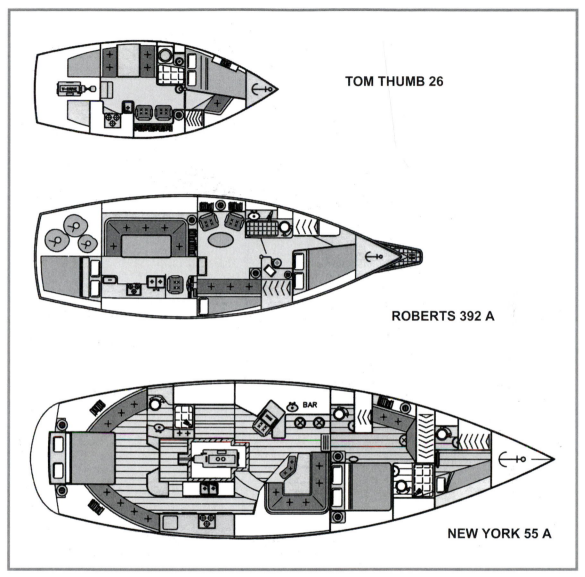

TOM THUMB 26

ROBERTS 392 A

NEW YORK 55 A

Accommodation plans for three different boats. The Tom Thumb 26 (top) is fine for two people, with room for the occasional guest or child. The Roberts 392 (center) has a pilothouse that determines how much space is available for other areas. The New York 55 (bottom) has plenty of room for all the elements of a comfortable, liveaboard cruising boat.

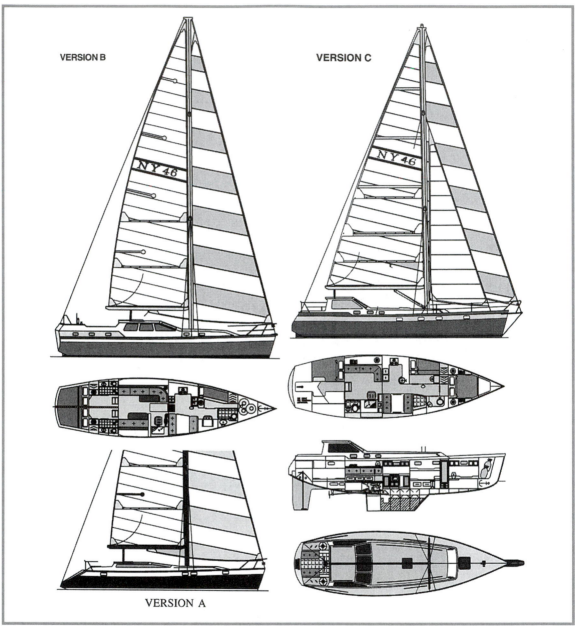

VERSION B

VERSION C

VERSION A

Three versions of the New York 46. Note the additional living space offered by a traditional transom; it accommodates twin double cabins in the stern. The smallest of the New York series, this design combines a fast hull with the ability to carry sufficient stores to qualify her as a proper cruising boat. There are several accommodation and deck layouts to choose from, and a variety of sail plans have already been designed for this boat. It can be built in aluminum, copper-nickel, or steel.

LOA	46'10" / 14.28 m
LWL	43'5" / 13.24 m
Beam	13'1" / 3.99 m
Draft	7'6" / 2.29 m
Displ.	42,972 lb. / 19,492 kg
Ballast	12,750 lb. / 5,783 kg
Sail area	1,200 sq. ft. / 111 sq. m
Aux. power	85 hp
D/L Ratio	235
S/A Displ. ratio	16.5

A multi-chine Roberts 43 surfing in moderate weather in the Pacific.

This steel, owner-built Roberts 432 is currently cruising in the Mediterranean.

This beautiful Roberts 434 radius-chine hull was built in the U.K.

This steel Roberts 43 was built in Germany by Willi Jansen and sailed to the U.S. Sequana is currently cruising in the Caribbean.

One of the most popular designs, the Roberts 432 makes an ideal family cruising boat. This design can be built in radius-chine or multi-chine steel or aluminum and comes in a variety of versions and accommodation layouts.

This design replaced the Mauritius and Norfolk 43, which were in production for over twenty years. This design is ideal for building in steel, copper-nickel, or aluminum and includes several versions featuring different accommodation and sail plans. The 432's long-keel configuration combined with a heel-supported rudder makes this boat eminently suitable for serious offshore cruising.

LOD	43'11" / 13.4 m
LWL	38'0" / 11.6 m
M	13'6" / 4.10 m
Shoal draft	5'3" / 1.60 m
Regular draft	6'0" / 1.80 m
Displ.	29,850 lb. / 13,539 kg

For those who prefer a short keel and separate skeg, the Roberts 434 is available in several versions and accommodation arrangements. It has been built in both steel and aluminum.

Over 500 Roberts 434 sailboats are in service around the world. Many of these boat have completed circumnavigations, including one sailed single-handedly by Major Pat Garnett, who completed his 27,000-mile (43,450 km) circumnavigation in only 218 days.

For those that prefer the medium fin–skeg arrangement, this is an excellent cruising boat that can be built in steel, aluminum, or copper-nickel.

LOD	*43'4" / 13.32 m*
LWL	*36'8" / 11.18 m*
Beam	*13'6" / 4.10 m*
Shoal draft	*5'0" / 1.52 mM*
Draft	*6'0" / 1.83 m*
Displ.	*29,859 lb. / 13,544 kg*

The Roberts 434 Baltic Rose *is one of many steel boats built by Put Veini in Riga, Latvia.*

This steel Roberts 44, Sifu, *was built in California, sailed to Florida, then crossed the Atlantic to Bristol, England, where it was refitted by its present owner John Clark.* Sifu *now has several Atlantic crossings to its credit, plus thousands of miles of island cruising.*

This steel, cutter-rigged, radius-chine Roberts 434 is another fine example of what can be achieved when building in metal.

Herbert and Petra Fritz, seen here during their successful circumnavigation. The happy smiles tell it all.

Any reasonably fit couple can handle this well-equipped Roberts 53 sailboat. Kallisto was built by Herbert and Petra Fritz, who sailed her around the world without assistance.

The steel Roberts 53 Henrike was built as a training ship for the Sea Scouts of Finland, who were more than satisfied with its 9-knot performance.

Another Roberts 53 radius-chine sailboat, built by Terry Erskine in Malta.

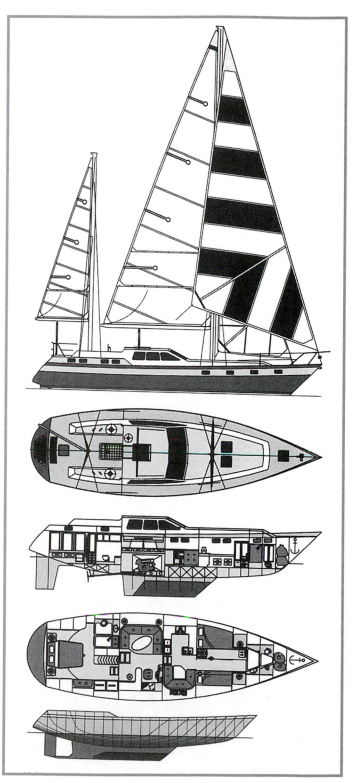

The Roberts 532 is the first of the Mark 2 versions of the ever-popular Roberts 53. It is available with a long cruising keel as well as the original long fin and separate skeg-and-rudder combination shown here. Both keel arrangements work well. You can build the 532 in steel, aluminum, or copper-nickel or a combination of these metals.

LOA	53'6" / 16.3 m
LWL	44'5" / 13.50 m
Beam	16'0" / 4.90 m
Shoal draft	5'6" / 1.68 m
Medium draft	6'0" / 1.83 m
Deep draft	7'0" / 2.13 m
Displ.	55,000 lb. / 24,950 kg

The radius-chine New York 55 is available in two versions and accommodation arrangements and has been built in both steel and aluminum. The hull design makes this is a very fast boat that will make extended passages with maximum speed and comfort.

LOA	55'8" / 16.97 m
LWL	50'10" / 15.50 m
Beam	16'7" / 5.05 m
Displ.	65,000 lb. / 29,484 kg
Sail area	1,420 sq. ft. / 132 sq. m
Aux. power	80–120 hp

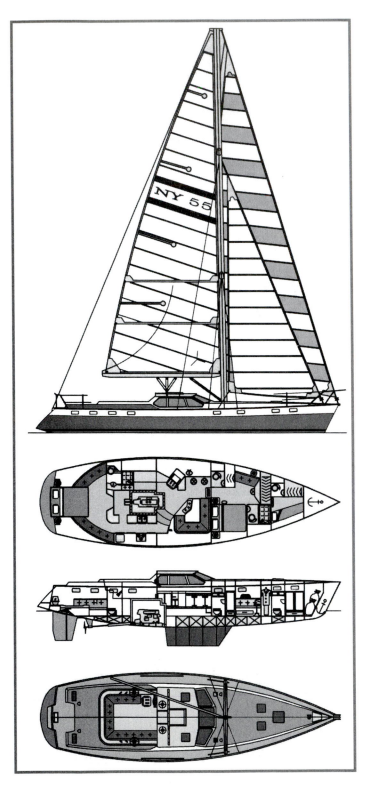

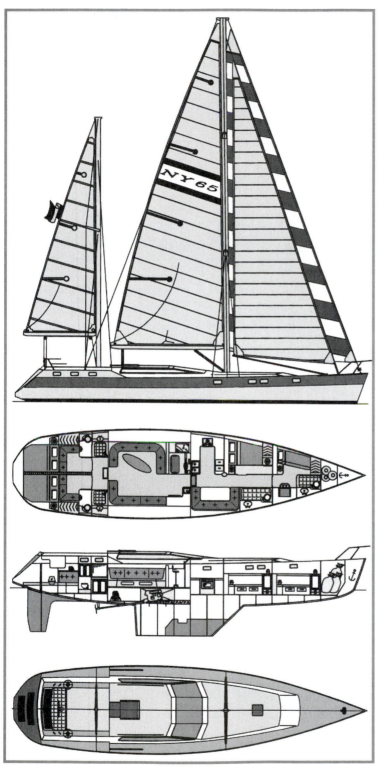

The radius-chine New York 65 has proved very popular, both as a live-aboard and a charter boat. Many have been built in radius-chine steel and aluminum. A kit version, known as the Voyager 655, is also available. This sailboat can be modified to suit a variety of sailing lifestyles. Both slimline and wide-body versions are available.

The prototype is the Omani 65. For fast family sailing, the New York 65 offers a variety of accommodation options and layouts.

LOA	65'0" / 19.81 m
LWL	60'8" / 18.53 m
Beam (Slimline)	12'6" / 3.81 m
Beam (Widebody)	16'0" / 4.88 m
Draft	various

17
CHOOSING THE DESIGN—POWERBOATS

As we get older, many of us consider moving across to power. If you're considering making this transition for any reason, you'll need to consider the relative merits of the different hull types.

Powerboat hulls are divided into three main types, namely, displacement, semidisplacement, and planing hulls. Each hull group can have many subtypes that are closer to one or other end of the spectrum. Considering each hull configuration in detail will reveal its benefits and disadvantages. Your choice will be influenced by your intended usage and the size of your wallet.

The size of your intended powerboat will also be a factor in your choice of hull type. If you're considering a large powerboat, then you will be less likely to choose a planing hull. Large fast, planing hulls require large expensive engines and use large amounts of fuel, so operat-

The builders of this Waverunner 24 stretched it to 26 feet and fitted it with a Dutch-style superstructure. The owners are delighted with this mini-cruiser.

ing costs are high. The long-distance cruiser may opt for a large displacement powerboat that travels efficiently at nonplaning speeds. Large powerboats require different skills and handling techniques, but the question of size is much the same as with a sailboat. Most craft up to 55 feet (16.76 m) can be handled by a couple. Again, our advice regarding practical size, cost, and maintenance requirements is the same. If possible, keep the size below 46 feet (14.02 m). If you're considering some serious long-distance cruising and need a boat with a minimum range of 3,000 nautical miles, then the 46-foot (14.02 m) boat can meet these requirements. But for various reasons you may want to go to 55 feet (16.76 m) and beyond. Once you've decided on a size of boat that will accommodate you and your intended regular crew, consider the "comfort factor." My advice is to figure out your current needs, think ahead to all the factors (such as your labor, the cost of maintenance, dock fees, and expected usage), then build as large as you can comfortably afford.

Potential speed will have a great bearing on which hull form you choose for your metal powerboat. If you want a boat that will achieve speeds of over 14 knots, you'll need to consider a planing hull. Some larger semidisplacement powerboats with waterlines of over 45 feet (13.72 m) can be made to perform at speeds of 16 knots but they do so at the cost of a great increase in fuel consumption.

Metal boats, including properly designed steel vessels, can plane. The Waverunner 342 is a good example of this. This all-steel boat of 36 feet (11 m) length on deck (LOD) weighs about 24,000 pounds (10,886 kg), and is powered by two 200 hp Volvo sterndrives. The Waverunner 342 cruises happily at 23 knots.

For economical cruising, consider the Waverunner 38. This is a semidisplacement hull that cruises at 6.8 knots and burns only 1.8 gallons (6.8 liters) per hour. At 8 knots, the fuel usage rises sharply to 6.6 gallons (25 liters) per hour. As you see, quite a price to pay for a small increase in performance.

DISPLACEMENT HULLS

Hulls at the displacement end of the range were the first to be developed and they go back to the beginning of time. As far as we know, the original log canoe and even the Ark were all displacement hulls.

The so-called heavy-displacement hulls include such craft as tugs and deep-sea trawlers. If you study these boats in profile, you'll notice that the stern rises above the waterline. The midsection of the hull is very full and deep in the water. The chine and buttock lines will reveal the full-bellied shape usually present in this type of hull. The heavy-displacement hull has to be able to carry great loads and, in the case of tugs, has to be able to get a great grip on the water in order to do its job properly. The hull speed of this type of vessel is generally less than that of other types.

The displacement hulls that concern us include most workboats, general fishing boats, and pleasure boats where speeds of 1.34 times the square root of the waterline length (or less) are sufficient to fulfill their operating requirements. For instance, let's consider a 40-foot (12.19 m) LOA motor cruiser with a waterline length of 36 feet (10.97 m). The square root of the waterline is 6, so multiply this by 1.34 and you arrive at a potential top speed of just over 8 knots. This is an economical speed for this vessel, taking into account the power required and the fuel used. Medium-displacement vessels can only exceed the 1.34 rule by adding excessive amounts of power.

If you already own an engine that has more horsepower than falls within the 1.34 calculation, then consider building a longer hull or one that employs semidisplacement-hull characteristics. Our own interest in displacement powerboat hulls goes back to the time we spent as young men in the Royal Australian Navy. We would often observe commercial fisherman out in weather that was uncomfortable even in our much larger naval vessel. These commercial trawlers were special. These observations were to stand us in good stead when later we designed many commercial fishing trawlers that were built to operate in the often very rough conditions off the Australian coast. These boats had to be capable of handling all types of wind and sea conditions and were often required to cross the shifting sand bars that are a feature of the entrances to many Australian ports and harbors. Bumping over sand bars in boisterous sea conditions and breaking waves was, and is, a way of life for the boats and the crews who fish these areas. Commercial trawlers have to be tough. We've used the same design philosophy and practice when designing offshore powerboats and trawler yachts.

When considering the various materials suitable for building your trawler yacht, the following are our thoughts on the matter. First, aluminum is often considered, and many fine boats have been built from this material. If you have a special case where the weight has to be kept low, then aluminum is worth your consideration.

Powering any displacement-hulled motor vessel follows much the same rules as those used to calculate the requirements for sailboats. The exception is that while the sailboat has its sails to

use in an emergency, the displacement motorboat totally relies on its engine. Most displacement powerboats are fitted with only one main power plant, so you should select yours with care. To estimate the horsepower requirements, start with an estimate of two horsepower per 1,000 pounds (454 kg) displacement. This should be taken as the minimum requirement.

You can gear your engine down to give *maximum performance at lower speeds* and reduce the number of horsepower required to drive your vessel. This option results in a larger-diameter propeller and there may not be room for it. There are other disadvantages to taking this minimum-power route. One day you may need extra power to get out of a sticky situation or tow another vessel. Conversely, a diesel engine likes to be worked moderately hard so it's not advisable to have an installation where only 50 percent or less of the power can be used without driving the stern down to an unacceptable level. If you want more power, then you may wish to consider a semidisplacement hull that can make better use of additional horsepower.

This steel Coastworker 30 is one of over 150 that have been built as commercial fishing boats.

SEMIDISPLACEMENT HULLS

As the name suggests, these hulls fit neatly in between the displacement and the planing-hull types. The stern of the semidisplacement hull is lower and designed to be always below water level. The hull can be the round-bilge form, but it's generally of the hard chine type. These hulls have less fullness than a full displacement hull. The chine line runs aft with a small curve from where it enters the water and

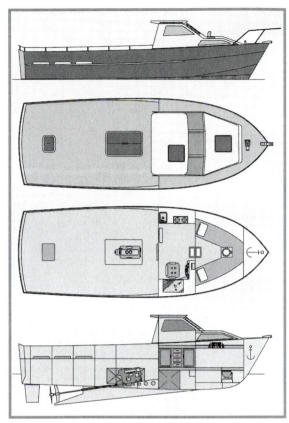

The Coastworker 25 and 30 are similar designs that can be built in aluminum or steel. There are trailerable versions as well as a choice between planing hulls and semidisplacement models. With all these choices, it's not surprising that one of these boats has made an excellent first metal boat building project for so many people.

on back to the transom. The hull sections are moderately V'd.

The semidisplacement hull will outperform the displacement hull-speed rules, and can accept additional power that it will convert to additional speed. There are limits to this benefit, however. Generally speaking, for vessels with waterline lengths of 30 to 60 feet (9.1 to 18.3 m), you should only consider semidisplacement hulls if your speed requirements do not exceed 12 to 18 knots.

As you have seen with displacement hulls, additional power is wasted. However, with semidisplacement hulls, the extra power may *often* be utilized to advantage. If you already have access

to a certain size of engine, or you already own the engine(s), then this factor may assist you in making the decision as to which type of hull best suits your situation.

As with displacement hulls, semidisplacement hulls can be driven harder, but at the expense of greater fuel consumption; and, again, the stern will tend to dig in at higher speeds. Existing semidisplacement hulls can be made to go faster with the same horsepower by adding trim tabs or planing wedges at the stern. The trim tabs and the wedges will be fixed after trials are completed to establish the best angle. In no case should you try to improve the performance of your hull in this manner without professional advice.

If you're building a semidisplacement hull, you should try to keep the weight down to reasonable levels. The semidisplacement hull is a good weight carrier, but it takes additional power and fuel to get the best out of an overweight boat of this type.

It requires excessive power to drive a semidisplacement hull faster than 1.5 times the square root of the waterline length in feet. For example, this type of hull measuring 36 feet (10.97 m) on the waterline would have a square

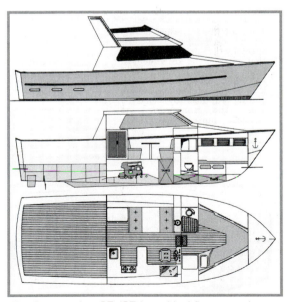

The Coastworker 35/37 is an ideal first powerboat project for any aspiring metal boat builder.

Another steel Coastworker 30; this one was built in Canada as a general-purpose workboat.

This Waverunner 28 was built by Put Veini, in Riga, Latvia, and is proof that smaller steel boats can be very successful. The WR28 low-profile motor cruiser features a moderately fast semiplaning hull that when correctly powered will perform best at speeds between 10 and 14 knots. The construction techniques to build this boat in aluminum, steel, or copper-nickel have been kept simple and are ideal for a first-time builder.

LOD	28'7" / 8.70 m
LWL	25'0" / 7.60 m
Beam	10'2" / 3.10 m
Draft	3'0" / 0.90 m
Hull form	semidisplacement

This Waverunner 342 was built by Filmar Engineering and achieved 23 knots with twin 200 hp Volvo stern-drives. The WR342 can be built as a semidisplacement or planing hull fast cruiser in steel or aluminum. This boat handles well under all conditions and makes a fine family boat.

LOD	35'11" / 11.0 m
LWL	32'0" / 9.75 m
Beam	12'3" / 3.73 m
Draft	2'3" / 0.68 m

root of 6. So, 6 times 1.5 equals 9 knots. A broad definition of planing is when a boat reaches a speed of twice the square root of its waterline length. Taking the 36-foot (10.97 m) example above, the square root (6) multiplied by 2 gives us a 12-knot planing speed. At this speed, the necessary horsepower and fuel requirements will turn a comfortable, economical cruising boat into an expensive proposition. Please note that the formula of twice the square root of the waterline is only the *start* of planing, and to make a semidisplacement hull reach a full (near-level) planing attitude will take considerably more

power and use more fuel than consumed by a similar-sized planing hull. The point is that it makes no sense to grossly overpower any semi-displacement hull. Figuratively speaking, you'll be just spinning your wheels. Or, in this case, your propellers.

Next, we have to consider the weight of the vessel. Weight in this instance means loaded displacement. This includes not only the weight of the finished boat but also that of fuel, water, stores, and people. In addition, you must include all those items that you bring aboard for a particular use or occasion, and which never leave the boat.

The many semidisplacement hulls range from a near-displacement vessel to almost a full-planing hull. The degree of rise in the chine or buttock lines aft will determine how fast the hull may be driven. Simply put, the more stern there is in the water at rest, the faster the hull may be driven. Overpowering a hull will cause the stern to drop and create a large stern wave. In certain instances, this wave can overwhelm the vessel.

PLANING HULLS

The planing hull is recognized by the straight run of the chine and buttock lines from amidships aft. The chine and the bottom of the hull V will generally run parallel to the waterline. The V in section will generally be constant from just aft of amidships to the stem. The angle between the baseline and the bottom of the V will be in the range of 12 to 20 degrees at the transom. As with other types of hulls, there's a great range of planing-hull variations. Usually, there's a planing strake or flat at the chine and often several planing strakes on the bottom of the hull.

You'll often hear the terms deep-V or moderate-V. They are meant to convey the amount of V, or deadrise, at the transom, and in addition to this they describe two different types of hull. A true deep-V hull will have 20 to 24 degrees of V at the transom, while a moderate-V hull is one with around 15 degrees of deadrise at the transom. Hulls with between 16 and 19 degrees can be described either way. Suffice to say that a hull with a transom deadrise of 20 degrees or over can be safely classified as a deep-V, and in our opinion should not be described as a long-distance or passagemaking cruising powerboat. Except for the boats in a few well-publicized ocean-crossing adventures by the very wealthy, boats *other* than those fitted with deep-V hulls have made most long-distance passagemaking cruises.

When deep-V hulls were introduced, they were touted as the last word in planing-hull design. These hulls do perform well at high speeds in rough water, which is one reason why they are so successful as racing powerboats. Deep-V planing hulls, depending on the particular design, can be driven at speeds in excess of 50 knots; however, most are designed to cruise at speeds between

The Waverunner 38 is a popular design for building in metal. This boat has been successfully built in aluminum and steel. Both the semidisplacement and planing-hull versions have been built in numbers exceeding 200 each. The new Euro 12 M was developed from this design.

30 and 35 knots. Modern computers can accurately estimate the power requirements and speed expectations of all hull types and are especially helpful in deciding the power needed for individual planing hulls.

Planing hulls are very popular. They make great pleasure boats if you are prepared to install sufficient power and pay the larger fuel bills. *Planing hulls do not like being operated at low speeds* as they throw a most unfriendly bow wave. Planing hulls are not the best of sea boats, especially in severe conditions.

This steel Waverunner 44 built in Oman, Arabia, as a fisheries patrol vessel illustrates the planing flat at the chine.

The Waverunner 44 has been built in many configurations, including as a fisheries patrol vessel in Oman, a drug enforcement patrol boat in the U.S., and of course as a family pleasure cruiser. It is ideal for building in steel, aluminum, or copper-nickel.

Shown here, the Waverunner Version B was used as the basic design for the Euro 14 M kit. You can build the WR 44 with the aft cockpit or aft cabin layout; both allow various accommodations. Additional versions are included in the basic plan and full-size pattern package. You can choose between semidisplacement or planing hulls. Over 250 boats of this design are already in service worldwide.

LOD	44'9" / 13.60 m
LWL	41'2" / 12.50 m
Beam	15'3" / 4.65 m
Draft	3'3" / 1.00 m

LOD	51'9" / 15.77 m
LWL	46'2" / 14.06 m
Beam	16'1" / 4.90 m
Draft	3'6" / 1.00 m

The semidisplacement hull form was chosen by the owner of this steel Waverunner 52. I have cruised on this boat and was favorably impressed by its acceleration.

The WR52 can be built with aft cockpit or aft cabin layouts. Also included in the plans are trawler yacht and sport fisherman versions. Within these four basic configurations, a number of variations are possible. It can be built in any of the three metals. With over 200 WR52s in service, this is a well-proven design. This boat can easily be handled by a couple and it is ideal for charter or family cruising.

For local and coastal cruising, it's worth noting that a planing hull may allow you to get home before the bad weather arrives. If your type of cruising lends itself to the advantages of a planing hull and if the disadvantages of the high cost of operation do not bother you, then by all means consider this type. In this case, a moderate-V hull is recommended. On no account select a planing hull if you intend to operate your boat in the canal systems of the U.S. or Europe. These hulls are not suitable if your cruising area is restricted to low-speed operation.

tude. It's our opinion that chine flats are desirable on all planing craft. Intermediate planing strakes may not be worthwhile on boats intended to perform at less than 30 knots. Planing chines or flats, will start with little or no flat at, or near, the bow and the width of the flat will gradually increase until it reaches its widest point somewhere just aft of amidships and maintains this width through

PLANING FLATS AND STRAKES

Almost all planing power-boat hulls are of single-chine configuration. Most have chine flats or planing chines (and, occasionally, planing strakes) that assist the boat to get onto, and maintain, the planing atti-

The Euro 16 is ideal as a family liveaboard or corporate motor yacht, and is available as a cut-to-size steel or aluminum kit.

The Waverunner 65 was used to develop the Euro 20 and several other larger designs and kits.

to the stern. The efficiency of the chine flat may be improved by canting it downward by, say, 2 to 4 degrees throughout its length.

Only a few years ago, it was thought impossible to build a *successful* small-to-medium-sized *steel* planing hull. Fortunately, modern building techniques and technical advances in design have not only made it possible, but practical as well. As mentioned above, planing occurs when the boat reaches a speed equal to twice the square root of

Another version of the Waverunner 65 that can be built in steel or aluminum.

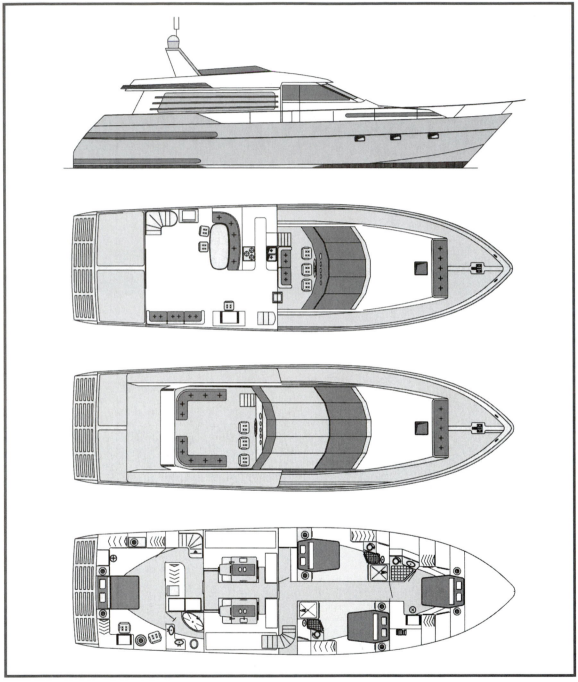

This version B of the Waverunner 65 can be built in steel or aluminum with a choice of planing or displacement hulls. This model was used as the basis for the Euro 20 kit; there are now several larger versions of this design. Plans are available in both stock and semicustom versions.

LOA	65'6" / 20.0 m
LWL	57'6" / 17.5 m
Beam	19'6" / 5.9 m
Draft	3'0" / 0.80 m

the waterline length in feet. A planing hull will then make the transition from "just planing" to "full planing" with less extra horsepower and less extra fuel than a similarly sized and equipped semi-displacement hull or semiplaning hull would need.

Aluminum has been used to build hundreds of thousands of small, medium, and large planing hulls. Although at first glance this material may appear to be the ideal metal for a fast hull, we have reservations about using it for hull construction, preferring to recommend it for decks and superstructures. You'll find this refrain scattered through this book, so it's not necessary to repeat it here.

Those of you who do intend to build in aluminum, however, will find that the performance of planing hulls is related to weight versus power. Unlike displacement hulls and, to a lesser extent, semidisplacement boats, waterline length plays a smaller part in the performance characteristics of a planing hull.

In simple terms, the more power and the less weight you have in your planing hull, the faster it will go. Fortunately for designers like us, it's not that simple. A well-designed planing hull equipped with modest power will outperform an overpowered, poorly designed vessel.

ROUND-BILGE HULLS

Powerboats intended for passagemaking will often have round-bilge hulls. It's possible to design a semidisplacement, round-bilge hull, but the semidisplacement type is more suited to the *chine* hull configuration. Round-bilge can be used for any displacement hull, especially those used for long-distance voyaging. One area we're exploring is the design of steel, radius-chine powerboat hulls, and we believe that this idea is worth further investigation. If you're planning to use active stabilizers or outrigger fins, you might want to consider this type of hull. Round-bilge hulls roll more than chine hulls, and for this reason they're ideally suited to roll correction because active stabilizers work best when the round-bilge hull form allows for a natural, easy rolling motion.

The Euro 26 M/Waverunner 85 is the ultimate metal boat building project. The first example of this design is being built in aluminum in Vancouver, British Columbia.

RADIUS-CHINE HULLS

We have developed new radius-chine steel techniques that produce beautiful round-bilge steel or aluminum hulls. These boats are easy to build and exhibit all of the advantages of both chine and round-bilge hull forms. These newly developed radius-chine hulls have been made possible by modern, computer-assisted yacht design. These soft-chine hulls offer the soft ride that we have often desired in a round-bilge or chine hull form, but seldom achieved. These hulls are designed to eliminate the firm ride of a chine hull. They also help with the installation of active antiroll fins. Our wide experience in using the radius-chine hull form in our designs has established that this hull form is ideal for all types of displacement off-shore vessels, including trawler yachts.

This radius chine method is ideal for building a round-bilge hull in either steel or aluminum. This method is very easy to execute and ideal for constructing either displacement power or sailboat hulls.

18
PASSAGEMAKING POWERBOATS

There are many differences between a true passagemaker and a regular powerboat. The cruising powerboat that you find at most boat shows may be designed for cruising over hundreds of miles. A true passagemaking powerboat must be capable of cruising at least 3,000 nautical miles without refueling. This vessel must also be capable of carrying sufficient stores for the voyage. Watermakers have largely solved the problems of carrying sufficient water. Passagemakers must be truly self-sufficient, and good weight carriers. If passagemaking is to be included in your boating future, you'll need to consider a custom-designed and custom-built powerboat unless you purchase one of the very few suitable vessels currently available.

Over recent years, interest in this type of cruising powerboat has increased to such a degree as to warrant a chapter on this very special type of cruising vessel. There are a few boats available that are suitable for modifying, fitting out, and equipping for this purpose. Most of these will need extensive modification if they are to meet the requirements of a true passagemaker.

HISTORY

When one thinks of the history of small-boat passagemaking, the first name that springs to mind is that of Robert P. Beebe, a well-known pioneer of passagemaking under power. However, Beebe was not the first to successfully undertake long ocean passages under power.

In 1902, a 38-foot (11.58 m) vessel called *Abiel Abbot Low*, powered by a kerosene engine, made the crossing from New York to Falmouth, England, in 38 days. The next recorded crossing was made in 1912 by the *Detroit*, a 35-foot (10.67 m) vessel powered by gasoline (petrol), that made the trip in 28 days. The sheer fortitude of the owners and crews of these vessels cannot be overstated. Using the primitive equipment of the time fitted into hulls that we would consider totally unsuitable for the purpose today, they achieved if not the impossible, then certainly the improbable, feat of crossing a major ocean in a small boat under power alone. If you want to read a more detailed report of these early crossings plus more about Capt. Robert Beebe, then we recommend Beebe's revised book, *Voyaging under Power*. See appendix 1.

More recently, there have been many long-distance passagemaking voyages under power, including several round-the-world epics. In 1983–84, Dutchman Kasemier Eilco made a 200-day circumnavigation from Plymouth, England, back to Plymouth. He did it in the 39-foot (11.88 m) aluminum displacement power cruiser *Bylgia 2 of Sneek*.

HULL DESIGN

If you're planning on building or buying a true passagemaker, then you'll need to accept the fact that only a displacement hull will be capable of delivering the performance over the distances involved. You'll need to carefully balance the factors that go into designing a hull capable of carrying you and your crew over vast distances economically and safely to your destination. The factors are displacement-to-length ratio; speed-to-length ratio; above-water/below-water area ratio; and the prismatic coefficient. All of these factors, together with other hull-design parameters, are discussed in chapter 16. Taking these parameters in turn, let's consider the effects they will have on a vessel intended to serve as a passagemaker.

■ **Displacement-to-length ratio (D/L).** Derived from the designer's calculations, displacement length ratio is used to compare one vessel against another. For instance , if a vessel has a D/L of under 200, it would be considered *light displacement* and a D/L of about 400 would be considered *heavy displacement*. In the case of cruising powerboats, I consider a D/L of between 280 and 350 to be about right. As with any design, there are several aspects to consider: the smaller the boat, the larger the D/L required in order to allow that vessel to carry sufficient stores and fuel to make meaningful passagemaking a reality.

■ **Speed-to-length ratio (S/L).** Speed length ratio is the speed of the vessel in knots, divided by the square root of the waterline length in feet. This ratio is important because to achieve your goal of creating a true passagemaker, you need to pay considerable attention to this parameter. It will be necessary to fit this figure in carefully with the other ratios to achieve the correct balance you need between speed, distance, and fuel used, to make it possible to cross an ocean. For long passages, a S/L of between 1.1 and 1.2 would seem the optimum; however, the vessel needs to be capable of running economically at the higher S/L of 1.34 (normal full displacement speeds) when cruising the

coastal areas where diesel fuel is readily available. The design for every potential passagemaker needs to be carefully evaluated to get the best balance between attained speed and fuel usage.

■ **Area above water/area below water (AB).** The AB ratio has everything to do with stability and safety. In most boats, the smaller this number the better the boat. In a design intended for use as a passagemaker, it's advisable that a number smaller than 2.5 be achieved. For coastal cruisers, 3.5 is a satisfactory ratio. There are other calculations, such as the one used by the Coast Guard, to estimate vessel stability in side winds of up to 80 knots. Adjusting the amount and location of ballast can assist in providing additional stability in this situation.

■ **Prismatic coefficient (PC).** Tank-testing and practical tests have proved that for any given S/L there is a correct PC. The correct combination will provide a hull that will achieve the designed hull speed with the minimum of power and consequently the most efficient usage of fuel. You can see why these design parameters must be carefully balanced to provide you with a hull capable of true passagemaking. Refer to chapter 16 for more details.

ENGINEERING

All the systems in a passagemaker will need to be extremely well thought out and reliable. Less-than-perfect installations and engineering practices that may be acceptable (by some) for coastal and local cruising cannot be tolerated in a cruising powerboat intended for ocean crossing. All the features and good practices detailed in this book that we've considered *desirable* are in fact *essential* in a passagemaker.

There's general agreement from those with experience of passagemaking that a single engine is the only answer to powering a successful vessel of this type. Twin engines are inefficient, and while they offer some security, this is far out-weighed by the need for efficient fuel usage when crossing oceans.

The addition of a "wing" engine, of modest power but capable of driving the vessel in an emergency, is recommended not only in a passagemaking vessel but also in any other single-engine powerboat. It may surprise many to know how little power is needed to drive a displacement hull at modest speeds, and a wing engine can provide it with acceptable costs. It has often been suggested that the wing engine can double as a power plant to drive the generating set. This may make sense in vessels of over 55 feet (16.76 m) where the expected usage of AC power justifies the size of an engine capable of providing power to drive the hull as well as driving the AC generator. Other suggestions have included using the gen-set to power an electric drive, either through the main shaft or through a specially installed wing shaft.

There are many ways to provide the security of alternate propulsion in the event of terminal failure of the main engine. One thing to keep in mind is that it's very rare for a well-serviced diesel engine to fail. Usually, there's a simple reason why any diesel engine ceases to operate. Any person with a reasonable knowledge of diesel engines can remedy these problems on the spot.

Fuel management is a primary concern. Dirty fuel, water in the fuel, and air in the fuel system can stop any diesel. Well-designed tanks, care in taking fuel on board (always filter), twin-filter systems, adequate spare filters, and constant monitoring of the systems will go a long way to ensuring that your diesel engine keeps running under all conditions. It's obvious that you'll need sufficient fuel to reach your destination (plus a reasonable reserve) but what may be not so apparent is that you'll need to *manage* your fuel supply carefully. For instance, when you start the voyage, you'll have full tanks and probably be modestly overloaded; however, as the voyage progresses and the tanks start to empty, the trim and stability of the vessel will change.

How it changes will affect the stability of your passagemaker, and you must ensure that these changes are allowed for in the design and loading of the vessel. Moderate-to-heavy-displacement cruising powerboats have the advantage that changes in trim brought about by changes in loading will be minimal compared to those experienced by a lighter-displacement vessel.

The other aspect of management affects fuel usage. For instance, weather can play an important part in the amount of fuel actually consumed, versus your best-case estimates. You'll have noted that slowing down can greatly decrease the amount of fuel used over the same distance. In fine weather, you want to put your foot down to cover as much distance as possible while the conditions are favorable; conversely, when the

The Voyager Trawler Yacht 43 carries some ballast and is designed for serious cruising; this boat is available as a steel cut-to-size kit or as plans and cutting files.

going's rough, slowing down will not only generally make the motion more acceptable but it will conserve fuel. It's common practice for those undertaking passagemaking voyages to monitor the daily fuel usage carefully against expected usage, and to adjust the speed accordingly.

To monitor your fuel successfully, you'll need some better method than simply relying on the regular fuel gauges. Sight gauges consisting of clear glass tubes that run down the side of the tank are one solution; however, current thinking is against such devices because they can break, especially in the case of fire in the engine room. The calibrated dipstick is hard to beat. Whatever method you use to establish the current rate of usage and the amount of fuel remaining, you'll need to ensure that it's accurate, and you'll need to record the results regularly.

SAIL ASSISTANCE

There are those who swear by sail for auxiliary power, and value it as a fail-safe propulsion system. There are others who decry its use. This is another case of whatever decision you make, you'll have a good proportion of the "experts" agreeing with your choice. One thought worth exploring is the fact that you'll most probably have outrigger masts to support your antiroll "flopper-stopper" system; why not try to work an auxiliary sail plan into this arrangement? This may provide you with food for thought.

As all passagemaking powerboats will have some form of projection above deck level, it's worthwhile working in some form of sail plan to be used when conditions are suitable, or when emergency propulsion is a necessity. A considerable amount of long-distance voyaging is planned to take advantage of favorable winds; this makes the consideration of sail assistance a sensible option.

STABILIZING EQUIPMENT

The best hull form for long distance passagemaking is the round-bilge or radius-chine type. These hull forms, when used in powerboats, are the most likely to have a predictable rolling action. Rolling motion can be very tiring to the crew, but fortunately there are methods to reduce and almost eliminate rolling. In the past, if your boat was on the smaller end of the recommended size—say under 50 feet (15 m)—the decision was a simple one: you had to opt for a passive device such as bilge plates, keel plates, or a pair of flopper-stoppers. More recently, devices such as activated fins are available to suit smaller hulls, so you should explore these options. There's another feature that can greatly reduce rolling and that is the use of auxiliary sails. Other devices, such as free-surface tanks, are more suited to large ships and will not be considered here. Note that the more easily a boat rolls, the more positive the effect an antirolling device will have on it.

Flopper-stoppers are one of the more affordable of your antiroll options but there are advantages and drawbacks to using either flopper-stoppers or active-fin devices. You will need to study the benefits and disadvantages of both systems. This rig is not mechanical, so it's less likely to break down; in addition, it will cost less than fitting activated fins.

For those not familiar with these devices, here's a brief description. Flopper-stoppers is the name generally given to a device that has been successfully used by long-distance powerboats to reduce rolling. The rig consists of twin triangular devices, each of about 1 square foot (0.09 square meter) that are suspended by wires from the poles so that the "fins" are sufficiently below water level to act as stabilizers. The rigs generally resemble those seen on prawn or shrimp trawlers, except that the boards are replaced with the fins.

Flopper-stoppers have a good reputation. They work well on all headings and are particularly effective when running before a gale at lower-than-normal speeds. These devices can be used in conjunction with "anchoring flopper-stoppers" that will reduce rolling while at anchor. Another advantage is that they can, and usually are, taken on board when they're not needed.

Of course, nothing is perfect, and some of the disadvantages of these devices are that the

The Voyager Trawler Yacht 55 will make a great liveaboard; this boat is available as a steel cut-to-size kit or as plans and cutting files.

boat will have to be strengthened in certain areas to accept the strains imposed by the rig. The rigging arrangements will need to be designed especially for your boat. The rig takes time and effort to set, and this can be difficult in heavy weather. Care must be taken when launching and retrieving the fins, so they don't damage the sides of the vessel. It has been reported that the drag caused by working flopper-stoppers costs the average passagemaker between 0.5 and 0.75 of a knot. Incidentally, these devices are noisy; however, by adding some chain to the rig the harmonic vibrations can be reduced, if not eliminated altogether. Stabilizer fins do create some drag and will effect fuel consumption. If you are planning a long voyage, you should run tests to ascertin exactly how much fuel you will use when the fins are in operation.

Appendix 1
RECOMMENDED READING

Brewer, Ted. *Understanding Boat Design.* Camden ME: International Marine, 1994.

Calder, Nigel. *Boatowner's Mechanical and Electrical Manual: How to Maintain, Repair, and Improve Your Boat's Essential Systems.* Camden ME: International Marine, 1996. How to maintain and repair your boat's essential systems. This is a good book to have on board.

Collier, Everett. *The Boatowner's Guide to Corrosion: A Complete Reference for Boatowners and Marine Professionals.* Camden ME: International Marine, 2001.

Colvin, Thomas E. *Steel Boat Building.* Camden ME: International Marine, 1992.

Gerr, Dave. *The Elements of Boat Strength: For Builders, Designers, and Owners.* Camden ME: International Marine, 2000. Rule-of-thumb and precise calculations for amateur and professional builders of boats, including metal boats.

Gougeon, Meade. *The Gougeon Brothers on Boat Construction: Wood and West System Materials.* Bay City MI: Gougeon Bros., 1985. This book is available from any Bruce Roberts Design office. There is also a German-language version of this title. If you're planning to add a timber-and-plywood deck and/or superstructure to your metal boat, this book will be a great help.

Pollard, Stephen F. *Boatbuilding with Aluminum.* Camden ME: International Marine, 1993.

Roberts-Goodson, Bruce. *Choosing for Cruising: How to Select and Equip the Perfect Cruising Yacht.* Dobbs Ferry NY. This book covers all aspects of choosing a cruising sailboat and is recommended to those who wish to expand their technical knowledge in sailboat design and associated subjects.

Roberts-Goodson, Bruce. *Spray: The Ultimate Cruising Boat.* Dobbs Ferry NY: Sheridan House, 1995. *Spray* was the first boat ever sailed single-handedly around the world, over 100 years ago. *Spray* and her skipper, Joshua Slocum, have become legendary in the annals of small-boat sailing; *Spray* is the mother of all cruising boats. This book covers the original voyage around the world and includes illustrations and photographs many of the over 1,000 replicas and copies of *Spray.* Included are details of current and past voyages and exploits of those who sail in copies of this wonderful boat.

Scott, Ken. *Metal Boats.* Dobbs Ferry NY: Sheridan House, 1999.

Sims, Ernest H. *Aluminum Boatbuilding.* Dobbs Ferry NY: Sheridan House, 2000.

Slocum, Joshua. *Sailing Alone Around the World.* West Dennis MA: Peninsula Press, 1995. Classic reading for all cruising sailors, but especially for those building the popular *Spray* replica designs.

Smith, Lecain, and Sheila Moir. *Steel Away: A Guidebook to the World of Steel Sailboats.* Port Townsend WA: Windrose Productions, 1986.

Vigor, John. *Boatowner's Handbook: Reference Data for Maintenance, Repair, Navigation, and Seamanship.* Camden ME: International Marine, 2000.

Appendix 2
SOURCES FOR BOATBUILDERS

Ambassador Marine Ltd.
252 Hursley
Winchester
Hampshire SO21 2JJ
UNITED KINGDOM
44 (0)1962 775 405
Fax 44 (0)1962 775 250
"The Stripper" shaft rope cutters.

ABYC (American Boat and Yacht Council)
3069 Solomons Island Rd.
Edgewater MD 21307
410 956 1050
Fax 410 956 2737
Construction standards for small craft.

American Boat Builders and Repairers
Association
345 Pier One Road, Ste. 106
Stevensville MD 21666
410 604 0060
Trade association for improving methods of boat building and repair. Adjudicates disputes between owners and the marine trade.

Apollo
833 W. 17th St., No. 3
Costa Mesa CA 92627
714 650 1240
Fax 714 650 2519
Twelve-volt and 120-volt generating sets.

Balmar
27010 12th· Ave. NW
Stanwood WA 98292
360 629 6100
Fax 360 629 3210
Twelve-volt DC high-capacity generating sets.

Boat Owners Association of the United States
880 S. Pickett St.
Alexandria VA 22304
703 461 2864
Lobbies Congress on behalf of boaters. Adjudicates disputes. Publishes BOAT/U.S. Reports.

Bruce Roberts Designs (Australia)
P.O. Box 9045
Burnett Heads
Queensland 4670
AUSTRALIA
61 (0)7 41511740
E-mail: phil@bruceroberts.com.au

Bruce Roberts Designs (UK)
3 Elm Close
Acle, Norfolk NR13 3EU
ENGLAND
44 (0)1493 751 779
E-mail: mike@topsail.co.uk

Bruce Roberts Designs (USA)
P.O. Box 1086
Severna Park MD 21146
410 349 2743
Fax 410 349 2744
E-mail: bruce@bruceroberts.com
Cruising boat plans and custom designs.

Canadian Coast Guard
200 Kent St.
Ottawa ON K1A OE6
CANADA
www.ccg-gcc.gc.ca
Safety material and free information on boating courses.

Copper Development Association (UK)
Orchard House
Mutton Lane
Potters Barr
Herefordshire EN6 3AP
ENGLAND
44 (0)1707 642 769
Fax 44 (0)1707 624 2749
Copper-nickel information.

Copper Development Association (USA)
260 Madison Ave.
New York NY 10016
212 251 7214
Fax 212 251 7234
Copper-nickel information; contact Dale T. Peters, VP.

Cruising Equipment Company
315 Seaview Ave. NW
Seattle WA 9807
Fax 206 782 4336
E-Meter and battery monitoring devices and services.

Dickinson Stoves (Canada)
407–204 Cayer St.
Coquitlam BC V3K 5B1
CANADA
605 525 6444
Diesel-powered galley and heating stoves.

Environmental Solutions International
11002 Racoon Ridge
Reston VA 22091
800 411 3284
Fax 703 620 2815
De-Bug microorganism fuel filters.

Ericson Safety Pump Corporation
435 Roosevelt Blvd.
Tarpon Springs FL 34689
Fax 813 934 6890
Bilge pumps.

Exide Batteries Ltd.
Gate No. 3
Pontselyn Industrial Estate
Pontypool NP4 5DG
UNITED KINGDOM
44 (0)1495 750 075
Marine batteries.

Float-Pac Pty. Ltd.
Unit 4/31 Wentworth St.
Greenacre NSW 2190
Australia
Fax 61 2 742 5565
Air bags.

Forespar
22322 Gilberto
Rancho Santa Margarita CA 92688
714 858 8820
Fax 714 858 0505
Lightning Master and other marine products.

Good Old Boat Magazine
7340 Niagara Lane N.
Maple Grove MN 55311-2655
763 420 8923
Fax 763 420 8921
www.goodoldboat.com
Lists sources of hard-to-find boat equipment. Comprehensive website links to boating associations, bulletin boards, and small manufacturers.

Halyard Marine Ltd.
Whaddon Business Park
Southampton Rd.
Whaddon, Nr. Salisbury SP5 3HF
ENGLAND
44 (0)1722 710 922
Fax 44 (0)710 975
HMI shaft seal, exhaust systems, engine insulation.

Heart Interface Corp.
21440 68th Ave.e S.
Kent WA 98032
Fax 206 872 3412
Battery chargers, inverters and battery monitors.

HFL Industrial and Marine Ltd.
HFL House
Lockfield Ave.
Enfield, Middlesex EN3 7PX
ENGLAND
44 (0)181 805 9088
Fax 44 (0)181 805 2440
AC generating sets.

Hypertherm Inc.
P.O. Box 5010
Hanover NH 03755
800 643 0030, 603 643 3441
Fax 603 643 5352
Powermax plasma cutters.

Kolstrand
4739 Ballard Ave. NW
Seattle WA 98107
Flopper stoppers.

Lancing Marine
51 Victoria Rd.
Portslade, Sussex BN41 1XY
ENGLAND
44 (0)1273 410025
Fax 44 (0)1273 430 290
Marine diesel engines, rebuild kits etc.

Lestek Manufacturing Inc.
6542 Baker Blvd.
Fort Worth TX 76118
Fax 817 284 2153
"Brute" high-output alternators.

Lugger/Northern Lights
206 789 3880
Fax 206 782 5455
Northern Lights generating sets.

Marine Retailers Association of America
155 N. Michigan Ave., Ste. 5230
Chicago IL 60611
312 938 0359
Information about hard-to-find parts and gear.

Marinetics Inc.
P.O. Box 2676
Newport Beach CA 92663
714 646 8889, 714 642 8627
Electrical panels.

Mastervolt
Unit D5, Premier Center
Abbey Park Industrial Estate
Romsey, Hampshire SO5 19AQ
ENGLAND

44 (0)1794 516 443
Fax 44 (0) 11794 516 453
Heart inverters, battery monitors, electrical panels.

Merlin Equipment
Unit 1 Hithercroft Court
Lupton Road
Wallingford
Oxfordshire OX10 9BT
ENGLAND
Fax 44 (0)1491 824466
E-Meter/Heart Link 10.

M. G. Duff Marine Ltd.
Unit 2 West
68 Bognor Rd.
Chichester
West Sussex PO19 2NS
ENGLAND
44 (0)1243 533 336
Fax 44 (0)1243 533 422
Zinc and magnesium anodes.

Morglasco Ltd.
Bosboa
Mount George Rd.
Penelewey, Feock
Truro, Cornwall TR3 6QX
ENGLAND
Phone/Fax +44 (0)1872 870 139
Person overboard recovery slings.

Nickel Development Institute
14 King St. West, Ste. 510
Toronto, Ontario M5H 3S6
CANADA
416 591 7999
Fax 416 591 7987
Information on copper-nickel and stainless steels.

Nickel Development Institute
European Technical Information Centre
The Holloway
Alvechurch, Birmingham B48 7QB
ENGLAND
+44 (0) 1527 584 777
Fax +44 (0) 1527 585 562
Information on copper-nickel and stainless steels.

Norseman Gibb Ltd.
Ollerton Rd.
Ordsall, Retford
Nottinghamshire DN22 7TG
ENGLAND
+44 (0)1777 706 465
Fax +44 (0)1777 860 346
E-mail: 10723.2744@compuserve.com
Norseman fittings.

Ocean Safety
Centurion Industrial Park
Bitterne Rd. West
Southampton SO18 1UB
ENGLAND
+44 (0)1703 333 334
Fax +44 (0)1703 333 360
Lightweight life rafts.

Porta-Bote
The Barn Snowdrop Cottage
Winchester Rd.
Kings Somborne, Stockbridge
Hampshire SO20 6NY
ENGLAND
Phone/Fax +44 (0)1794 388046
Folding dinghies.

Put Veini Ltd.
P.O. LV1015 Box 2,
Riga
Latvia
+371 2 349 543
Fax +371 7 353 831
Builders of steel boats at a favorable price.

Registrar of British Ships
P.O. Box 165
Cardiff CF4 5FU
UNITED KINGDOM
+44 (0)1222 747333
Small-ships register (SSR).

Rolls Battery Engineering
8 Proctor St.
Salem MA 01970
508 745 3333
Heavy-duty, deep-cycle batteries.

Rule Industries Inc.
Cape Ann Industrial Park
Gloucester MA 01930
508 281 0440
All types of marine pumps.

Royal Yachting Association
RYA House
Romsey Rd.
Eastleigh
Hampshire SO5O 9YA
ENGLAND
+44 (0)1703 629 962
Fax +44 (0)1703 629 924

Scanmar International
432 South 1st St.
Richmond CA 94804
510 215 2010
Fax 510 215 5005
Self-steering windvanes.

Solpower Corp.
7309 E. Stetson Dr., Ste. 102
Scottsdale AZ 85251
480 947 6366, 888 289 8866
Fax 480 947 6324
www.solpower.com

Southwester Ltd.
Stinsford Rd.
Poole, Dorset BH17 7EU
ENGLAND
+44 (0)1202 667 700
Fax +44 (0)668 585
Deep Sea Seals and other marine gear.

Sure Marine Services, Inc.
5320 28th Ave. NW
Seattle WA 98107
800 562 7797
206 784 9903
Diesel hot-air systems and water-heating systems.

Swiftlik
1325 E State St.
Trenton NJ 08609
609 587 3300
Fax 609 586 6647
Affordable coastal life raft/rescue pod.

Terry Erskine Boatbuilder
1 Glendower,
Gonvena Hill
Wadebridge PL27 6DQ
UNITED KINGDOM
+44 (0)1208 815 862
Mobile phone 0370 613 914
Builder of fine steel boats.

U.S. Coast Guard
Marine Safety Center
400 7th St. SW
Washington DC 20590
202 366 6480
www.uscgboating.org
Information on safety, drugs, marine sanitation devices.

United States Sailing Association (U.S. Sailing)
P.O. Box 1260
Portsmouth RI 02871
401 683 0800
www.ussailing.org

Vetus Den Ouden
38 South Hampshire Industrial Park
Totton-Southampton
Hampshire SO40 3SA
ENGLAND
+44 (0)1703 861 033
Fax +44 (0)1703 663 142
Marine equipment, gen-sets, engines, tanks, ventilators.

Vetus Den Ouden
Fokkerstraat 571 3125 BD
Schiedam
THE NETHERLANDS
+31 10 437 7700
Fax +31 10 415 2634
Marine equipment, gen-sets, engines, tanks, ventilators.

Vetus Den Ouden
P.O. Box 8712
Baltimore MD 21240
410 712 0740
Fax 410 712 0985
Marine equipment, gen-sets, engines, tanks, ventilators.

Village Marine Tech.
2000 W. 135th St.
Gardenia CA 90249
Fax 310 538 3048
Watermakers.

COPPER-NICKEL PRODUCERS IN THE UNITED STATES

Hussy Copper Ltd.
800 733 8866, 412 266 8430
Fax 412 857 4243

Olin Brass
618 258 2000
Fax 618 258 2777

PMX Industries Inc.
800 531 5468, 319 368 7700
Fax 319 368 7721

Revere Copper Products Inc.
800 448 1776, 315 338 2022
Fax 315 338 2224

Appendix 3
GLOSSARY

abaft—Behind or toward the rear.

abeam—A point beside the boat; usually refers to a point relative to the boat such as "abeam of midships" or abeam of the bow, close abeam, etc.

ABL, or Above the Baseline—Usually given as a measurement, for example: Stem is 6 feet, 6 inches (1.98 m) above the baseline.

AB ratio—Area of side view of vessel above and below the water. In most vessels except submarines, the amount above the water will be greater. A number between 2 and 3 is desirable.

AC Electrode—Welding rod.

AH (amp-hour)capacity—The ability of a fully charged battery to deliver a specified amount of electricity at a given rate for a definite period of time. This number may give a false impression because you cannot use all of the AH or you will flatten the battery, and the AH capacity of any battery will vary with age and condition.

alternating current (AC)—Household and shore electrical power of 220 or 240-volts in Europe, Australia, etc., or 120 volts in North America. It's also the type of power usually supplied by your generating set. Some generating sets can supply 12-volt DC power. See Direct Current.

ampere, amp, or A—Unit of measure of flow rate of current through a circuit.

ampere-hour, amp-hour or AH—A unit of measure of the battery's electrical storage capacity, obtained by multiplying the current in amperes by the time in hours of the discharge.

angle—A term used to describe L-shaped bar.

arc radius—The radius used to draw an arc of a circle, quoted when discussing radius-chine construction.

athwartships—Across the boat. For example: The webs are mostly athwartships, when located in the keel.

backbone—Another name for the centerline bar that runs most of the length of a hull and could include the stem and the aft centerline bar.

back-chipping—The techniques used to remove unwanted weld metal. Usually undertaken between weld passes. Usually achieved with a chisel or special tool, by hand or using mechanical means. On aluminum welds, a power saw may be used with care.

back gouging—Grinding back on opposite side of plate or back of weld to find root of weld material.

back-step welding—Welding from unwelded join are back to previous welded area.

baseline (BL)—A line that runs parallel to the waterline. It's used on some plans and drawings as a common reference line. The baseline may sometimes be above the hull, but more usually the bottom of the keel acts as a baseline.

batten—A long piece of fine-grained timber, plastic, or steel used for fairing purposes. The timber variety are used by loftsman as an aid to drawing the long waterlines and buttocks on the loft floor. Shorter versions are used for drawing the frame sections. Before the advent of computer design, naval architects used miniature versions called splines for the same purpose.

beam—The width of the boat at any given point. Usually given as a measurement at the maximum width of the hull (beam overall, the widest beam) or waterline beam (beam at the waterline).

bedlogs—Used when setting up hulls upside down. Can be steel I beams or 6- by 2-inch (150 by 100 mm) timber or similar. See *I beam*.

body plan—Also referred to as "stations," or "sections," this is the drawing of the hull divided into stations, usually equally spaced, and may actually represent the frames. The waterline length is divided into a number of equal stations (usually 10) and the 90-degree view of these, plus the ones at the bow and stern, are shown in the body plan. In most cases the forward stations are shown to the right of the centerline and those aft of the centerline are shown on the left.

boottop—A decorative stripe painted parallel to and about 6 inches (150 mm) above the waterline. This stripe separates the topside and bottom paints. It is wise not to paint this line until your boat has been launched and loaded for cruising.

bracing—Extra bar across, or vertically installed on, frames as a temporary measure to stiffen them until the hull is completed; it stops stringers deforming the frames at an early stage of construction and is also used to support frames or other members of the hull during the setting-up stage.

brazing—Usually done with oxyacetylene equipment and is used to join two light metals.

breakwater—A vertical bulkhead above the deck, usually located ahead of the wheelhouse. As the name implies, the breakwater deflects the force of any water or spray that may wash onto or over the foredeck.

bulkhead or blkd—Any "wall" in a boat. May run longitudinally or athwartships (fore and aft, or across the boat).

bulwark—Topsides that extend above the main deck. Can be combined with liferails to provide security for the crew. Usually extend from bow to stern. Can be any height from 4 inches (100 mm) to 36 inches (914 mm).

buttock line—A line dividing the hull longitudinally and vertically. When viewed in profile can reveal a considerable amount of information about the shape of the hull. They appear as straight lines in the body and plan views of the hull and as curved lines on the profile view. Used by loftsman as another set of reference lines when lofting a hull full-size.

butt weld—Used to join two pieces of plate or bar edge to edge.

CAD—Computer-assisted drafting.

camber—Denotes the amount of upward curve in the deck, cabintop, and transom. For decks, a common amount of camber is ⅜ inch (10 mm) for every 12 inches (305 mm) of beam. Sailboat cabintops tend to have more camber; powerboats with flying bridges tend to have less, pilothouses have more, and so forth. If the plans include camber patterns (as ours do) or specify cambers, do not change them without consulting the designer.

camber pattern—See Camber. Patterns are supplied, or you need to make your own from measurements supplied with your plans.

castles—Steel forms used in setting up steel kit building jigs.

ceiling—Longitudinal planking attached to the inside of the frames. In traditional timber boats, this inside planking was installed to add strength to the hull. In modern boats, the ceiling planks are about 1½ by ⅜ inch (35 by 10 mm) and are intended only as a lining material.

centerboard—A device used in sailboats to reduce draft while reducing leeway. Used in place of a deep keel. See also *drop keel*.

centerline (C/L)—An imaginary line running down the center of the vessel; also a line drawn on the plan view and body plan of the designer's plans.

centerline bar—The bar on edge that runs long the centerline of a metal boat. The stem is usually part of the centerline bar, as is the bar running from the aft end of the keel to the stern. On some powerboats, especially planing hulls, the centerline bar runs full length.

chainplate—These days seldom used for chain, this is the tang on the hull to which the turnbuckles or rigging screws are attached. Part of the rigging setup on a sailboat.

chine—This, when used alone, generally refers to a "hard" chine, or abrupt change of direction between the sides and bottom of the hull. In general terms, a chine is the point where the hull bottom and sides meet in a "chine boat." A hull can have more than one chine (double-chine), or several chines (multi-chine). See also *radius chine* and *knuckle*.

Chine flat—The area at the chine on a planing powerboat that is parallel or near parallel to the waterline. The forward end deflects spray while mid and after parts are under water and provide additional lift.

chord—A straight line joining two points on an arc, curve, or circumference.

circuit—The path of an electric current; a closed circuit has a complete path, and an open circuit has a broken or disconnected path.

collar—The lining of a hole through a bulkhead (short length of pipe) so electrical cables or other similar items that penetrate a bulkhead do not chafe on the sharp edges.

compound curvature—A surface that has curvature in more than one direction is said to have compound curvature. A regular round-bilge hull has a considerable amount of compound curvature.

computer lofting—Drawing out the boat full-size in the computer and then plotting patterns for the frames, stem, keel, deck beams, etc. See also *lofting*.

conical developed or developed surface—A surface that is part of a cone or several interconnected cones, so that a flat sheet of metal or plywood will "drape" over the surface. Many modern powerboat designs have computer-generated developed hull surfaces.

construction drawing—A single sheet of drawings, measurements, and written instructions that usually forms part of a set of drawings. The construction drawings are usually prepared by the designer but additional drawings may be prepared by the builder, marine electrical engineer, or marine plumber.

consumable—Welding rod or electrode or welding wire or other metal that is used in welding and joining two pieces of metal.

copper-nickel—Alloy metal consisting of mainly copper and a smaller amount of nickel. Often described as 70/30 or 90/10 to indicate the percentage of copper (first number) and nickel (second number).

crevice corrosion—Cracks that often appear in stainless-steel rudder shafts and other stainless parts that are underwater and suffer from oxygen starvation. In simple terms, stainless steel needs to breathe.

current (electrial)—Rate of flow that is best described by comparing it to a stream of water; the unit of measure is an ampere.

curve of areas—A line plotted by the designer from measurements taken from the lines plan. The curve represents the areas of the vessel's immersed sections and provides information to the designer about the shape of the hull. The computer now generates this line that was not, and is not, used for lofting.

custom-built—Any boat that is not built in series production may be one-off or could be part of a series of boats built one at a time with special features to suit individual owners.

cycle—One discharge, plus one recharge, is one battery cycle.

deadrise (hull deadrise)—The change in elevation in relation to the horizontal plane of the bottom of the hull. Most often used to describe the angle of V in the bottom of a powerboat hull. Deadrise is often quoted at the transom, say 18 degrees of V or 18 degrees deadrise. The deadrise in a boats hull usually increases towards the bow.

deck plan—Drawing of the deck, cabin, etc., looking down from above.

deck stringer—The stringer that intersects the

hull and the deck and is used to accept the deck plating and the outboard ends of the deck beams.

descaling—Removing mill scale and other impurities from the surface of metal may be done chemically or mechanically.

dipswitches—A series of small switches used for alternate programming in all types of electrical and electronic devices.

direct current (DC)—Electric power from a battery, generator or a 12V battery charger.

discharge—When a battery is delivering current it is said to be discharging.

D/L ratio—Uses a formula to compare the displacement versus the waterline length.

designed waterline (DWL)—The line around the hull where the designer expects, hopes, or predicts that the boat will float when completed and launched; stores, half the fuel, water, and crew should all be aboard when the boat floats on this line.

developed or developable surface—Any surface that can be constructed from a flat plate. See also *conical developed surface*.

diagonal—Another line used by the designer to fair round-bilge lines at the design stage. Generally not used for lofting.

displacement—True displacement equals the actual weight of the vessel when in cruising trim. This is turn equals the weight of the amount of water displaced by the vessel.

down-hand welding—Welding from above.

drop keel—A ballasted centerboard. Often airfoil-shaped, it is pivoted on a strong pin and can be raised and lowered as required. For safety's sake, it should be capable of being locked in the down position.

ductile—Easily stretched, bent, or formed without breaking.

elevation—A flat scale drawing of the front, rear, or side of an object.

engine beds or bearers—The longitudinal bearers or girders on which the engine is mounted, usually via flexible mountings.

equalizing charge—A controlled overcharge of the batteries that brings all cells up to the same voltage.

fair line, faired surface, to fair—A curved line or surface devoid of humps and hollows; to fair is to take some action to achieve this end.

fillet weld—The weld on the intersection where the end of one piece of metal rests at an angle on a flat plate. The weld in the corner is termed a fillet weld.

flare—The outward slope of a hull above the waterline. Also used to describe the hollow seen in the bow of some fiberglass powerboats. Example: the boat has a flared bow. The opposite of tumblehome. See *tumblehome*.

flat bar—Metal formed or cut into strips. For example, ¼-inch (6 mm) plate that is only 2 to 8 inches wide (50 to 205 mm). After that, it may be called *sheet*. Flat bar can be any thickness.

flux coating—The coating on some welding rods.

frame—A structural member, usually on the same plane as a station.

frameless—Some smaller metal boats are frameless, which is really a misnomer as the stringers and chine bars are longitudinal framing.

framing—The structure inside the hull. Transverse framing is generally known as the *frames*, whereas longitudinal framing is known as the *stringers*.

freeboard—The height of the boat's side above the water. Often quoted at various parts of the hull, usually the lowest freeboard is quoted as "the" freeboard measurement.

freeing port—An opening in the side of the hull above the deck (usually through a bulwark) to allow the surface water from the deck to flow overboard.

full-size patterns, or FSP—Patterns of the frames, stem, deck beams, and other construction members that have been obtained by manual lofting or computer fairing and lofting. Can be supplied on paper or Mylar film. A great aid to getting on with the job and highly recommended by this writer.

galvanic action—Similar to corrosion and caused when two dissimilar metals are joined and unprotected by coatings or other methods. Especially prevalent in a saltwater environment.

garage (for main hatch)—See *turtle*.

gel-cell battery—A type of battery that has the electrolyte in gel form.

girth—A measurement around a curved surface or arc.

good boatbuilding practice—A recognised standard among boatbuilders that denotes good-quality workmanship and the use of good-quality materials. The opposite of shoddy practice.

gouging rods—Very high carbon used with high power to gouge out bad welds.

grid—All the straight and parallel lines used by loftsmen to prepare a loft floor for drawing up a set of lines. The grid includes the baseline, waterlines, and buttocks.

ground—To ground is to connect an electrical conductor to the ground, or the water, so that it becomes a part of the circuit and is at the earth's potential or voltage. A ground is any part of an electrical circuit that joins to the circuit to the ground or water. In electronics, automobiles, and sometimes boats there are often "pseudo grounds" (a chassis, a frame, or even an engine block, where all wires of one polarity are connected) that float at some potential other than the earth's.

gusset—A bracket connnecting two parts to reinforce a join, usually at a 45-degree angle. Similar to a knee in a timber boat.

half breadth—The distance from any point of the hull to the centerline, when taken horizontally and parallel to the DWL. All symmetrical hulls have the same half breadths for each side.

headstock—A length of L-angle or timber installed across the frames and used as part of the bracing and setting-up procedure.

heat-weld puddle—The pool of molten metal or consumable that is present prior to cooling of weld.

house—As in deck house, doghouse, or cabin.

hydrogen embrittlement—Caused by incorrectly matching electrodes and metal to be welded results in poor ductility and hairline cracks.

I beam—A steel section shaped like an "I" and used in the construction industry. This type of beam is used as a setting-up base for kits and when setting up the frames in hulls that are built upside down.

inboard profile—Elevation drawing, usually showing one half of the accommodation viewed in profile (a slice from bow to stern along the centerline).

initial (or form) stability—The shape of a hull as a form of stability as opposed to ballast-induced stability.

intercostal—Fore-and-aft stiffener inserted between frames or deck beams, as opposed to a continuous stiffener or stringer.

ISO—The International Standards Organization.

jerry-built—Unacceptable or shoddy workmanship.

jig—An arrangement specially made to hold parts of an object in a certain way until they can be permanently assembled. For example, if you were building a number of similar hulls, you may have a building jig for forming up parts of the hulls or superstructure. A temporary framework as used in frameless construction is a building jig.

keel and ballast keel—The lowest portion of the hull; may hang well below, as in a fin keel, or may run almost the full length, as in traditional boats like the *Spray*. There are long keels, three-quarter keels, fin keels, bulb keels, and wing keels.

keelson—The inner keel; usually runs the full length of the hull, from the stem aft to the transom. More applicable to timber boats, but the centerline bar in a metal boat may be thought of as the keelson.

knuckle—A definite change of direction in the hull plating or other surface. In true terms, a chine is a knuckle. The change in direction is usually not as abrupt as with a chine. See also *chine*.

ladder—As in ship's ladder or boat ladder; another term for a set of stairs or steps, usually more vertical than either of the latter.

laid deck—A timber-planked deck usually installed over a regular deck, for instance over a metal deck. Depending on the thickness of the timber planks, this deck can contribute to the strength of the decks and the vessel.

lay-back—Used to describe or measure the angle the front of the cabin is angled from the vertical, usually expressed in degrees.

lay-in—Used to describe or measure the angle the cabin or pilothouse sides are angled from the vertical, usually expressed in degrees.

laying out—Measuring and locating a point on a drawing, loft floor, or on a boat.

LED—A light-emitting diode, often used as an indicator light.

lightening hole—A single hole or a series of circular holes cut in a web or similar beam to reduce the weight without materially reducing the strength. Often arranged to allow the passage of cables and plumbing beneath the sole.

limber hole—A hole cut in the bottom of a frame or web or elsewhere to allow the passage of water between frames or webs. In wooden boats, a light chain was lead through the series of limber holes to clear accumulated rubbish preventing drainage to the lowest point of the bilge.

lines drawing, or lines—The original drawing of the hull, made by the designer or naval architect, that presents the hull in plan view, profile, and sectional view (stations). The hull is faired on the drawing board, today in the computer, by using waterlines, buttock lines, and stations. From the lines plan the designer takes off a set of offsets that are used by the loftsman, or computer, to draw out the hull full-size on the loft floor, or by plotting on a printer/plotter.

LOA—Length overall, including bowsprits and other appendages.

LOD—Length on deck; this figure is often shown as the LOA, but should not include bowsprits, etc.

loft floor—An area of floor that has been prepared for drawing out the lines full size. Usually painted off-white to allow a clearer view of the various lines to be drawn, seen, and identified. A small version of this floor is useful for transferring Mylar or paper full-size patterns to a semipermanent surface.

lofting or computer lofting—Drawing out the boat full-size on the loft floor so as to provide patterns for the frames, stem, keel, deck beams, etc. Today, the lofting is more likely to be done in the computer.

longitudinal—Fore and aft; for instance, a longitudinal, when discussing framing of a hull, usually refers to a fore-and-aft stringer.

margin plate—A narrow plate welded inside the hull at the deckline to accept a timber and plywood deck. This plate is located in the same position and would replace the deck stringer.

midships (amidships)—Around the center of the hull in the fore-and-aft plane; for instance, midships cabin, midships steering, or something is located midships.

MIG—An abbreviation for the Metal Inert Gas welding process.

mullion—The narrow space or post between windows.

NC cutting—Computer-controlled cutting of metal, used to cut out metal parts from sheet material in a semiautomatic operation.

negative—The negative terminal is the point from which electrons flow during discharge.

nibbed—The way ends of deck planking are fitted to king plank or covering board.

ni-cad battery—Nickel-cadmium battery, rechargeable and used in small appliances; larger varieties are too expensive for most boats.

offsets, or table of offsets—The figures or dimensions shown on a lines plan, these are offset from a known point such as a centerline or baseline.

ohm—A unit of electrical resistance.

outboard profile—Side view of the boat as seen from outside.

pad eye—A small metal plate welded to a plate or structure. It has either an eye or a hole to which a line or chain can be attached for lifting the plate or structure.

passagemaker—A term, popularized by Robert P. Beebe, meaning a long-distance ocean-crossing powerboat.

passageway—Space between bulkheads or joinery used as access, usually fore and aft.

pickling—One method of cleaning metal by the application of acids to copper-nickel and other metals to remove impurities.

planing chine—A surface running mostly parallel to the waterline and longitudinally where the sides and bottom of the hull join that assists in lifting the hull on to a plane.

planing strake—Angled surface on the bottom of a planing hull added to assist the boat in getting on to and remaining in a planing attitude. Very effective on boats that perform at less than 30 knots.

plate-mill stock—Plate that is supplied flat and has never been coiled.

plug welding—Welding through slots or holes; for instance, when attaching the outside shell of a keel to the inside webs, where access from inside is not possible. Also used to weld one plate on top of another; not recommended, at least for steel, due to potential corrosion problems.

plumb bob—A pointed weight on a string line; used from above a frame or other section to ensure that the frame is truly vertical or plumb.

porosity—Used to describe welds that have small voids or are porous.

port—To the left when looking forward, as in port side, left side. Any window in a boat can be termed as a port. Large ports are now usually referred to as windows.

portlight—Another boating term for window.

pulsed-arc transfer—Welding at low heat; usually done with automatic welding equipment.

radius chine—A chine formed by part of a circle, where the radius is constant from the stern right through to the bow. Most radius-chine boats are designed with complex yacht-design computer software. The amount of arc may vary in a radius-chine boat, but the radius remains constant. The largest amount of arc is at the stern, tapering right through to the bow.

scale—Ratio of size relative to actual size; for example, a scale of ½ inch equals 1 foot means one half inch on the drawing equals one foot on the boat. In drawings prepared the metric scale, 1=50 would mean that one unit on the drawing equals 50 on the actual boat.

scale, on steel—Generally referred to as *mill scale*, impurities usually on the surface of the steel left over from the steel manufacturing process.

scantlings—Sizes and dimensions of materials used to build the boat. The thickness and other dimensions shown on the list of materials are the scantlings.

seacock—A tap or valve used to shut off a flow of water or other liquid into and out of the hull. Drains, inlet pipes, and other pipes that pierce the hull surface should all be fitted with seacocks.

shaft horsepower—The horsepower actually available at the propeller.

sheer, or sheerline—The top of the hull, viewed in profile.

shell—The outer skin of the hull; as in shell plating.

shoal draft—A boat with shallow draft is said to be a shoal-draft vessel.

shotblasted—Steel that has been blasted with either sand, grit or small shot to remove impurities and/or rust from the surface of the steel, brings steel back to bright metal.

shroud—A side stay or wire support for the mast.

S/L ratio—Speed length ratio is the speed of the vessel in knots, divided by the square root of the waterline length in feet.

slag—Impurities that form on a weld and need to be removed as part of the welding process.

sniping, or to snipe—To cut off the ends of a stringer or similar member at a 3:1 angle, leaving about one quarter of the width as a right-angle cut.

Spanish windlass—A loop of rope or wire twisted with a stick or rod to draw in one surface or section to another.

stanchion—The posts around the edge of the deck are known as *stanchions*.

starboard or stbd—To the right when looking forward, as in starboard side.

station or stn—A slice through the hull from side to side. Usually, there are 10 stations dividing up the waterline.

stay—Fore-and-aft wire supporting the mast; as in forestay or backstay.

steel, low-carbon—This is steel with a low carbon content, generally speaking steel with carbon content of between 0.15 and 0.28% can be described in the way.

steel, mild—This is a generic term for general-purpose low-carbon steel.

stem—The vertical forward end of the boat.

stern—The aft end of the boat; as in counter stern (a long overhanging stern), transom stern (a squared-off after end of the hull), and canoe stern (when the aft end of the hull comes to a point similar to that of the bow).

stiffener—Frames, stringers, and chine bars are all stiffeners. A stiffener supports an area of the hull from inside and breaks up areas of hull shell into smaller stiffened or supported areas.

strake—A stiffener or stringer on the outside of the hull. Traditional timber boats often have strakes on the outside to add strength. Workboats have strakes to protect the hull against fishing gear, etc. Modern planing hulls have planing strakes to assist them in reaching and maintaining the planing attitude.

stringer—A fore-and-aft stiffener, as in hull or deck stringer.

strip-mill stock—Steel that has been coiled after production and is then uncoiled to be sold as flat plate. Can have a "memory" so should not be your first choice for boatbuilding material.

strongback—A jig used to set up the frames during the initial setting up of the hull.

stuffing box—A packing gland used to keep the water from entering the hull from the stern or rudder tube.

superstructure—On a boat the cabin, pilothouse, deckhouse and other structures above the deck are collectively known as the 'superstructure'.

T-bar—A bar shaped like a T and used for transverse frames, deck beams, and other structural members in a metal boat.

tack-weld—To apply a small spot of weld to temporarily hold two pieces of metal in place. This has many uses and all steel boats are best tack-welded together before any permanent welding is undertaken.

tang—A strap or flat bar, usually at a point on the mast where the rigging is attached. Can be used elsewhere on the boat.

temper—To treat metals with heat to change their mechanical qualities; for example, to make a metal more or less ductile.

template—A pattern. A plate template is a pattern made directly off the framework of the hull. It is then transferred to the plate, which it cut to the exact shape and installed on the hull.

TIG or Tungsten Inert Gas—A welding process suitable for most metals; uses a nonconsumable electrode and a shielding gas.

transom—A form of stern. A transom stern is squared-off. Reverse transoms are seen on many modern sailboats.

transverse—Across the boat at 90 degrees to the centerline.

transverse profile jig—Used to support the bottom plates when setting up a hull using a precut kit.

tumblehome—The inward inclination of a boat's sides from the widest part of the hull to the sheerline.

turtle—A low boxlike structure that covers the main sliding hatch when the hatch is open. Acts as a spray delfector.

unfair (hull)—This means a hull or other part of the boat that does not present a smooth and fair exterior. Often caused by using incorrect sequences of welding and by overwelding.

ultimate stablity—This is the factor that measures will the hull return to its upright position from a complete capsize. This factor is more related to positive stability than to the form stability.

volt—A unit of electric potential.

waterline (WL)—The line the water describes around a floating hull. The *designed* waterline is where the designer *hopes* it will float. On a lines drawing, waterlines are drawn at regular intervals above and below the true waterline.

watt—A unit of electrical power. Volts times amps.

wet-cell battery—A battery that uses liquid electrolyte.

wheel—A boating term for the propeller.

work hardening—Making metal harder by hammering, or a similar method.

Appendix 4
OTHER DESIGNS AVAILABLE AS KITS

DESIGNING AND CUTTING PRECUT METAL BOAT KITS

Many of you may be surprised that it's not possible to take a regular boat plan—even one that is already prepared using the latest computer-aided design techniques—and use it for automatic computer-controlled cutting. There are many steps between creating the original design and having the boat cut out on a computerized plasma-oxygen cutter. If a particular design is to be sold as a precut steel or aluminum hull, deck, and superstructure package, then this should be decided at an early design stage. Some designs can be converted, but it is preferable to start with automatic cutting in mind.

The main steps in preparing a new design for a boat that is destined to be cut out by a computerized plasma-oxygen cutter is as follows. It is usually the customer who gets the process started by contacting the designer with a brief outline of what they have in mind. Further correspondence quickly establishes the client's "wish list." The list usually includes things such as type and style of boat, intended usage, overall length and beam. Draft limitations should be specified at this stage.

Accommodation requirements, including the number of regular crew versus occasional guests, should be defined. Speed requirements are important, as are the client's attitude to fuel costs. This list may need some refining as some elements may conflict one with the other. The designer's brief ensures that client ends up with a boat that meets most if not all their desires and overall requirements. So far the process is very similar to what would be followed no matter which material or building method was used to construct the vessel.

The client and designer then enter into what can be a simple agreement where the designer agrees to prepare preliminary plans for the proposed vessel for a reasonable (a relative term!) fee. In our office we consider the preliminary plan to include lines plan, general arrangement drawings consisting of exterior profile, deck plan, accommodation profile, and plan views, plus sufficient calculations to ensure that the final design can meet the client's requirements.

Before a preliminary plan is produced, the designer produces a 3D computer-generated model of at least the hull of the vessel. Once the preliminary plans are completed and both the designer and the client are satisfied with the overall concept and layout of the vessel, complete plans for the vessel are prepared.

A comprehensive 3D computer model must now be completed that includes all parts of the hull, transom, keel, and rudder, all decks, cockpits, complete superstructure, main interior bulkheads, and any other features such as fly bridge, radar arch, and exhaust stack. Special items such as transom steps and other similar features are included in the comprehensive 3D model. Depending on the complexity of the design, this process can take between 80 and 200 hours.

From this model, all of the salient hydrostatics such as detailed weight calculations to enable material requirements and final displacement are calculated; stability calculations are also made at this time. During this process fine-tuning of the model can be undertaken to make sure that the finished vessel will meet all the design requirements.

When the comprehensive 3D model is completed and checked, copies are provided to a team of specialized designers who prepare the final model that includes all the scantlings such as

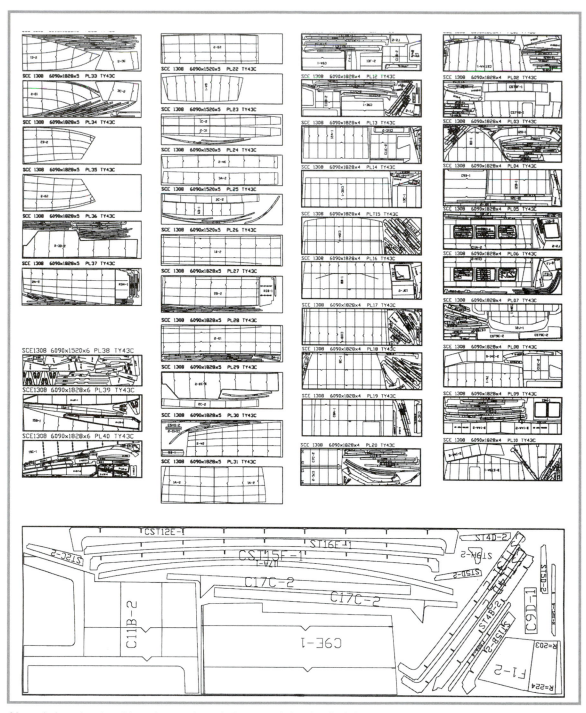

Nested plate drawing. Note the number of sheets and the detail of the parts.

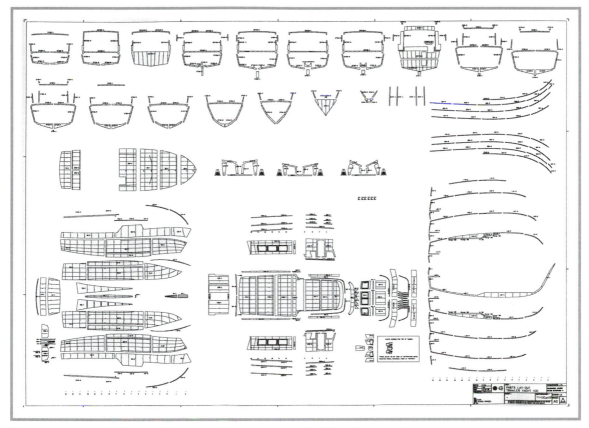

Here we see a typical layout of the parts for a powerboat kit. Note the cut stringers.

transverse and longditunal framing, sole bearers, deck beams, and engine beds. This team separates out all the parts for the frames, stringers, engine beds, bulkheads, hull, deck and superstructure plating etc., and add notches to the frames and bulkheads before "nesting" the parts on plates.

The design team numbers each item and draws reference lines on each part to represent frame locations, etc (the numbers help builders identify each part, and the lines are used during the assembly process to locate frames and other structural members).

The designer then works out a "path" for the computerized plasma-oxygen cutting machine. The path is the point at which the cutter enters the plate and starts to cut the parts. In addition, the path has to determine which part is cut next and so forth. This is all necessary so that the parts are cut in the correct order. For instance, if a window has to be cut from a cabin side, then the window aperture must be cut before the larger cabin side part is cut otherwise any movement in the cabin side after cutting could cause the window to be cut in an incorrect location.

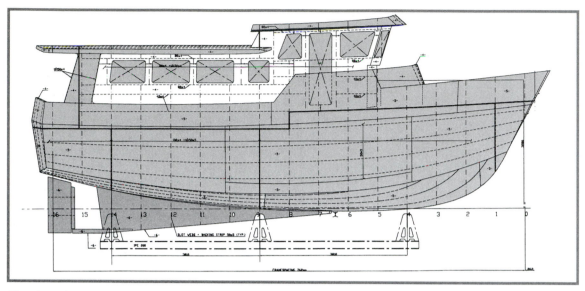

The plans that come with the kits include detailed measurements.

Several sheets of assembly drawings are now prepared, for instance, each frame is shown separately with all parts are clearly numbered and measurements are given to assist in welding up the frames.

Other drawings show how to set up the building jig that is supplied with the kits. The location of every part that forms the competed hull deck and superstructure is shown in the various assembly drawings supplied with the kit. Finally, all the parts are listed in a spreadsheet program and checked against the drawings and cutting files. Another designer is simultaneously working on the engineering drawings for engine room layout.

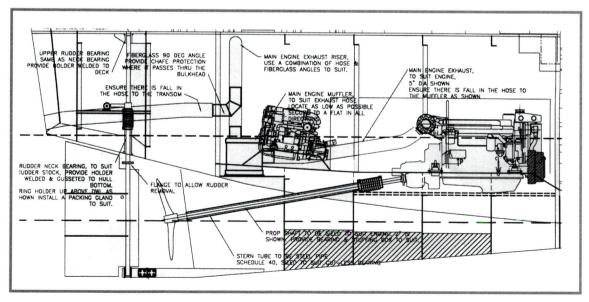

Part of an engineering drawing.

Battery placement, drive train and bearing location and sizes, exhaust system, fuel tank sizes and placement, and battery location are shown in these drawings.

Of course all the above steps have to be carefully checked and the whole design package coordinated before the cutting files are released to the client (to have the kit cut locally) or sent to the cutting shop that produces our kits. In terms of investment we figure that each set of cutting files and associated plans for a boat of between 36 and 65 ft. costs the originating design office between $35,000 and $50,000. Because this figure is too great an individual customer, we try to group orders for similar kits as well as treat a large part of the cost as investment against the future kit orders.

VOYAGER TRAWLER YACHT SERIES

My interest in trawlers goes back to my time spent as a young naval rating in the Royal Australian Navy. I would often observe commercial fisherman out in weather that was more than a little uncomfortable even in our much larger naval vessel. These trawlers were very special.

These observations were to stand me in good stead when later I designed many commercial fishing trawlers built to operate in the rough conditions off the Australian coast. These boats had to be able to handle all types of wind and sea conditions and were often required to cross the shifting sand bars that are a feature of the entrances to many Australian ports and harbors. Because umping over sand bars in boisterous sea conditions and breaking waves was and is a way of

life for the boats and the crews who fish these areas, commercial trawlers have to be tough. I have carried the same design philosophy and practice into our range of Voyager Trawler Yachts.

Aluminum is often considered among the various suitable materials for trawler yachts, and many fine boats have been built from that material. If you have a special case where the weight has to be kept low, then aluminum is worth consideration. My personal choice for an offshore cruising powerboat is an all-steel vessel. Trawler Yachts are by design medium-displacement vessels. The modest difference in the all up weight between a fiberglass or aluminum trawler and an all-steel one can work in favor of the steel boat.

The Voyager Trawler Yacht series is based on our successful Waverunner Trawler Yacht 40/42 and Trawler Yacht 45. Over 300 of these boats have been built worldwide. These boats are available as a steel or aluminum kits, and the interior can be customized.

The smallest steel trawler yacht with a raised pilothouse configuration where there is accommodation under the pilothouse should be in the range of 40 ft. If you require a smaller metal raised pilothouse vessel, then it will be necessary to use aluminum at least for the decks and superstructure. In that case 32 ft is about the minimum size.

Stability is a very important factor with any trawler yacht design. We subject our designs to extensive calculations that are now much easier to undertake thanks to the computer software that has become available in recent years. Ballast is required in most trawler yachts and especially in the smaller boats as well as in the long-range versions of the Voyager trawler yacht series.

VOYAGER TRAWLER YACHT 41
This design is based on our successful Waverunner 40/42. This boat is available as a steel or aluminum kit, and the interior can be customized.

LOA	41' 6" / 12.65 m
LWL	35' 9" / 10.90 m
Beam	14' 0" / 4.27 m
Draft	4' 9" / 1.45 m
Power	100 hp
Speed	8 knots

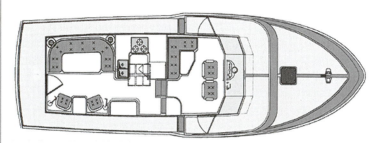

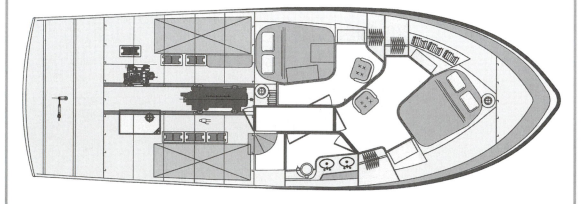

VOYAGER TRAWLER YACHT 43
Full-width saloon shown, other versions feature regular side decks.

LOA	43' 10" / 13.35 m
LWL	36" 9" / 11.20 m
Beam	15' 0" / 4.57 m
Draft	5' 0" / 1.52 m
Power	120 hp
Speed	9 knots
Sail assist	optional
WP area	375 sq. ft./34.84 m
PC	0.647
D/L ratio	398

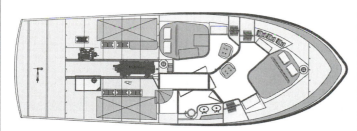

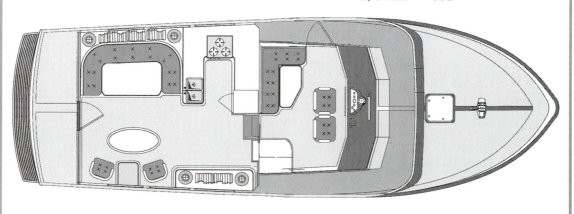

VOYAGER TRAWLER YACHT 55

LOA	55' 0" / 16.76 m
LWL	54' 4" / 16.56 m
Beam	18' 0" / 4.87 m
Power	250 hp
Displ.	91,500 lb/ 41,500 kg
WP area	718 sq. ft. / 66.70 s/m
Prismatic	0.638
Block	0.338 (incl. keel)
Displ./Length	270
Mom. to heel 1 deg.	7,650 ft. lb.
Mom. trim 1 deg.	140,000 ft. lb.

The Trawler Yacht 55 is designed to be built in steel or aluminum. This boat can be ordered as a kit, as partially built, or as a complete boat. Several varied accommodation layouts are possible.

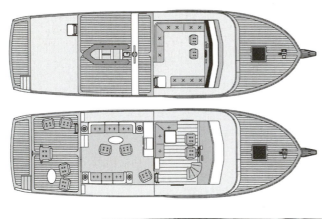

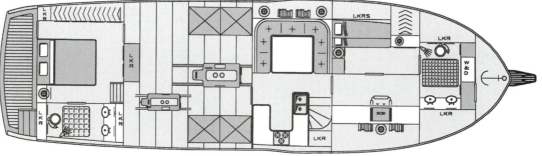

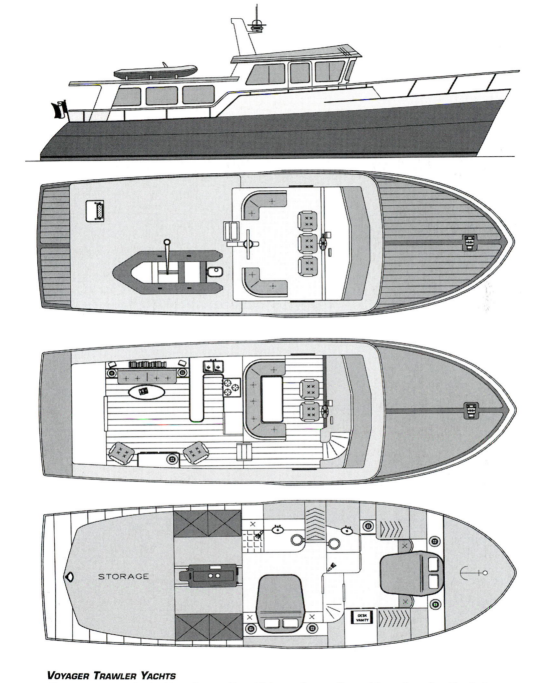

VOYAGER TRAWLER YACHTS

Above we see a typical trawler yacht, which can be configured in various lengths between 47 and 65 feet. The accommodation plans can be expanded into multiple cabins as required.

SPRAY TRAWLER YACHT SERIES

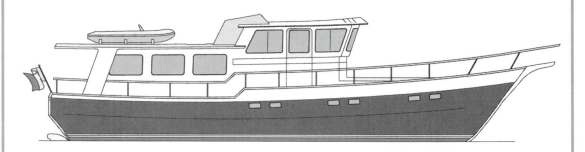

The first Spray 52 Trawler Yacht is being designed to U.S. Coast Guard T boat regulations for Edmond Badham and will be used for passenger-carrying charter. Another version is being designed for charter operations in the Caribbean.

The large flush deck areas will provide adequate stowage for dinghy and various deck boxes and other stowage as required. The moderate size bulwarks combined with sturdy pipe life rails provide some security for offshore cruising.

These designs lend themselves to many different accommodation arrangements. The two shown here are for the Spray TY 52 and the larger Spray TY 58. Both versions feature full standing headroom throughout the accommodation areas. The

on-deck pilothouse could be increased in size without compromising the stability of this vessel. Note that the present A/B ratio is a very favorable 1.75. Another possibility in either vessel would be to have a grand saloon aft. The voluminous engine room is accessible from both forward and aft accommodation areas and features full standing headroom throughout. There is adequate room to install a workbench as well as all of the machinery and equipment necessary in a long-distance passagemaker.

We are preparing plans and cutting files for the Spray Trawler Yacht 45. Although smaller Sprays can be configured as Trawler Yachts, we consider 45 feet (13.72 m) the minimum size for serious world voyaging.

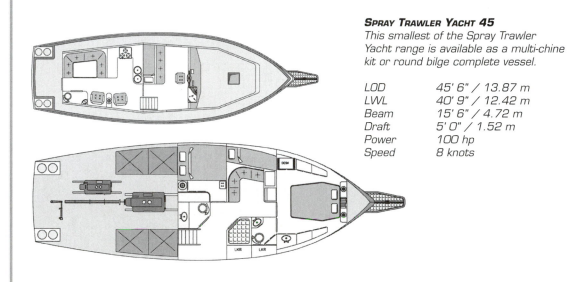

SPRAY TRAWLER YACHT 45
This smallest of the Spray Trawler Yacht range is available as a multi-chine kit or round bilge complete vessel.

LOD	45' 6" / 13.87 m
LWL	40' 9" / 12.42 m
Beam	15' 6" / 4.72 m
Draft	5' 0" / 1.52 m
Power	100 hp
Speed	8 knots

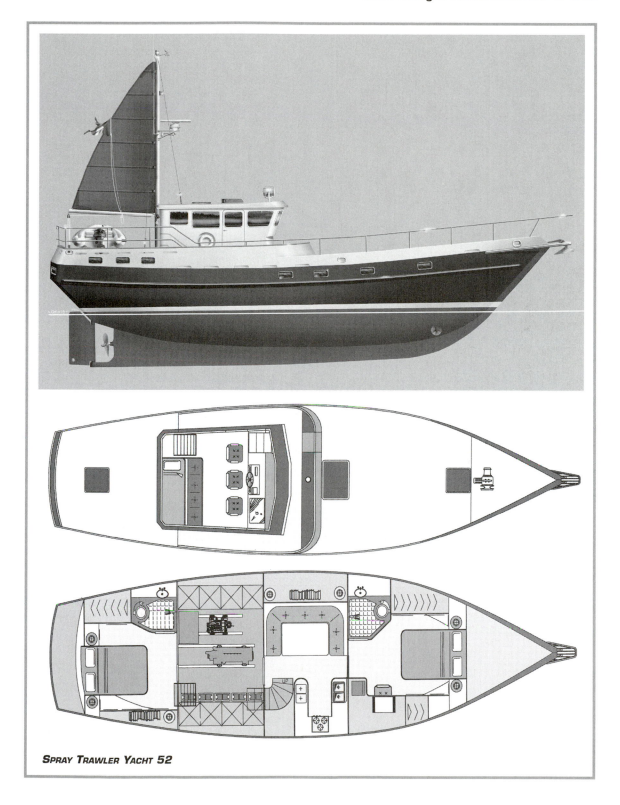

SPRAY TRAWLER YACHT 52

SPRAY 52 SAILBOAT
Flush deck version also available.

Kits are available for this full sailboat design.
You can also choose between gaff and Bermudan
rigs.

LOD	52' 0" / 15.85 m
LWL	42' 8" / 13.00 m
Beam	(Wide Body).17' 0" / 5.18 m
Beam	(Slim line).15' 0" / 4.57 m
Draft	0.5' 4" / 1.63 m
Displacement	67,500 lb. / 30,618 kg
Power	225 hp
Construction	multi-chine
Fuel	1,800 U.S. gal
Water	450 U.S. gal
Range under power	3,500 miles
A/B Ratio	1.75
D/L Ratio	.387
PC	654

SPRAY 58 TRAWLER YACHT

Flush deck version also available.

LOD	*57' 9" / 17.60 m*
LWL	*47' 8" / 14.53 m*
Beam	*0.18' 9" / 5.72 m*
Draft	*0.6' 0" / 1.83 m*
Displacement.	*85,500 lb. / 30,618 kg*
Power	*225 hp*
Fuel	*2,500 U.S. gal*
Water	*450 U.S. gal*
Range under power	*3,500 miles*
A/B Ratio	*1.75*
D/L Ratio	*.387*
PC	*654*

Kits available for this full sailboat design include a choice between gaff and Bermudan rigs. This new design is now available as a cut-to-size kit or cutting files.

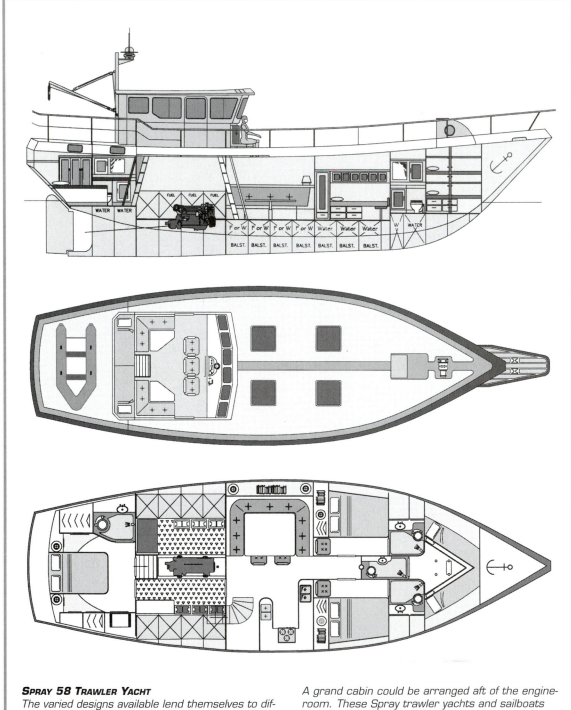

SPRAY 58 TRAWLER YACHT
The varied designs available lend themselves to different accommodation arrangements. For instance, you may decide to have the galley in the pilothouse.

A grand cabin could be arranged aft of the engine-room. These Spray trawler yachts and sailboats are serious ocean crossing vessels and are well proven by many circumnavigations.

VOYAGER 388
Radius-chine kit

LOH	39' 0" / 11.89 m
LWL	4' 10" / 10.63 m
Beam	13' 2" / 4.02 m
Draft (deep)	6' 0" / 1.83 m
Draft (shoal)	5' 6" / 1.71 m

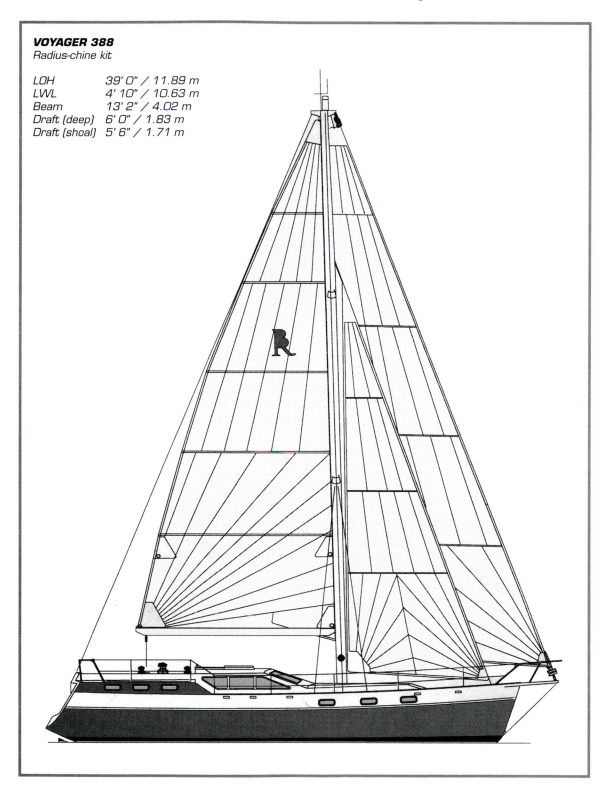

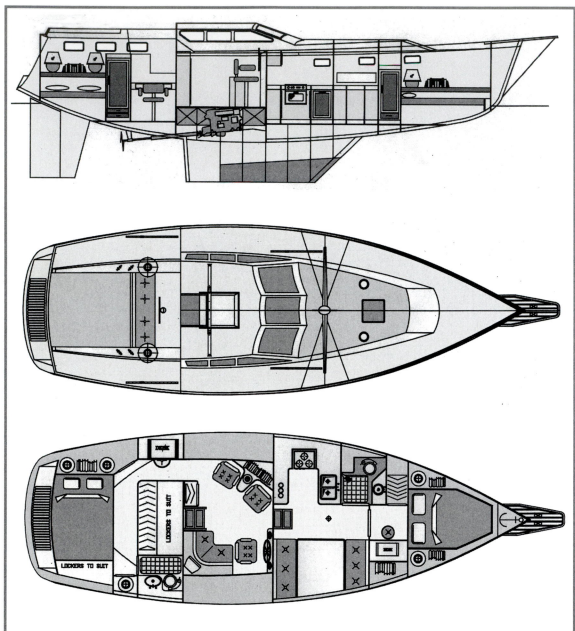

This new radius-chine kit boat is based on our highly successful Roberts 370 and Roberts 392 designs. Over 200 of these designs are sailing the oceans of the world. This new design is available in kit form. The VOYAGER 388 is slightly longer than the R370. We have taken the opportunity to heighten the cabin roof to give a greater feeling of spaciousness below. This new design features full headroom throughout. Accommodations can be rearranged to suit the client's needs. All radius chine kits supplied by Bruce Roberts include all the radius panels bent to exact shape and ready to fit in position on the hull.

VOYAGER 495
Long- and short-keel models are available for
this design.

Radius-chine kit.

LOA	49' 4" / 15.03 m
LWL	43' 5" / 13.24 m
Beam	14' 8" / 4.47 m
Draft	shoal 5' 8" / 1.73 m
Draft	deep 6' 9" / 2.06 m
SAILS	1,392 sq. ft. / 129.32 sq. m

This new design has all of the features that
make a great cruising boat. The radius chine
kit is simple to assemble. Partially built and
complete boats are also available. There are
a variety of accommodation plans that can
be used in this versatile radius-chine
sailboat.

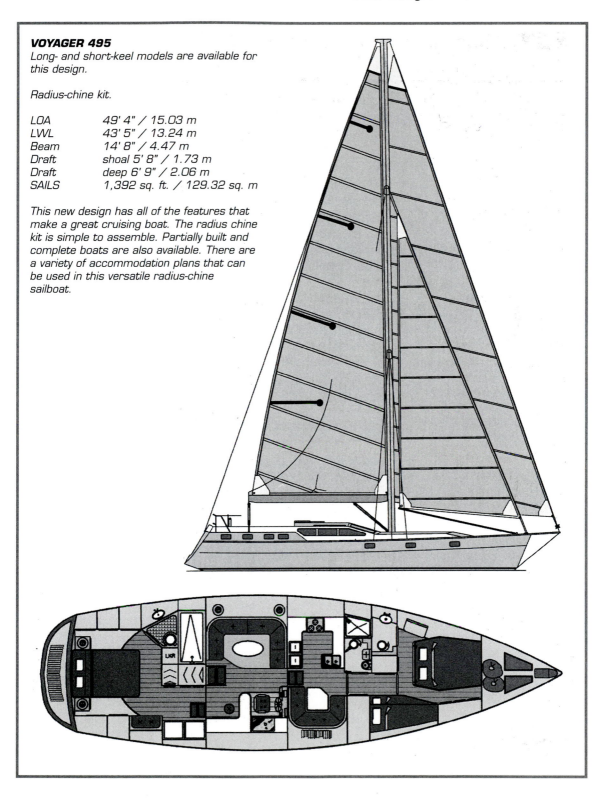

VOYAGER 655

Long and short keel models available.

Radius-chine kit.

LOA	66' 9" / 20.34 m
LWL	60' 8" / 18.50 m
Beam	16' 6" / 5.03 m
Draft	8' 0" / 2.44 m
Displ.	80,000 lb. / 36,286 kg
Sails	2,025 sq. ft./ 188 sq. m

The Voyager 655 is the kit version of the very popular New York 65

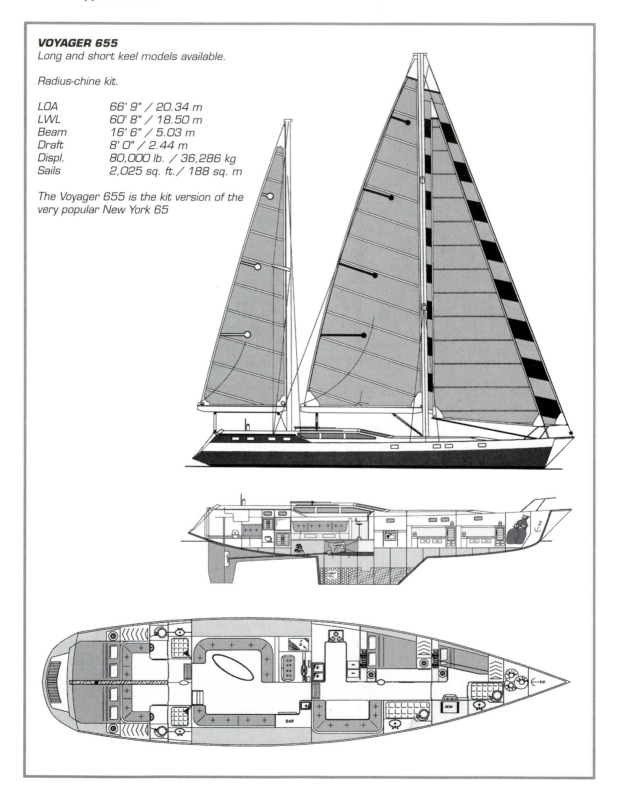

INDEX